D1616065

6/9/16

GRIMM PICTURES

GRIMM PICTURES

*Fairy Tale Archetypes
in Eight Horror
and Suspense Films*

Walter Rankin

McFarland & Company, Inc., Publishers
Jefferson, North Carolina, and London

LIBRARY OF CONGRESS CATALOGUING-IN-PUBLICATION DATA

Rankin, Walter, 1969–
    Grimm pictures : fairy tale archetypes in eight horror and
suspense films / Walter Rankin.
        p.   cm.
    Includes bibliographical references and index.

    ISBN-13: 978-0-7864-3174-8
    softcover : 50# alkaline paper ∞

    1. Horror films—United States—History and criticism.
2. Thrillers (Motion pictures, television, etc.)—United States—
History and criticism.   3. Fairy tales—History and criticism.
I. Title.
PN1995.9.H6R35 2007
791.43'6164—dc22
                                                    2007026245

British Library cataloguing data are available

On the cover: Samara (Daveigh Chase) in an asylum from *The Ring,*
2002 (The Kobal Collection/Dreamworks LLC); (inset) Rapunzel
illustration (E. H. Wehnert from *Household Stories Collected by the
Brothers Grimm*, London: Routledge and Sons, 1880)

Manufactured in the United States of America

*McFarland & Company, Inc., Publishers
    Box 611, Jefferson, North Carolina 28640
    www.mcfarlandpub.com*

Table of Contents

5

Preface

Fairy tale horrors, oddly enough, comprise some of my earliest, most beloved memories. As my mother prepared me for bed each night, she'd take out her well-worn copy of the *Fairy Tales of the Brothers Grimm* and select a good-night story. I would drift off to sleep hearing about the adventures of Little Red Cap, Cinderella, and Snow White. However, these heroines were no mere damsels in distress awaiting rescue by some tale-hopping, nameless Prince Charming. Some manly intervention may have come into play, but these ladies fought back, too, and in truly creative ways: That little red-capped girl cut open the wolf and stuffed his tummy with rocks; the new princess Cindy brought her stepsisters to her wedding so that they would get their eyes poked out; and Snow revealed a vengeful streak under her whitened veneer, having red hot iron boots strapped to her stepmother's legs and forcing her to dance to death at her wedding. Such was my introduction to the fairy tales. For the record, my mother also made ice cream floats, painted sunny murals on my bedroom wall, and made me an Uncle Sam costume for a school play.

I have an older, protective sister, and my favorite tales involved siblings who stuck together. I was horrified by a Hans Christian Andersen tale called "Snow Queen" in which an enchanted mirror breaks, sending shards of glass throughout the land. A tiny fragment lands in the eye and heart of a little boy who turns on his sister. That story bothered me so much that my mother never read me another tale by Andersen, sticking instead to the reliable Grimms who collected a variety of supportive-sibling tales. Everyone knows about resourceful Hansel and Gretel, a devoted duo who managed to kill a witch, take her treasure, and find their way back home out of the dark forest.

My sister played a vital role in getting me to link fairy tales and horror films early on: As the older one, she could go see R-rated films like *Halloween* and *Friday the 13th*. When she would get home, my friends and I would beg her to tell us what happened, and she'd cover the bloody events in detail. Despite the heavy death toll in these films, there was always a bit of hope that the good, smart kids could survive the masked killer. Jamie Lee Curtis' babysitter fends off Michael Myers with knitting needles, a hanger, and even his own knife, saving herself and the children without any help from a boyfriend. (For now, we'll forget that Michael ends up being her psycho brother.) My sister had to serve as my brave babysitter several times after *Halloween* came out, and we lived in one of those rambling houses out in the country with too many glass doors and windows with faulty locks. It never took long to imagine that crazed killer making his way into the house. When my parents arrived home one evening, they found me asleep in my sister's lap in the den. She was still awake, holding our biggest kitchen knife.

By the time I was old enough to watch and appreciate horror films, they had mostly devolved into the hack-and-slash genre parodied so well by Kevin Williamson and Wes Craven in *Scream*. Every holiday and teen event had been taken over (*Slumber Party Massacre; Happy Birthday to Me; Prom Night; Final Exam; Silent Night, Deadly Night; My Bloody Valentine*), and the villain Jason was still dispatching those nubile camp counselors who kept going outside to investigate a scary noise. I stayed away from horror films until my junior year of college when Jonathan Demme's *The Silence of the Lambs*, easily the most frightening film I had (and have) ever seen, was released. From the opening credits that show Agent Starling running alone down a forest path, to the creepy underworld cell of Hannibal Lecter, to the showdown between Starling and Buffalo Bill in his pitch-black basement, this film caused a purely visceral, physical reaction in me. By the end of the film, I had pulled my legs up to my chest to sit in an awkward fetal position, and I was biting my thumbnail. For the first time, I had felt what Noël Carroll describes as the emotion of "art-horror" in his outstanding book, *The Philosophy of Horror or Paradoxes of the Heart* (1990): "And though it need not be the case that our hair must literally stand on end when we are art-horrified, it is important to stress that the original conception of the word connected it with an abnormal (from the subject's point of view) physiological state of agitation" (p. 25).

I chose the other films for this study because they inspired similar reactions when I first saw them. With the exception of *Rosemary's Baby*, I saw each of them as a regular filmgoer looking for entertainment when they premiered. For some reason, the films stuck with me even after I left the theater and the adrenaline wore off. I may like the films personally and enjoy watching them for a jolt, but I also believe that they are well-made films with extra layers of depth worthy of analysis. This argument is easy to make with an Academy Award winner like *The Silence of the Lambs*, but not all of these films were so well received by the critics. For example, the more I watched *What Lies Beneath*, the least critically praised film in this text, the more convinced I became that it will stand as a remarkably well-crafted and satisfying thriller. In the process of writing this book, I have been most pleasantly surprised by the number of people—friends, family, and colleagues, but also new acquaintances at office get-togethers— who have shared their passion for these films with me. Everyone loves a good story, and that's exactly what these films provide.

Some excellent authors and critics have tied fairy tales to horror films in their own way. In his chapter "The Modern American Horror Movie— Text and Subtext" from *Danse Macabre* (1981), the master of horror writing himself, Stephen King, suggests that most great horror films can be summarized "with that wonderful fairy-tale door-opener, 'Once upon a time'" (p. 176). He then briefly reviews films like *Coma, The Birds, The Omen*, and *Deliverance* as condensed fairy tales. King does not tie the films to particular fairy tales, however, instead arguing more globally about their common structure. In *Nightmares in Red, White and Blue: The Evolution of the American Horror Film* (2004), Joseph Maddrey points out the "Hansel and Gretel" leitmotif that runs through a number of Wes Craven's films, including *Flowers in the Attic* and *Wes Craven's New Nightmare*. And in *Offensive Films: Toward an Anthropology of Cinéma Vomitif* (1997), Mikita Brottman focuses on the common narrative structure shared by fairy tales and horror films. She also links themes and images from a variety of fairy tales, including "Jack and the Beanstalk," "Goldilocks and the Three Bears," "Beauty and the Beast," "Little Red Riding Hood," and "Hansel and Gretel" to similar ideas in *The Texas Chainsaw Massacre*.

In this text, I take a more direct approach, specifically pairing a single Grimm Brothers fairy tale with a horror/suspense film. I discuss structural similarities but also look at the ways certain themes, motifs, images, and even dialogue emerge uniquely in both works within each chapter. At the start of each chapter, I categorize the primary tale with similar Grimm tales based upon an archetypical villain (cannibal; serial killer; freak-of-nature; vampire; manmade monster; witch; or devil), and I place each villain in the historical and societal context of the Grimm Brothers. In the conclusion, I examine how the Grimm tales can also be interpreted as various representations of the reader-writer relationship. The analysis of the fairy tale is as important to me as the analysis of its connection to the film. To that end, I have also included research from some of the most prominent scholars of the Grimm tales, including Jack Zipes, Maria Tatar, Ruth Bottigheimer, Bruno Bettelheim, and James McGlathery, among others. Their love and respect for these tales comes through in their books and articles, and I hope to follow their example in the chapters to come.

Woodcut illustrations in the text are by E. H. Wehnert and reproduced from *Household Stories Collected by the Brothers Grimm* (London: Routledge and Sons, 1880).

I owe special thanks—along with a special dinner of fava beans and a nice Chianti—to my family and to my partner, Chris, for their support throughout this endeavor, particularly as my books, DVDs, and other research made their way out of my office like Rapunzel's tendrils, extending wildly into all parts of the house. I am also indebted to Dr. Doris Bitler and Dr. Donna Fox, my partners in mystery, madness, and murder.

Branding the Grimm Brothers

From the Black Forest to the Hollywood Hills

When Jacob and Wilhelm Grimm began collecting fairy tales in nineteenth-century Germany, they could never have foreseen the reach those stories would have in our twentieth- and twenty-first-century popular culture. The Grimm Brothers have attained such iconic status that they are essentially a brand name associated with an array of cultural genres and products far removed from the wolves and witches of the Black Forest. The toy maker X-Concepts has marketed hybrid toys called *Grimm Dudes* (a spin-off of their popular Tech Deck Dudes) that feature characters like Prince Harming and Big Bad Wolf on skateboards (along with the Toof Fairy and Peter Rottentail). In the music world, Bad Mutha Goose and the Brothers Grimm produced a couple of albums like *Tower of Babel* and *Jump the Funk* in the late 1980s. From 1972 to 1982, Gold Key produced the comic book series *Grimm's Ghost Stories* which centered largely on stories of the occult. Mike Peters' comic strip *Mother Goose and Grimm* appears in over 800 newspapers worldwide. While Peters occasionally satirizes our world through fairy tales, as in his January 1, 2006 panel depicting "Disney's Desperate Housewives," most of his strips center on the

11

antics of a mischievous dog named Grimm. And a 2001 paperback titled *Dr. Who: Grimm Reality* transports the time-traveling doctor to a dangerous fairy tale world.

These items often have little to do with the tales or lives of the Grimm Brothers, and their association serves primarily as a convenient marketing tool. However, this strategy also reveals their incredible name cachet in contrast to other famed fairy tale collectors like Charles Perrault, Hans Christian Andersen, and Joseph Jacobs. That the Grimm Brothers have come to be associated with the bizarre, strange, mystical, and macabre can no doubt be attributed in part to their name which lends itself to plays on the word grim, as seen above and in such scholarly works as Maria Tatar's *Grimm's Grimmest*, a collection of their most gruesome tales. There is no denying, however, that their fairy tale collection also remains the most enduringly popular: Amazon.com recently ranked several versions of their complete fairy tales as high as 9,146 (a Pantheon Books version originally translated by Margaret Hunt) in comparison to Perrault's complete tales which came in at a high of 220,601 (a Clarion Books translation by Neil Philip).

It is well documented that cultures all over the world have their own versions of the most famous tales, particularly most of the ones chosen for this text: "Little Red Cap," "Brier Rose (Sleeping Beauty)," "Little Snow White," "Rapunzel," "Cinderella," "Rumpelstiltskin," and "Hansel and Gretel." And despite their claims to have assembled purely Germanic folktales, the Grimm Brothers collected some of their best-known tales from storytellers like the Hassenpflug family, French-speaking Hugeunots who were familiar with Charles Perrault's earlier versions of "Red Riding Hood" and "Cinderella" (Zipes, 1988; Tatar, 2003). Through various editions, the Brothers edited and revised the tales, increasing their "Germanness" by emphasizing elements like the dark forest and incorporating strict moral lessons. Their versions are also pointedly grim, and even the most beloved stories involve intense images of torture, cannibalism, and dismemberment. Snow White's wicked stepmother greedily consumes what she believes are the lung and liver of her young rival, and she is forced to dance until dead in red-hot iron boots at her stepdaughter's wedding; meanwhile, after years of abuse at the hands of her own stepmother and stepsisters, Cinderella, Snow White's equally famous canonical cousin, invites her stepsisters to her wedding where their eyes are poked out by her guardian birds. Tatar (1997) remarks that "violent endings for fairy tales are peculiar to the Grimms' collection" when compared to similar tales from other cultures, and she argues that their tales "were designed to keep audiences awake, alert, attentive, and engaged in the intricacies of their plot.... Like horror films, folktales trade in the sensational—breaking taboos and enacting the forbidden with uninhibited energy" (pp. 9–10). This violence coupled with a strong moral ties the Grimm tales to our modern horror and suspense films in provocative and profound ways.

Some films directly link themselves to the Grimm fairy tale world. For example, Henry Levin and George Pal's *The Wonderful World of the Brothers Grimm* (1962) focuses on three of the lesser-known Grimm tales, while Terry Gilliam's *The Brothers Grimm* (2005) transforms the siblings into scamming con men, played by Matt Damon and Heath Ledger, who become lost among special effects. One of the posters for Gilliam's film shows Little Red Cap walking along an ominous path. The tag line reads, "This isn't the way to grandmother's house." Michael Cohn's made-for-cable *Snow White: A Tale of Terror* (1997) gives story credit to the Grimm Brothers, and his pointed mentioning of terror in the title indicates that the Grimm tale differs greatly in tone from the Disney version. Caroline Thompson's *Snow White: The Fairest of Them All* (2001) likewise credits the Grimms, and the DVD cover claims, "There is perhaps no more beloved Brothers Grimm fairy tale than the legend of a beautiful young girl fleeing her home because of a jealous stepmother." Her version freely adapts the text, however, even humanizing the wicked stepmother and vindicating Snow White's absent father. Films like Matthew Bright's *Freeway* (1996), starring Reese Witherspoon as a gun-wielding Red Riding Hood who encounters Kiefer Sutherland's big, bad Bob Wolverton on the way to her grandmother's trailer, give modern twists to the tales while honoring their violent core.

For the purposes of this discussion, I have chosen eight horror and suspense films that are, upon first viewing, not linked so noticeably to the Grimm Brothers' world: In order of analysis, *The Silence of the Lambs* (1991), *Scream* (1996), *The Ring* (2002), *The Talented Mr. Ripley* (1999), *Aliens* (1986), *Rosemary's Baby* (1968), *What Lies Beneath* (2000), and *Misery* (1990). Their appeal to both young audiences and parents, however, allows us to draw an immediate parallel to the attractions of the Grimm tales. All of these films received an R-rating with the exception of the PG-13 assigned to *What Lies Beneath* and *The Ring*. *Scream* was named Best Film at the 1997 MTV Movie Awards; Matt Damon's Tom Ripley was nominated for Best Villain at the 2000 MTV Movie Awards, while his film was nominated for Best Drama at the Teen Choice Awards; and *The Ring* received similar dual nominations for Best Villain at the 2003 MTV Movie Awards and Best Horror/Thriller at the Teen Choice Awards. The MTV Movie Awards have been awarded since 1992, while the Teen Choice Awards were sponsored by *Seventeen Magazine* until 1999 when *Teen People* took over the ballot process. *The Silence of the Lambs, Aliens, Rosemary's Baby,* and *Misery* were released before these award shows came along. Otherwise, we can be assured that Hannibal Lecter, the Alien Queen, Satan, and Annie Wilkes would have earned their own Best Villain nominations. In fact, Anthony Hopkins' Lecter finally did receive such a nomination in 2002 for his work in *Hannibal* (2001).

In celebration of its 100th birthday, the American Film Institute (AFI) named its top fifty heroes and villains. For voting purposes, the institute defined a hero as "a character(s) who prevails in extreme circumstances and dramatizes a sense of morality, courage, and purpose. Though they may be ambiguous and flawed, they often sacrifice themselves to show humanity at its best." A villain was described as "a character(s) whose wickedness of mind, selfishness of character and will to power are sometimes masked by beauty and nobility, while others may rage unmasked. They can be horribly evil or grandiosely funny, but are ultimately tragic." Clarice Starling (number six) and Ellen Ripley (number eight) made the list of heroes while the Alien Queen (number fourteen) and Annie Wilkes (number seventeen) were among the top-ranked villains. Outranking them all, however, was Dr. Hannibal Lecter at number one. The heroes and villains thrilling us in the other films analyzed in this text all exemplify similar qualities of courage and purpose, of masked wickedness and tragedy, as do our fairy tale heroes and villains.

The films chosen for this study provide scares, screams, jumps, and jolts that stem from our understanding of Grimm fairy tale archetypes. We know almost instinctively what to expect from our heroes and villains. As Jodie Foster's agent-in-training Clarice Starling jogs alone down an ominous forest path during the opening credits of *The Silence of the Lambs,* we know that symbolic wolves can and will emerge on her journey. Like the dozing Brier Rose, *Scream's* Sydney Prescott must constantly be on guard against her relentless male stalkers until she finally wakes up to the truth of her past. A pre-pubescent girl is locked away in a barn loft and then thrown into a well, forming her seemingly inescapable inverted tower, in *The Ring*. A jealous Tom Ripley almost magically assumes the identity of the ever-lovely Dickie Greenleaf after bathing metaphorically in his blood. A young girl who has lost her entire family must fight an indomitable new mother looking out for her own offspring in *Aliens*. Fears of parenthood, empty nests, and spousal trust arise in the complementary films *Rosemary's Baby* and *What Lies Beneath* as unsuspecting parents confront deception in their own homes. And a powerful woman determines the fates of her author's best and least-loved creations in *Misery*, destroying the former while obsessively praising the latter.

In "The Golden Key," the 200th tale in the Grimm Brothers' final collection, a poor boy finds a golden key under the snow. He digs deeper into the ground and finds a small iron casket with a tiny keyhole. He inserts the key and as he unlocks the box, the tale ends as we are told that we will have to wait to discover what kinds of wonderful things he found therein. It is no wonder that the Pulitzer Prize–winning Anne Sexton chose this particular tale to begin her collection of deliciously revised Grimm tales, *Transformations* (1971), in which the boy's turn of the key "opens this book of odd tales / which transform the Brothers Grimm" (p. 2). In each of the films analyzed in this text, the Brothers find their tales transformed once again, celluloid creations unleashed as we open that little casket and peer inside the darkness.

ONE

The Path
of Beast Resistance

"Little Red Cap" and
The Silence of the Lambs

A GRIMM VIEW OF THE FAIRY TALE CANNIBAL

Cannibalism appears both metaphorically and literally in a number of the Grimm Brothers' fairy tales, and not simply for its shock value. The Germany of the early nineteenth century did not provide an easy life for most of its residents, and true stories of infanticide and child abandonment among the poor were not considered uncommon (Tatar, 2003, pp. 49–50). Poverty and hunger were known to the Brothers Grimm as well, and for a time after their mother's death in 1808, Jacob was the sole provider to his five siblings. According to O'Neill (1999), when the fairy tales were first published in 1812, the Grimm family was surviving on one meal a day.

Due to the economic and social realities of the time, it would not have seemed impossible for little Hansel and Gretel to learn that their step-mother and father intend on abandoning them in the wilderness since there is not enough food to eat, and the children are blamed for eating them out of house and home. They eventually stumble upon an edible gingerbread house that is used as a trap by an evil witch who captures them. She forces Gretel into servitude, and cages Hansel, whom she intends to fatten up for a hearty meal. Clever Gretel, however, is able to trick the witch into falling into her own oven, thereby getting roasted in her own juices.

The ever-jealous stepmother of Snow White sends our young heroine out into the wilderness as well; however, she does not simply want her to be lost and alone. She has a hunter accompany her and gives him instructions to bring back the lung and liver as proof of her death. Although he carries her into the woods as commanded, he cannot bring himself to kill her and leaves her to be eaten by the wild animals. To placate his queen, he brings her the lung and liver of a young doe. The queen then has these organs cooked in salt for her dinner, gobbling them up and consulting her mirror to see if she is now the fairest in the land.

Walt Disney would likely never have considered a film devoted to "Fundevogel," whose name literally translates as "Found-Bird." In this tale of sibling devotion, a forester finds a little child up in a tree where it was kept by a bird of prey. He rescues the child and brings him home to be a brother to his daughter Lina. One day Lina learns that the cook, old Sanna, is planning to boil him up in a pot of water. The two escape, but the cook and some servants chase after them. Fundevogel and Lina avoid detection by transforming themselves into a rose on a rosebush, a chandelier in a church, and a duck in a fishpond. In their latter forms, Lina pulls the cook into the water with her beak, thereby drowning her and saving Fundevogel from a boiling pot.

In the lesser known "The Six Swans," a young queen must remain mute for six years to lift a curse on her six brothers, who have been transformed into swans, while her wicked mother-in-law devises a scheme to rid herself of her rival. After the birth of each of the queen's three children, the mother-in-law hides the newborn and smears blood upon the mouth of the sleeping mother. She then accuses the queen of having feasted on her own children during the night. The king defends his wife after the first two disappearances, but he cannot bring himself to do so for a third time, and he sentences his wife to be burned at the stake. The day of her burning coincides with the last day of her muted sentence, and she is finally able to speak against the actions of her mother-in-law. Her brothers become men once more, her children are recovered, and the mother-in-law is burnt to ashes.

The young bride-to-be in "The Robber Bridegroom" is filled with

Naïve Little Red Cap glances warily behind her, sensing the approach of the hungry wolf as she begins her journey in the woods. (Illustration by E. H. Wehnert from *Household Stories Collected by the Brothers Grimm.* London: Routledge and Sons, 1880.)

dread every time she thinks about her insistent suitor. When he finally convinces her to visit his house, she arrives early and encounters an old woman boiling a pot of water. The old woman warns her that her intended is a murderer and a cannibal, explaining that he and his men plan on chopping her up for a cold-blooded meal. Fortunately for the girl, the old woman takes pity on her and helps her escape. On the day of their wedding celebration, she reveals her wicked groom's true nature, and he and his band of robbers are executed.

"The Juniper Tree" is perhaps one of the most disturbing and violent of all the Grimm tales dealing with cannibalism. Here we are told of a stepmother who comes to detest her stepson so much that she decapitates him and feeds him to his own father in a stew. The father devours his dinner, complimenting his wife on her recipe and asking for a second helping. He tosses the bones under the table, and his daughter gathers the bones and buries them under a juniper tree. Her brother appears as a bird, singing throughout the land that his stepmother killed him, and his father ate him. He finally gets his revenge by dropping a millstone on top of his murderer, crushing her to death. Thereafter, he is magically transformed into a human again, and he joins his sister and father at the table for dinner.

What separates Little Red Cap from Hansel, Gretel, Snow White, Fundevogel, the children of the mute queen, and the robber's bride is that she is, in fact, eaten. Her story also has a clear and valuable lesson in contrast to that of the poor son in "The Juniper Tree." She undergoes the unimaginable journey into the belly of the wolf, and she emerges from it, smarter and more resourceful. Her tale is actually comprised of a brief, often ignored, second journey to her grandmother's cottage to show that she is no longer the simple girl who can be fooled by any wolf that comes along. When she is confronted by another wolf, she hides and makes her way quickly to her grandmother's house. They lock the door and await the wolf's arrival. Like the wolf before him, he comes to the door pretending to be the visiting granddaughter, but this time they are wise to his wicked words, and they remain silent. The wolf decides to wait on the roof, planning to attack little Red on her way home that evening. The grandmother boils sausages, and she has little Red pour the sausage water into the trough. The wolf is so drawn to the aroma that he falls from the roof into the trough and drowns. And little Red goes happily home, never to be hurt by anyone again.

A HOLLYWOOD VIEW OF "LITTLE RED CAP"

In contrast to Cinderella and Snow White, most Hollywood versions of our red-capped heroine have been geared more to an adult market. Walt Disney produced a 1922 black-and-white short (*Little Red Riding Hood and the Big Bad Wolf*) but did not revisit the tale with the lavish feature-length treatment given to other fairy tale heroines. Other animated shorts by Fritz Freleng (1944's *Little Red Riding Rabbit*) and Tex Avery (1939's *Little Red Walking Hood*; 1943's *Red Hot Riding Hood*; and 1949's *Little Rural Riding Hood*) kept the character very much in the adult realm, particularly Avery's sexualized, scantily clad version (no doubt the inspiration for Jessica Rabbit who explains, "I'm not bad—I'm just drawn that way" in 1988's *Who Framed Roger Rabbit?*), a long-legged chanteuse who makes the eyes pop out of leering, panting wolves. In Cory and Todd Edwards' satirical *Hoodwinked* (2005), Red and her tough-talking granny are criminal suspects along with the wolf and woodsman as they all recount their version of events in a pop culture environment.

With its overtones of sexuality, gender-crossing, and cannibalism, the tale of Little Red Cap is certainly well-suited to suspense films, particularly those centering on dangerous male-female relationships. Alfred Hitchcock's *Psycho* (1960) features a young woman (Janet Leigh) who has veered off the right path, figuratively after stealing funds from her office, and literally as she ends up at the isolated Bates Motel. Anthony Perkin's Norman Bates is a gentle and charming motel manager, luring his guest into a sense of security before assuming his mother's murderous form. In Wes Craven's *Red Eye* (2005), a lovely hotel executive (Rachel McAdams) returning from her grandmother's funeral encounters handsome Jack Rippner (Cillian Murphy), a professional stalker of sorts who makes certain to end up behind her in line and then in the seat next to her on the flight. He threatens to have her father killed if she does not place a powerful politician in a specific hotel room to aid in his assassination; despite his attempts, she is able to get back onto the right path to foil his plans.

A number of films take their cues directly from Little Red Cap's journey, in their plotlines and marketing. Neil Jordan's *The Company of Wolves* (1984) features Angela Lansbury as a grandmother who tells her maturing granddaughter (Sarah Patterson) terrifying tales of men and wolves. The cover art for the film poster shows the girl wearing the traditional red cloak while carrying a basket and walking through the woods. A half-dressed man transforming into a wolf under a full moon is in the foreground.[1] The opening credits of Matthew Bright's *Freeway* (1996) feature an animated wolf chasing after a series of provocative Little Red Caps before delving into the story of Vanessa Lutz (Reese Witherspoon), a teenager trying to find her grandmother while avoiding the predatory Bob Wolverton (Kiefer Sutherland). When she finally arrives at her grandmother's trailer, she discovers Bob dressed in the old woman's clothing and hiding in her bed, telling him, "Them some big ugly fuckin' teeth you got there, Bob." He attacks, but she is able to subdue and kill him without the aid of any woodsmen. David Slade gives us a similarly resilient youth in *Hard Candy* (2005). Hayley Stark (Ellen Paige) is a fourteen-year-old girl who decides to meet the pedophile photographer (Patrick Wilson) with whom she's been talking online. Once she gains access to his home and studio, she reveals that she is not a helpless, clueless babe in the woods. The striking film poster centers on a red-hooded girl, her back to the viewer, standing in the middle of a giant bear (wolf) trap.

REVISING THE OFT-TOLD TALE

By most accounts (Dundes, 1989; Mcglathery, 1993; Tatar, 1999; Willard, 2002), the Grimm version of "Little Red Cap" is based upon Charles Perrault's French version, "Little Red Riding Hood," which is, in turn, based upon an oral fairy tale called "The False Grandmother." Ashliman (2004) points out that, while the tale is known through most of the English-speaking world by Perrault's title, it is most associated with the Grimm Brothers' version. Perrault made a special point of altering the tale to reduce a number of its cruder elements for his audience in the French Royal Court (Willard, 2002). For our purposes, the original tale includes a particularly disturbing scene that is of merit: When the young girl—she does not yet have a name, nor does she wear a red cap—encounters the wolf (a werewolf, actually) on the path, he races to her grandmother's home and devours the old woman quickly. He puts pieces of her flesh and blood aside, however, and then has the granddaughter prepare and eat them when she arrives. After he has deceived her into becoming a cannibal, he tries to get her into bed, but she outsmarts him and manages to escape on her own.

Perrault added the red cap and deleted the girl's cannibalistic scene. He also allowed the wolf to eat her at the end of the tale—with no hope of reemergence—and concluded with an obvious moral that young girls should watch out for wolves and never invite them into their homes, no matter how kindly they might appear. The Grimms, who likely heard the story from a French-speaking family friend, Marie Hassenpflug, adjusted the tale again, giving it a happy ending as Red and the grandmother both get to live, and the wicked wolf gets his comeuppance, verifying the educational value of punishment as a tool for education (Shavit, 1989). As critics like Murphy (2000) and Vaz da Silva (2002) point out, the Grimms connect back to the imagery of cannibalism by having Red carry bread and wine to her grandmother. These symbols of the Eucharist summon up ideas of flesh and blood once again, although in a strictly Christian sense in this retelling. At the conclusion of the Grimm tale, the grandmother regains her health only after partaking of the bread and wine, essentially taking communion.

The resourceful heroine and cannibalistic villain of Thomas Harris's *The Silence of the Lambs* must similarly relive an altered version of their tale as it is transformed from novel to film. As in Red's second journey to her grandmother's house, the filmed version is shorter than the original tale, and it has been streamlined considerably to emphasize the heroine's abilities and ingenuity. For example, Ted Tally's Oscar-winning screenplay eliminates the subplot of Crawford's terminally ill wife while editing greatly Clarice Starling's backstory and uncomfortable interactions with Senator Ruth Martin. By making these substantial changes to improve the flow of the story, Tally also increases the parallels between Harris's work and the Grimm tale. In the film, the focus is now more clearly centered on the interplay between Starling and Lecter, an inquisitive Red to a calculating wolf. Crawford also becomes more one-dimensional, like the Grimm wood-cutter who saves Red in the first tale but not in the other, while Starling's interactions with the lone mother figure, Senator Martin, are excised alto-gether. Thus, our film Lecter feeds off of the mother's pain and Starling's in separate interactions much like the Grimm wolf gobbles up the grand-mother and Red individually. In both tellings, the consumption of the tough, older woman serves as an appetizer for the evil epicure's tender, main course.

Symbolically and metaphorically, two other changes are of signifi-cance between the novel and the film. Although Harris tells us frequently that Starling is quite attractive—and aware of her attractiveness, since one of his first lines describing her inner thoughts reads, "She knew she could look all right without primping" (p. 1)—he does not give us a full descrip-tion of her physically. For the film, however, we must see her, and the final choice of actress and wardrobe form an indelible image: Jodie Foster, red hair perfectly framing a delicate, wide-eyed face like a protective cap with a slight build that contrasts the hulking men around her. In the DVD doc-umentary *Inside the Labyrinth: The Making of The Silence of the Lambs*, Tally explains that he wrote the role specifically with Foster in mind, although he knew that Jonathan Demme's first choice was Michelle Pfeiffer. He also reinforces the idea that the story is, at its center, a kind of fairy tale, commenting, "Any good story reduces to sort of mythic elements and reduces to a kind of fable.... The character that she [Foster] plays goes into the dark forest of evil and ignorance in order to rescue a princess and come out on the other side with greater wisdom." It is important to note that the opening scene of the film, with Starling running alone along a path in the woods, appears neither in the novel nor in Tally's final screenplay.

Another alteration from the novel to film lies in Starling's defining psychological moment—trying to silence the screaming lambs of her childhood. In the novel, young Starling awakens to the sound of lambs being led to the slaughter; however, she does not try to rescue them. Rather, she is focused on saving her horse, Hannah. Harris's Starling lives with her aunt and uncle on a ranch where horses are slaughtered for glue, fertilizer, and dog food. When she is awakened by the lambs one evening, she decides to rescue her horse. After she rides away, she ends up living at an orphanage with a barn where they let her keep the horse, and she tells Lecter that it lived about twenty-two years.

Tally's screenplay eliminates the horse and shifts the focus solely to Starling's desire to save the sacrificial lambs themselves. She tells Lecter, "First I tried to free them ... I opened the gate of their pen—but they wouldn't run. They just stood there, confused. They wouldn't run...." She attempts to save the smallest one but laments, "I thought, I thought if I could save just one, but he was so heavy, he was so heavy." Her voice trails off in disappointment and sadness. The young Starling is soon caught while trying to carry it away to freedom; thus, her first attempt to save a life ends in haunting failure. By tying Starling's destiny to that of the slaughtered lambs, Tally brings up a natural association to the iconic image of the wolf hunting its prey.

Despite these changes, there are some noteworthy similarities between Harris's novel and the Grimm fairy tale as well, particularly Harris's physical descriptions of Lecter. While we learn little about Starling's appearance in the novel, Lecter is described precisely; thus, we know that he is "small and sleek" with small, white teeth, and his eyes are "maroon and they reflect the light in pinpoints of red" (p. 16). In an odd aside, we are also told that he has six fingers on his left hand. He seems not quite human, a ferocious animal masked by his education and uncommon courtesy. In Chapter 36, when Lecter plots his escape from the courthouse after Starling has finally shared her tale of the doomed lambs with him, Harris describes the doctor with the attributes that are most commonly linked to Red's lupine lothario in drag—with his big ears, hands, and terribly big mouth:

> He [Lecter] nodded along, his tongue moving over the edges of his *teeth*.... Carefully, with his *powerful hands*, he bent the metal and it was coming. Now. The minute strip of metal was ... a handcuff key.... He heard Pembry behind him now ... Dr. Lecter *heard* the clink of the key ring as Pembry took it from the desk drawer.... [Lecter] sank his teeth in Pembry's face ... his nose and upper lip caught between *tearing teeth* [emphasis added; pp. 235–238].

Intriguingly, when Lecter has finished his attack, we are told, "Dr. Lecter's pulse was elevated to more than one hundred by the exercise, but quickly slowed to normal. He turned off the music and listened" (p. 239). His desire to rest after sating his appetite mirrors the Grimm wolf's actions after he gobbles up the grandmother and Red: "After the wolf had satisfied his desires, he lay down in bed again, fell asleep, and began to snore very loudly" (p. 95).

RUNNING DOWN THE FOREST PATH

In *The Trials and Tribulations of Little Red Riding Hood*, Jack Zipes (1993) details cultural and literary retellings of the tale from various countries. He explains that this tale has been altered rather drastically with regard to content (for example, in Charles Perrault's French version, our heroine is eaten and dies, while the Grimm version has a happy ending for everyone except the wolf), but the title character herself "has always been used as a warning to children, particularly girls, a symbol and embodiment of what might happen if they are disobedient and careless" (p. 17). Likewise, in *Little Red Riding Hood Uncloaked*, Orenstein (2002) reviews transformations of the tale from its origins through present-day representations. She asserts:

> Over the years, scholars have piled an entire cosmos of meanings on this small girl's shoulders. Some call her a seasonal myth, an allegory of the sun swallowed by night, or the personification of Good triumphing over Evil.... From a structural perspective, the plot is powerfully simple. Opposites collide—good and evil, beast and human, male and female. How the heroine negotiates this clash determines her fate [p. 4].

These interpretations of our fairy tale neophyte can readily be applied to Clarice Starling, the FBI agent-in-training portrayed by Jodie Foster in Jonathan Demme's Oscar-winning *The Silence of the Lambs* (1991).[2] The story, based upon Thomas Harris's novel of the same name, vividly shows the importance of women being neither careless nor disobedient in life. Structurally, the plot is as simple as the one described by Orenstein, as the primal opposites of good and evil, beast and human, male and female confront each other onscreen. Smith (1991) notes, "In cinematic terms, it pre-

cisely inverts the psycho-chases-girl format, in accordance with Harris'
novel" (p. 29), while Sundelson (1993), Simpson (2000), and Johnson
(2001) all argue that the film can be construed as a (post)modern fairy tale
with Johnson claiming, "*Silence* is fundamentally a fairytale which comments knowingly and ironically on the genre" (p. 28). Although the film
ostensibly revolves around a young agent on the trail of "Buffalo Bill"
(Ted Levine), a serial killer who has kidnapped a senator's daughter, the
most interesting parts of the film turn on this classic fairy tale relationship between agent Starling (an empowered Little Red Cap) and Anthony
Hopkins's Hannibal "The Cannibal" Lecter (a still very dangerous and
hungry wolf) as the captured psychiatrist who helps her construct a profile
of her psychopath.

The very first scene of *The Silence of the Lambs* transplants the viewer
into a forest setting that could have been envisioned by the Brothers
Grimm. Starling, a young, auburn-haired woman, is running alone along
a path while the camera tracks her from behind. We hear her breathing
heavily while Howard Shore's haunting score sets a tone of anxiety and
dread. This journey is interrupted mid-run when she is told to go see her
supervisor, Jack Crawford (Scott Glenn). As she makes her way out of the
forest, she jogs past a tree with five signs tacked on it. In order from top
to bottom, they read in all caps: "HURT," "AGONY," "PAIN," "LOVE-IT,"
and "PRIDE." These signs are obviously meant to serve as quick moments
of inspiration, placed strategically on the obstacle course. The first four
signs are easy-to-read; however, the pride-sign is so dirty and worn that it
is barely legible as if to say that pride will not be as easy for her to find
here as are the others.

"Little Red Cap" reveals the possible danger of wolves lurking just
off such paths in the dark woods; however, this film takes this warning and
carries it out of the forest and into "civilized" society. Starling's journey
to visit her supervisor, Jack Crawford, appears even more labyrinthine than
the obstacle course, for example, as she walks determinedly down angling
hallways and corridors that seem almost without end. At one point, Starling enters an elevator surrounded by a large group of much taller men
who are all wearing identical red polo shirts. She stands quietly in her grey
sweats as the elevator doors loudly shut. In this particular moment, she
appears just as isolated personally as when she was running alone physically, her femininity at risk of being completely devoured within this largely
masculine world.

Demme returns to this theme later in the film, as he shows Starling get purposefully and publicly ignored by a small-town sheriff and his group of police officers who prefer to talk solely with Crawford about the female body they have recently found. Crawford leads the sheriff and a male agent into a separate room, leaving Starling alone in the middle of another large group of much taller men, this time officers who are all dressed in identical police uniforms and matching hats. There is nothing distinctive about any one of them other than their surrounding male presence as they form a pack of wolves posturing for an alpha position in the presence of a suspicious stranger.

As agent-in-training Clarice Starling (Jodie Foster) cautiously faces the cannibalistic Dr. Lecter (Anthony Hopkins), his image is ominously reflected behind her in *The Silence of the Lambs* (Orion, 1991). *The Kobal Collection,* Ken Regan

CONVERSING AND DINING WITH THE WOLF

The DVD chapter that marks Starling's initial conversation with Crawford is entitled "An Interesting Errand." He tells her that the FBI is trying to create a general psycho-behavioral profile of serial killers and asks her to interview Hannibal "The Cannibal" Lecter, the notorious and brilliant psychiatrist known for eating his victims.[3] Crawford says that he does not expect Lecter to talk to her, and if he will not cooperate, Crawford asks that she simply report on what he and his cell look like. The supposed simplicity of this errand mirrors the one Little Red Cap's mother gives her to visit her ill grandmother with some cake and wine. The mother instructs her daughter very specifically:

> Get an early start, before it becomes hot, and when you're out in the woods, be nice and good and don't stray from the path, otherwise you'll fall and break the glass, and your grandmother will get nothing. And when you enter her room, don't forget to say good morning, and don't go peeping in all the corners [Grimm & Grimm, 2003, p. 93].

Much like Little Red Cap's mother, Crawford offers definitive guidance to his charge as well:

> I want your full attention, Starling. Be very careful with Hannibal Lecter. Dr. Chilton at the asylum will go over all the physical procedures used with him. Do not deviate from them for any reason whatsoever. And you're to tell him nothing personal, Starling. Believe me, you don't want Hannibal Lecter inside your head. Just do your job, but never forget what he is [Demme, 1991].

When she first encounters the wolf on the path, we are told that Little Red Cap naively answers all of his questions, because she does not know that he is a wicked animal that she should fear and avoid. When she later confronts the wolf dressed in her grandmother's nightgown, it is therefore not surprising that she is so quickly gobbled up. In marked contrast, Starling knows from the beginning that she will be visiting "a monster, pure psychopath"; however, she does not know the real reason for her visit. Crawford has actually sent her in as blindly as possible so that she can get information about Buffalo Bill. When Starling later questions him about why he kept this purpose from her, Crawford explains, "If I'd sent you in there with an actual agenda, Lecter would have known it instantly. He would have toyed with you, then turned to stone." Crawford realizes that a certain genuine innocence is necessary for her to build trust with Lecter, and Starling's inexperience and openness draw him to her.

As he leads her down to Lecter's cell, Dr. Chilton (Anthony Heald) smiles lasciviously, telling Starling, "And, oh, are you ever his taste." Despite the nearby presence of armed guards and a cell wall separating her from Lecter, Starling's first meeting with him is as tense as Little Red Cap's with her wolf. As she did when visiting Crawford, Starling must again make her way down a long series of passageways until she comes to Lecter's dark, windowless cell at the very end. He is standing behind a thick glass wall with air holes at the top, smiling politely and waiting patiently. He asks for her credentials and bids her, wolf-like, to come, "Closer, please. Closer." He gazes directly into her eyes, whiffs the air, and tells her the soap and perfume she uses.

When he learns that Crawford has sent a trainee, Lecter immediately becomes incredulous. Starling assures him, "Yes, I'm a student. I'm here to learn from you. Maybe you can decide for yourself if I'm qualified enough to do that." She engages him in some small talk, commenting on his detailed etchings of Florence before trying to get him to fill out her irrelevant questionnaire. Lecter chastises her, "Oh, no, no, no, no. You were doing fine. You'd been courteous and receptive to courtesy. You had established trust with the embarrassing truth about Miggs. And now this hamhanded segue into your questionnaire. It won't do." After she pushes him too firmly, he chillingly retorts, "A census taker once tried to test me. I ate his liver with some fava beans and a nice Chianti," revealing the wolf disguised under pleasantries.

Although Lecter is a cannibal in the truest sense, he does not merely feast upon his victims' bodies and organs. As Bliss and Banks (1996) note, "Lecter enjoys others' pain, drinking it in" (p. 114). What he most longs to consume from Clarice are personal memories and intense, barely buried emotions, and he is willing to trade "his knowledge for a taste of her soul" (Murphy, 1991, p. 32). In the chapter titled "Quid Pro Quo," Lecter explains, "If I help you, Clarice, it will be turns with us, too. Quid pro quo. I tell you things, you tell me things. Not about this case, though, about yourself. Quid pro quo." Thus, Starling has to feed him stories about herself and her past if she wants him to feed her information to help her find the serial killer and Catherine (Brooke Smith), the girl he most recently abducted. From this point on, their conversations take on a markedly similar style to the simple question-and-answer session of Little Red Cap as she interrogates her "grandmother" about her unusual appearance. As Bliss and Banks (1996) point out, "All of *Silence of the Lambs*'s conversations center on sex and the use of language as determinants of social responsibility and status, and further reveal how strongly the film is concerned with investigating the manner in which women are manipulated" (pp. 111–112).

The two most arguably climatic emotional scenes of "Little Red Cap" and *The Silence of the Lambs* share much in common stylistically. In each scenario, our young heroine is trying to ascertain the truth from the dangerous creature sitting directly in front of her. The sentences are choppy and matter-of-fact, and these conversations merely serve as oral appetizers for the hungry beasts, a prelude to their feasts. In "Little Red Cap," the wolf counters each of Red's observations regarding his big ears, then his big hands, and finally his big mouth, forcing her to judge him more and more critically. Rather than simply gobble her up when she enters the house, he engages the young girl in a bizarre give-and-take conversation that heightens the tension of the scene while making her judge the situation and her surroundings more analytically. He makes her the ultimate object of each of his assertions—syntactically and physically subject to his control—as he tells her that his big, masculine parts will allow him to better hear, grab, and, ultimately, eat her. Once his desires have been satisfied, he is ready for a good, long nap. In *The Silence of the Lambs*, Lecter engages Starling in a similar exchange:

LECTER: Of each particular thing, ask, what is it in itself? What is its nature? What does he do, this man you seek?

STARLING: He kills women.

LECTER: No, that is incidental.... What needs does he serve by killing?

STARLING: Anger, um, social acceptance, and, um, sexual frustration.

LECTER: No, he covets. That is his nature. And how do we begin to covet, Clarice? Do we seek out things to covet? ... No, we begin by coveting what we see every day. Don't you feel eyes moving over your body, Clarice, and don't your eyes seek out the things you want?

Like the wolf, Lecter creates a discourse in which he is in complete control. He has the answers, he has the training, and his verbal acumen allows him to better hear, grab, and consume her metaphorically. Lecter even brings the conversation back to Starling's physical body and its effect on male figures.

Little Red Cap is consumed completely by the wolf. When she is finally rescued by the hunter, she tells him that how frightening it was to be immersed within the darkness of this beast. Clarice, too, is consumed by her wolf, this time emotionally, as "Lecter's lucid and twisted discourse engenders a kind of love-making with Clarice" (Johnson, 2001, p. 29). In an effort to convince Lecter to give her the name of the serial killer, she tells him her deepest secret—why she ran away from her uncle's ranch where she lived after her father died. She explains that she was awakened by the horrible screaming of the spring lambs as they were slaughtered. When she tried to rescue them, they would not move, so she tried to carry the smallest one away. It was too heavy for her to carry far, and she was quickly apprehended by the sheriff. Thereafter, she was sent to an orphanage; her lamb was slaughtered. As the camera pans closely in on his face, Dr. Lecter takes in each morsel of her story and concludes, "You still wake up sometimes, don't you? Wake up in the dark and hear the screaming of the lambs? And you think if you save poor Catherine, you could make them stop, don't you? You think if Catherine lives, you won't wake up in the dark ever again to that awful screaming of the lambs?" Like the wolf in grandmother's nightclothes who patiently awaits Red's arrival, Lecter has allowed himself to remain caged and restrained (as seemingly harmless as that old, sickly granny) for this single moment of ravenous revelation. As guards come to escort Starling from the building, she breaks free of their grasp and races back to Lecter's cell to get her papers. As he passes them to her through the bars, his index finger lightly brushes against hers, a stolen moment of intimacy that signals the climax of their conversations. They will not talk again until the end of the film when he tells her that he has no plans to call on her.

Once the wolf has eaten the grandmother and Red, he falls asleep and lets his true nature show to the world and, arrogantly, to the woodsman passing by. He can discard his sartorial and mannerly disguise and once again be his true self after the feeding frenzy has finished. Similarly, Lecter can reveal himself after Starling serves up her childhood trauma. Once the guards have escorted her safely from the building, the symbolic equivalent of a waiter removing an empty plate following a first course, the DVD chapter segues to "His Second Meal," mirroring the wolf's two separate dinners. In all of his scenes leading up to this one, Lecter has appeared polite, calm, and cultivated—both physically and emotionally retrained. He is the embodiment of Walton's (2004) warning that, as a society, "we are becoming increasingly savage in our civility, to the point where our civility is actually beginning to consume us" (p. 34). In this gruesome chapter, the guards complain, "Son of a bitch demanded a second dinner, lamb chops, extra rare." Lecter expertly picks his handcuffs (using part of Dr. Chilton's stolen pen) and brutally attacks the unsuspecting guards, bludgeoning one to death and then eviscerating the other, hanging his flayed body in the center of the room like a work of perverse art.[4] Crane (1994) maintains that these "central set pieces celebrate the handiwork of the

killer in order to confirm for the audience that the multi-murderer on view
is a most talented specialist worthy of our undivided attention ... [We pay]
to see death choreographed by a master" (pp. 166–167). In both the novel
and the film, Lecter sits calmly in his open cell listening to his music following these attacks, his mouth covered in blood. Unlike the careless wolf,
however, this master killer knows that he must quickly assume another disguise if he is ever to caste off his chains—literally—and go into the world
of men. Wearing the uniform and face of the fallen Pembry, Lecter is
escorted from the building, loaded into an ambulance, and driven away.

TRYING ON GRANDMOTHER'S CLOTHES FOR SIZE

According to Orenstein (2002), one popular interpretation of "Little
Red Cap" claims that the title heroine, the wolf, and the grandmother ultimately form a single self, and they are all "multiple aliases for the same
body" (p. 241). *The Silence of the Lambs* plays with this idea, linking
Buffalo Bill, Lecter, and Starling thematically and symbolically. The opening menu of the DVD notably forms a bizarre composite picture focusing
on the top half of their faces, primarily the eyes, together with the moth
covering the lower half. The jumbled nature of identity is symbolized in
the film by Lecter's subtle clues and anagrams, like his "Your Self Storage" reference and his naming "Louis Friend," which forms an anagram
for the scientific name of fool's gold. Starling must listen carefully to his
every word and take in every intonation; thereafter, she must find the truth
hidden within his words. Indeed, as in "Little Red Cap," one of the major
themes of *The Silence of the Lambs* lies in understanding transformation
and in recognizing the true nature of others and oneself. When Lecter
decides to help Starling understand and find Buffalo Bill, he lectures, "First
principles, Clarice. Simplicity. Read Marcus Aurelius: Of each particular
thing ask, What is it in itself? What is its nature?" In Book II of the great
emperor's *Meditations*, Aurelius begins a discourse that could apply to the
journeys of Starling and Little Red Cap:

> When you wake up in the morning, tell yourself: The people I deal
> with today will be meddling, ungrateful, arrogant, dishonest, jealous,
> and surly. They are like this because they can't tell good from evil.
> But I have seen the beauty of good, and the ugliness of evil, and have
> recognized that the wrongdoer has a nature related to my own—not of

the same blood or birth, but the same mind, and possessing a share of the divine [p. 17].

When Red first bumps into the wolf, we learn that she has never been taught to fear the cunning wolf, and she cannot recognize his intrinsically evil nature. As far as her powers of perception go, the wolf is as innocent as she is. Lacking the ability to tell good from evil, Red blindly walks into her grandmother's house and into the wolf's ravenous trap. On a deeper level, Starling must learn not merely to recognize the various kinds of evil in the world, but also how connected good and evil can be.

During an autopsy of Buffalo Bill's first victim, Fredrica Bimmel, Starling finds the cocoon of an exotic moth lodged purposefully inside of her throat. When she discusses this unusual fact with Lecter, he explains, "The significance of the moth is change." He also corrects her immediate assumption that Buffalo Bill is a real transsexual or a man who truly even wants to become a woman. No, Lecter explains, "Billy hates his own identity" and this is what has led him to covet something specific about his innocent prey. As Demme explains in a 1991 interview with Gavin Smith, "This is someone who is so completely, completely horrified by who he is that his desperation to become someone completely other is manifested in his ill-guided attempts at transvestitism" (p. 37). Buffalo Bill's aliases, like John Grant, Jack Gordon, and Jame Gumb, have the same effect as Lecter's anagrams, names that are loosely tied together to his shaky identity.

In an early anthropological article entitled "The Cave Cannibals of South Africa" Bowker, Bleek, and Beddoe (1869) describe one means of common attack in which the cannibals craftily conceal their true intentions:

> If they saw a man going alone they went to him, they decoyed him, and made themselves out merciful people; they treated him kindly, and spoke gently with him; and appeared incapable of doing any evil. When the man was thus beguiled and entirely unsuspicious, regarding them as pleasant people only, they would then lay hold of him ... and carry him away to eat him [p. 126].

This same method of disguise is used by both Buffalo Bill and the wolf in "Little Red Cap." The wolf does not simply devour the young girl on the path as would be expected of a savage animal. With careful deliberation, he instead talks kindly to her, encouraging her to go off the path in search of flowers so that he can beat her to her destination, eat the grandmother, and disguise himself in her clothes.[5] Starling's profile of Buffalo Bill could easily be applied to the wolf, as she explains, "He's got real physical strength combined with an older man's self-control. He's cautious, precise. And he's never impulsive. He'll never stop. He's got *a real taste* for it now, and he's getting better at his work [emphasis added]." We should not assume that Little Red Cap is the wolf's first victim; clearly, he has been prowling these woods for a long time, and like Buffalo Bill, he too has a real taste for his work. When the hunter comes across the dozing wolf, he declares that he has found an old nemesis whom he has tracked for a long time. What makes the Grimm story of Little Red Cap so interesting is that she manages to escape while we assume that countless, nameless others were deceived, devoured, and digested.

Structurally, the scene of Catherine's abduction by Buffalo Bill is strikingly similar to that of Little Red Cap when she arrives at her grandmother's house. A kind of sixth sense warns her that something is not quite right as she approaches the house only to find the door already open. Rather than flee then and there, Little Red Cap still goes inside where she will have her infamous encounter. In order to trick Catherine, Buffalo Bill must pretend to be as helpless as an old woman; thus, he wears a fake cast on his arm instead of a grandmother's nightgown. He has beaten Catherine home from the grocery store, and he appears to be having great difficulty loading a sofa into his van outside of her apartment building. She is almost to her apartment door when she puts down her bag of groceries, hesitantly approaches him, and offers to help, telling him, "You look kind of handicapped." He angles the sofa just so and asks her to pull on it from inside the van. She looks a bit wary and seems to notice that no one is around. She glances to her apartment door and appears mildly comforted by her nearness to home. And so, like Little Red Cap, she acts against her better judgment and puts herself in direct danger. Buffalo Bill then reveals his true, able-bodied self, attacking her easily and out of sight.

The theme of evil hiding through the appearance of goodness is stunningly realized in a scene involving Lecter's escape from prison. With incredible speed and brutality he dispenses with the guards watching over him. After hanging one of the disemboweled guards from his cell, he then cunningly exchanges clothes with the other guard. Going a crucial step beyond the Grimm wolf, he severs the guard's face and uses it as a mask. As unsuspecting as Little Red Cap and Catherine, the other officers (and the audience) believe he is their fallen friend, and they remove him quickly to the safety of an ambulance. Meanwhile, we are led to believe that Lecter is still in the building, hiding on top of an elevator. Demme masterfully cuts between scenes of the officers firing bullets into the unmoving body of the officer in Lecter's clothes and of Lecter rising up in the ambulance and pulling off his human mask.[6] His disguise has worked as well as Buffalo Bill's, and his freedom is assured.

Both Sundelson (1993) and Badley (1995) postulate that Lecter's cannibalism transforms him in another primal manner: Consuming others allows him, in essence, to assume and pervert the role of mother. He literally takes life into his body, and through his education of Clarice, he even gives a kind of birth to a daughter who understands him. According to Badley, "It is Lecter's maternal qualities that give the film its final series of twists. Lecter avenges, protects, and instructs his/her protégé, however paradoxically, to 'save lives'" (p. 144). This theory ties nicely back to dear Little Red Cap who is both careless and reckless when she is eaten by the first wolf. When she jumps out of his stomach and back into the light, she is essentially reborn. Thus, when a second wolf hopes to trick her into leaving the path, Little Red Cap instead races directly to her grandmother's house to warn her about the beast and his intentions. She does not stop to chat, and she does not let herself be coerced into picking flowers. Starling, like the new Little Red Cap, comprehends the nature of the beast that has eaten her, and this knowledge can now serve and protect her.

Through all of their conversations, Lecter never gives Starling a simple answer to any of her questions. In this regard, their talks are like the fairy tales described by Bettelheim (1989), who claims, "It destroys the value of a fairy tale for the child if someone details its meaning for him" (p. 169). He provides his cryptic clues and anagrams for her to decipher, telling her during one crucial scene, "Look deep within yourself, Clarice Starling." She says that this reference to "yourself" seems "hokey" for Lecter, and she finds the "Your Self Storage" in Lecter's home city of Baltimore, Maryland that contains vital information. Nevertheless, in order for her to figure out Buffalo Bill's identity, she will have to look deep within herself and undergo the most fundamental, internal transformation in the film. At their first meeting, Lecter is not impressed with Starling, and he cuts through her professional manner by attacking her upbringing (in a put-on, southern accent oozing sarcasm):

> You know what you look like to me with your good bag and cheap
> shoes? You look like a rube, a well-scrubbed, hustling rube with a lit-
> tle taste. Good nutrition's given you some length of bone, but you're

not more than one generation from poor, white trash, are you Agent
Starling? And that accent you've tried so desperately to shed? Pure
West Virginia....

He becomes increasingly fascinated by her, however, particularly by the
reasons for her internal changes and growth since fleeing the ranch. He
comes to serve as a mentor of logic, and she feeds off of his knowledge
and intelligence just as he feeds off of her painful, personal memories. After
Lecter's escape, "Starling graduates from the role of passive interviewer
to dominant pursuer on a trail of horror" (Magill, 1991, p. 185), and she,
perhaps unconsciously, adopts his question-answer style to solve the case.
While talking with her FBI roommate, Ardelia Mapp (Kasi Lemmons),
Clarice returns to Lecter's interpretation of coveting that which we see every
day. The camera alternates in close-ups of her face and Ardelia's, (as it
had when Starling and Lector were talking). Starling actively assumes
Lecter's role of questioner, and Ardelia supplies logical answers. Together,
they surmise that the killer must have known his first victim, Fredrica Bimmel, an overweight girl who, like Little Red Cap's wolf, was found weighted
down and skinned. Starling drives to Bimmel's hometown in Ohio, continuing the investigation on her own and showing her development as an
independent investigator.

In another masterful juxtaposition of scenes, Demme again shows how
quickly appearances can deceive. Starling calls Crawford from Ohio to
inform him that Buffalo Bill is skinning his victims to make "a woman suit
out of real women," and she has a complete profile of him. Crawford cuts
her off in mid-sentence to say that they have located him and are on their
way to apprehend him. He tells her to stay there and finish up questioning
the locals while they go to Buffalo Bill's house in Illinois. Demme shows
Clarice learning that Bimmel did some sewing for an elderly woman named
Mrs. Lippmann, so she decides to go to her house. He parallel cuts to the
FBI approaching a small "grandmotherly" house and ringing the bell. He
then cuts to Buffalo Bill hearing a loud alarm in his basement. As the alarm
continues to ring, he begins to head upstairs. The FBI agents have surrounded a house and appear ready to apprehend him. When Buffalo Bill
opens the door, however, Agent Starling is standing outside quite alone. In
a cutaway scene, the FBI agents break through the door and windows of
the Illinois residence and discover an empty house. Now the audience and
Starling have taken on the role of Little Red Cap, having been falsely led
to believe that she would be safe on the path to visit old lady Lippmann.

EMERGING FROM THE DARK BELLY OF THE WOLF

Interspersed throughout the film are scenes of Starling going through physical training to become an agent. In addition to the obstacle course, she must handle one-on-one combat with male trainees and complete rigorous practice sessions. One of these sessions signals an important change from advice given to Little Red Cap by her mother. As Red prepares for her trip to grandmother's house, her mother reminds her not to waste time by looking into all of the corners of the old woman's house. Starling learns that peeping in all the corners is a necessity of her field, however. During one training session, a gun is placed to the back of her head, and she is pronounced dead. Her instructor asks, "Starling, where's your danger area?" Starling responds, "In the corner, sir." When asked if she checked her corner, she responds in the negative, and her instructor replies, "That's the reason you're dead."

In the DVD Chapter "Sniper in the Dark," Starling arrives at Ms. Lippman's house, never expecting that she will have to check any corners. Her training by both the FBI and Lecter now comes to completion as she questions Jame Gumb, aka Buffalo Bill, about Ms. Lippmann and Fredrica Bimmel. She notices sewing supplies throughout the house and then sees a moth land on a spindle of thread. As she prepares to draw her gun, Buffalo Bill realizes that she recognizes him as the killer, and he flees to his basement. The basement is as cavernous as the passageways leading to Crawford's office at the beginning of the film, and there are doors and rooms on all sides. As Murphy (1991) explains, "The process of filling her terrible emptiness, of silencing the lambs for good, is completed only when, through Starling's heroic descent into an actual hell, the real child in Jame Gumb's dark pit is released" (p. 32).

Starling checks every corner as she searches for the killer, and she blocks doors to limit Buffalo Bill's ability to maneuver. Then he cuts out the lights. She is now fully consumed by the darkness deep within the symbolic stomach of her wolf. He wears night-vision goggles and stalks her within arms reach, almost caressing her hair. We see her through his green lenses, terrified but thinking. In his interview with Smith, Demme seems particularly proud of this scene and its point-of-view:

> I relished that on a technique-of-making-a-movie level: the idea that we'll be predominantly in the shoes of the protagonist throughout, and then when she's deprived of her sight, we'll be in the shoes of the

killer. And perhaps that abandonment of Clarice's point of view will make the situation even more distressing on a certain dialectic level [p. 33].

When Buffalo Bill cocks his gun to shoot Starling, she reflexively turns and shoots a round of bullets through him and a basement window. Demme explains, "[W]hen Jodie finally shoots down Jame Gumb, I wanted to avoid the obligatory triumphant shot of Clarice's face. I wanted to respect her privacy at the moment of having just taken a life. And the camera doesn't travel to her. It goes in on Gumb" (p. 36). Light streams in, signaling that she and Catherine—like Little Red Cap and her grandmother—can now emerge, reborn smarter and stronger, into the sunshine. This scene can be tied to Bettelheim's (1989) interpretation of the Grimm fairy tale as well, as he explains, "Little Red Cap, having been projected into inner darkness (the darkness inside the wolf), becomes ready and appreciate of a new light, a better understanding of the emotional experiences she has to master" (p. 181).

After Little Red Cap dispenses with the second wolf, the Grimm Brothers assure us that she "went merrily on her way home, and no one harmed her" (p. 96). In much the same manner, Demme assures us that, although wolves like Lecter are still at-large, Starling has learned her lessons and is now safe as well. The film returns Starling to the academy, only instead of racing along an ominous obstacle course in a bulky sweatsuit, she is now walking across a stage in a tailored suit on her graduation day. In marked contrast to the touch stolen earlier by Lecter, Starling receives a lingering, respectful handshake from Crawford, the woodsman whose skills are no longer needed. He exits so that Starling can take an unexpected phone call from the wolf making another appearance. With seeming sincerity, Lecter asks, "Well, Clarice, have the lambs stopped screaming?" Starling is immediately on her guard and looks carefully around the corner, scanning the room. He continues, "I have no plans to call on you, Clarice. The world is more interesting with you in it. So you take care now to extend me the same courtesy.... I do wish we could chat longer, but I'm having an old friend for dinner. Bye." The camera pulls away from Starling's expression of horror, and her realization that she has stopped one predator while another more fearsome one remains on the loose, and cuts to a focused Lecter. Disguised under a blond wig and hat, and dressed in an all-white suit, he follows the vacationing Dr. Chilton as he exits a plane in the tropics. Sharrett (1993) argues that the film's ending shows "the inevitability of violence" in a world without simple endings, while Walton (2004) compellingly asserts that "the placement of the white Lecter in a white suit amid a sea of non-white faces spotlights him as the new savage" (pp. 145–146). Picart and Frank (2004) assert that Lecter's "subsequent disappearance into the anonymity of public space—the sphere of the normal, the visible, the known—also enacts the blurring of the two domains" of normal and otherness (p. 220). The credits begin to roll, and the audience walks out of the dark theater, having learned like Little Red Cap that cunning wolves cannot always be recognized, and that they can never be satisfied.

TWO

A Rose by
Any Other Name

"Brier Rose" and
Scream

A GRIMM VIEW OF THE FAIRY TALE
SERIAL KILLER

We can safely assume that Little Red Cap's wolf and Hansel and Gretel's witch spent years trapping such young prey in anticipation of enjoying yet another hearty meal. The primary concern of these storybook stalkers is for their culinary creations, and their life's purpose seems set on satisfying their epicurean endeavors. In addition to learning how important it is for them to stay on a clear and steady path, children also learn that gluttony leads to an inevitable, ironic downfall. The wolf's final meal of Little Red Cap and her grandmother is replaced with heavy stones, and the witch is baked alive in her own oven. In these stories, the children return home a bit more prepared to watch out for their own hunger as well as that of others.

Simpson (2000) notes that "tales of multiple murder have always attracted a disproportionate amount of public attention and often appear in oral folklore.... This may be so because folklore, essentially verbal in nature, considers repetition of key images and phrases a vital structural component to begin with, and so finds a metaphoric parallel to a series of murders" (p. 3). In her discussion of a specific type of serial murder, Maria Tatar (1995) defines the German term *Lustmord* as "sexual murder," noting, "the German term *Lust*—which implies desire and pleasure along with sexual gain—captures more precisely the multiple dimensions of the motives driving this type of killing" (pp. 7–8). The Grimm Brothers give us several examples of this unique kind of stalker, one driven by passions of the heart rather than pangs of the stomach. In most of these tales, the victims are brutally slain when they fail to complete a nearly impossible task to win the hand—if not always the heart—of a beautiful maiden. What makes these tales truly compelling is that, although the relentless stalkers are always dispensable, interchangeable males, their killers are always singularly beautiful females who collect dead suitors as greedily as the forest wolf seeks out his next underage happy meal. We are treated to a sly role reversal in which the woman wields the ultimate authority, that is, until she is forced to yield her independence to that one victorious man.

In "The Six Servants," we learn of an old queen who uses her daughter's beauty to lure many young men to their doom. She tells the would-be suitors that they must perform a specific and extraordinary task. When they fail, they must kneel down and have their heads chopped off. A prince decides to try his luck and travels to the queen. Along the way, he picks up six servants with bizarre abilities to grow fatter; to hear everything in the world; to grow taller; to shatter anything with a look; to freeze in heat and become hot in the cold; and to see anything in the world. Each of these servants allows him to complete an otherwise impossible task devised by the queen, and he is eventually awarded her daughter.

In the similarly themed, "The White Snake," a handsome servant tastes the secret dish of his king—the white snake of the title—and is given the power to communicate with animals. He makes his way into the world and saves the lives of three fish, an army of ants, and some young ravens. All promise to repay his kindness. He later learns of a king who has, not surprisingly, a beautiful daughter looking for a husband. Her suitors must complete a difficult task, and when they do not, they are put to death. With the help of his animal friends, he is able to retrieve a ring from the sea, pick up scattered millet, and fetch an apple from the Tree of Life in order to prove his worth to the proud king's daughter. The two finally marry and live in peace and happiness.

Like the two stories above, "The Riddle," also centers on a young man who will try courting a lovely, deadly maiden. This particular tale is divided into two distinct sections, however. In the first part, our fearless prince encounters a witch who tries to poison him. She gives a tainted drink to his servant, but the glass breaks and its evil contents spill on his horse, which dies instantly. A raven begins eating the horse, and the servant kills it for later. He and the prince then happen upon a tavern frequented by twelve murderers. They are fed infected raven soup and all die. In the second section, the prince and his servant learn of a beautiful, intelligent princess who will only accept as her husband the man who can devise a riddle that she cannot solve. Having failed in this task, nine men have already been beheaded by the time this prince arrives. His riddle ties back to his first adventure, as he asks her, "What is it that slew nobody and yet slew twelve?" She is only able to solve the riddle by questioning him asleep; however, he grasps her cloak and is able to prove to the judges that she cheated. Thus, she must marry him, wearing her cloak as a wedding dress.

Each of these tales features a male protagonist on a mission to win himself a bride of renowned beauty. The bride-to-be is a reluctant—and dangerous—wife, however, portrayed as a proud and haughty prize. As Tatar (2003) explains, "In short, male heroes demonstrate from the start a meekness and humility that qualify them for an ascent to wealth, the exercise of power, and happiness crowned by wedded bliss; their female counterparts undergo a process of humiliation and defeat that ... signals a loss of pride and the abdication of power" (p. 95). Stripped of their fairy tale allure and inevitable happy endings, these tales feature relentless stalking as their primary romantic gesture. Prior to being "won," the female figure endures the apparently unwanted advances of countless, nameless young men. With each manly defeat that ends in death, her desirability reaches mythic levels, and as the body count rises, we learn that the only way to stop her bloody courtship is through a misogynistic marriage. As an unmarried, virginal, and beautiful young woman, she is repeatedly presented as a self-centered and maniacal monster, and we are taught to cheer her defeat.

"Brier Rose" (commonly called "Sleeping Beauty") possesses the same basic plot as these tales, but it does differ from them in several impor-

Opposite: **Unaware of the men who have died in the protective thorns surrounding her castle, young Brier Rose remains asleep as a prince approaches her bed. (Illustration by E. H. Wehnert from *Household Stories Collected by the Brothers Grimm*. London: Routledge and Sons, 1880.)**

tant areas. In this oft-told tale, the dozing bride is still a famously sought-after object of perfection whose reported beauty seduces foolish princes to their untimely deaths, this time in the impenetrable thorny brier surrounding her castle. However, she is not a willing—or even knowing—participant in these ritual courtship slayings. It appears that she is completely unaware of the spell cast upon her (and her kingdom) to fall into a sleep of 100 years upon her fifteenth birthday, and when she awakens coincidentally to the kiss of a fortunate prince, she is overjoyed to find a strange suitor at her bedside. Everyone awakens, completely unconcerned about the number of male corpses scattered outside the castle walls, and a wedding is celebrated in classic fairy tale style.

SOFTENING THE SPELL, PART I

The opening scene of Wes Craven's 1996 horror film *Scream* mimics the essential elements of "Brier Rose," as we are introduced to a teenage girl left home alone. In his screenplay for the film *Scream*, Kevin Williamson (1997) describes Casey Becker as "a young girl, no more than sixteen. A friendly face with innocent eyes" (p. 1), and as played by Drew Barrymore, she embodies these qualities as well as those used to describe the teen Brier Rose: "The girl was so beautiful, polite, kind, and sensible that whoever encountered her could not help but adore her" (Grimm & Grimm, 2003, p. 172). The audience needs to care about this young girl immediately, and Craven's use of an established young actress whom the audience has seen grow up is imperative.[1] Like Brier Rose, she lives in an enormous home, a kind of modern-day palace supposedly secluded from the dangers of the outside world, and she roams happily from room to room while preparing popcorn. As Clover (1992) notes in *Men, Women, and Chain Saws*, however, "The house or tunnel may at first seem a safe haven, but the same walls that promise to keep the killer out quickly become, once the killer penetrates them, the walls the hold the victim in" (p. 31). This idea harks back to Brier Rose's tale, as the heroine stumbles across danger within the confines of her own home.

Crane (2004b) points out that modern horror filmmakers often "employ new machinery to spindle and fold the flesh" of their young victims (p. 163). In *Scream*, the telephone replaces the spindle as a symbol of an everyday, practical object that ultimately bodes great pain and the possibility of death. Thus, the tone shifts dramatically when Casey receives a phone call from an unknown stranger. They flirt harmlessly at first and discuss scary movies from *Halloween* (1978) to *A Nightmare on Elm Street* (1984).[2] Much like Brier Rose, who has no idea that she is being watched and stalked in her slumber, Casey suddenly snaps out of her relaxed state when her unknown caller reveals that she is being watched. After she learns that her boyfriend is tied up outside, the assumed safety of her palace is called into question as "the terror occurs in an environment long familiar and secure, but now, suddenly, a perverse death-trap haunted by the unfamiliar" (Wilson, 1999, p. 152). When she pleads, "Why are you doing this,"

Scream (Miramax, 1996): Having witnessed her boyfriend's murder just outside her home, young Casey Becker (Drew Barrymore) prepares to defend herself against the masked killer with a sharp knife. *The Kobal Collection*

the caller insists that he wants to play a game. Again, like Brier Rose, she is not allowed to know the true purpose behind the stalking, and she is forced to play along in accordance with horror movie rules in place of fairy tale spells. When she incorrectly identifies the serial killer in the original *Friday the Thirteenth* (1980) as Jason (rather than Jason's psychotic mother), her boyfriend is brutally murdered outside the supposed safety of her home, and the killer continues to torment her, asking her to identify which door he is at as she cowers behind the television.

A chair is suddenly thrown through the patio doors, and our heroine flees through the kitchen and out the back door after grabbing a large butcher knife.[3] Still holding the phone, she tries to sneak to the front yard. She sees her parents driving up a long, lonely road. When it appears that she just might be able to signal them in time, the killer stabs her in the chest, but she is able to kick him off of her in a last-minute attempt to escape. Her parents arrive home and enter the house just as their defense-less daughter is about to reach them. The killer stabs her again and drags the near-lifeless Casey away while she clutches the phone. Inside the house, the panicked mother picks up the phone to call the police only to hear her dying daughter's final breaths. Like Brier Rose's parents, who oddly choose to leave their daughter alone even though they know what is to happen on her fifteenth birthday, they have arrived home *almost* in time to save her. Neither set of parents is able to prevent the inevitable attack.

In the Grimm fairy tale, a wise (but vengeful) woman who is furious at having not been invited to the royal daughter's birth casts a spell so that she will die by pricking her finger on a spindle on her fifteenth birthday. One of the invited wise women explains that she cannot undo this spell entirely, but she can soften it somewhat, and she commands that, instead of death, the princess will fall asleep for a period of one hundred years. The former, fatal spell can be viewed as the one that befalls poor Casey Becker; her death is unavoidable. The softened, sleeping spell can then be considered the one cast upon our principal heroine, Sidney Prescott (Neve Campbell), who will continue being stalked by a nameless, faceless killer as the body count increases throughout the film.

SLEEPING WITHOUT THE ENEMY

When we first meet Sidney, she is, appropriately enough, getting ready for bed. She is dressed in a flannel nightgown, and her hair is pulled back in a ponytail. Williamson describes her as "a young girl of seventeen, ... [s]harp and clever with deep, lonely eyes" (p 28). She hears a noise at the window of her second-story bedroom and is surprised by the appearance of her boyfriend, Billy (Skeet Ulrich), "[a] young, strapping boy of sev-enteen. Handsome and alluring. A star quarterback/class president type of guy. He sports a smile that could last for days" (p. 29). He appears prince-like by climbing through the window. During a fairly intimate kissing session, music plays in the background, as we hear a love song promising a man's fidelity to a young woman. Sidney stops Billy from going too far, and we learn that she is a virgin. Virginity seems equally fundamental to most fairy tale and horror film heroines, especially those who must be won by a prince. Thus Snow White remains chaste and unchanged in her glass coffin until the prince rescues her, while Brier Rose goes into her century-long sleep upon reaching puberty. Her sleeping becomes a metaphor for her purity, and she can only be reawakened as a woman when the time is exactly right (Ashliman, 2004).

In comparing horror films to fairy tales, Brottman (1997) suggests:

> Most traditional horror films share the functions of the fairy tale in that they serve to teach their (mainly adolescent) audience of the dangerous consequences of inappropriate sexual (and other) behavior, thereby serving as a ritual process of acculturation for the modern adolescent, just as the fairy tale helps the child come to terms with many of the psychological problems of growing up [p. 108].

Historically, traditional horror films have taught us that the "good" girl typically lives long enough to fight the villain (and usually to survive for the sequel) while the "bad" girl is usually killed along with her randy boyfriend shortly after they have consummated their relationship. The aptly-named Randy (Jamie Kennedy), the horror-film guru of *Scream*, explains that Jamie Lee Curtis's virginal heroine in such horror classics as the aforementioned *Halloween*, as well as *Prom Night* (1980) and *Terror Train* (1980), must remain pure in all of her horror films: "That's why she always outsmarted the killer in the big chase scene at the end. Only virgins can do that." He goes on to explain, "There are certain rules that one must abide by in order to successfully survive a horror movie. For instance, number one, you can never have sex. Big no-no! Big no-no! Sex equals death, ok?"

Throughout the film, Sidney's innocence is contrasted with her mother's overt sexuality and marital duplicity. Williamson describes a snapshot of her mother as "an older version of Sidney" (p. 46). We learn that her mother was murdered one year earlier, and that Sidney provided the eye-witness testimony that led to the (wrongful) conviction of Cotton Weary (Liev Schreiber). Since that time, she has lived in denial that her mother could have been the town adulteress. In the school bathroom, Sidney overhears a cheerleader (Leonora Scelfo) comment, "Maybe she's a slut, just like her mother." The cheerleader implies that Sidney could be the killer and explains, "Her mother's death leaves her disturbed and hostile in a cruel and inhumane world. She's delusional. Where's God, etcetera? Completely suicidal. One day, she snaps. She wants to kill herself, but she realizes teen suicide is out this year, and homicide is a much healthier, therapeutic expression." Preserving her virginity allows Sidney to protect her chaste maternal image from the rumors that pervade the town. At the same time, Sidney's reluctance to accept this painful truth leads her into a kind of somnambulistic state that prevents her from picking up on hidden clues to the killer. In the DVD commentary, Williamson posits that Sidney could likely figure out who the killer is if she could simply come to terms with the facts about her mother. Similarly, if Brier Rose were simply told the facts about her curse, then she might not rush up to the poisonous spindle so rapidly and vapidly. Both heroines must complete their personal journeys at their own pace and in their own time.

Although she is rewarded with a story named in her honor, Brier Rose at first appears to be the dullest of heroines, particularly when compared to some of the Grimms' other fearsome fiancées. After all, she is primarily known for sleeping. It is important to keep in mind, however, just how powerful she is, even while she appears quietly manipulated by circumstances beyond her control. After Brier Rose is pricked, her slumber infects all of those around her: The king, queen, servants, and even the animals and insects all fall asleep at exactly the same time and in the middle of their everyday tasks. The world really does await her awakening. Likewise, after Sidney is attacked in her own home, a deep sleep is thrust upon the town. The principal cancels all classes and sends the students home. A town-wide curfew is also put into effect, sequestering everyone into their homes for an early night's rest. As businesses close and cars drive home, the song "Red Right Hand" by Nick Cave and the Bad Seeds plays eerily in the background, suggesting that a communal sleep has overtaken the town, and that a mysterious man who is not quite what he appears will suddenly appear out of their nightmares and dreams. Noticing the quiet that envelopes her town at sunset, Sidney compares Woodsboro to *The Town that Dreaded Sundown* (1977), in which a character known as the Phantom terrorizes a small town. Sidney knows that the killings of her mother, Casey, and Steve are all linked to her in some way, but, unlike Brier Rose, she also witnesses the wide-ranging effects her circumstances have on the town around her.

Ascending the Winding Staircase

One of the more striking elements of "Brier Rose" lies in the inherent inevitability of the events that are to follow. Her father can have all of the spindles destroyed within his kingdom, and he can try his best to keep her safe within the confines of the castle, but he cannot stop the spell from coming to fruition. Tatar (2003) describes this aspect of the fairy tale as "prohibition/violation," arguing that "these paired functions stand as one of the fairy tale's most fundamental plot sequences. As soon as we learn about the dire consequences that will attend the mere touching of a spindle, we know that Brier Rose will somehow search out and find the only spindle left in her father's kingdom" (p. 165).[4] Craven and Williamson understand that this same inevitability must be played out in the so-called "slasher" film. The audience knows that the nubile and dispensable casts of *Halloween* and *Friday the Thirteenth* should never open that closet door, investigate that strange sound, or, heaven forbid, turn around with a sigh of relief, believing that the killer is really, really dead. They are bound by the confines of their genre, however, just like our sweet Brier Rose. Surely each child who hears the tale must wonder why her parents would decide to leave their daughter alone on the very day that the spell is to take effect. As teenagers, these same children would no doubt scream orders to the screen as another dumb teenager makes a foolish and fatal turn into Jason's axe. Yet they are like the obsessive princes who make their way towards Brier Rose, all the while knowing that death is more likely to greet them than a beautiful maiden.

The events leading to Brier Rose's finally pricking her finger build the same kind of suspense as a teenager on the run. We know what the outcome will be, and now we must simply wait as she meanders aimlessly around her home. She goes in and out of chambers and doors until she finally happens upon a tower room with a narrow, winding staircase leading to a hidden upper room. She heads up the stairs where finds an old woman—and her destiny—spinning away in a tiny room. This scene closely parallels Sidney at home alone on the day after her father has left town. She arrives home from school and casually walks up the back deck into the house. She goes through various rooms and opens the closet by the front door. Eventually, she lies down to take a nap. She is awakened when her friend Tatum (Rose McGowan) calls to say that she is coming over. Sidney hangs up, and the phone—again acting as the killer's pointed spindle—rings once more. She asks who is calling and says, "I have no idea" when asked to guess. When the killer refers to scary movies, she assumes that Randy has called from the video store. She answers without irony when the killer asks her why she doesn't like scary movies, calmly explaining one of the main plotlines: "It's just, what's the point? They're all the same. Some stupid killer stalking some big-breasted girl who can't act, who's always running up the stairs when she should be going out the front door. It's insulting."

We know that Brier Rose must ascend the tower staircase and go into the hidden room with the spinning wheel. Like all maidens, she must meet her fate in order to mature fully into womanhood and earn her happy ending. In *Scream*, Sidney must largely follow the rules of her genre as well, even though she knows how to subvert them. In her critique of horror films, Dika (1990) claims, "Moreover, the central question asked by the stalker film game is not so much Will he win? but *Where is the killer?* and *When will he strike?* [emphasis added]" (p. 22). *Scream* directly addresses this issue in the introductory scene when the killer tells the unsuspecting Casey, "I want to know who I'm looking at" and then demands that she guess behind which door he's lurking before he finally attacks. Sidney carries on her conversation with the killer calmly and nonchalantly, even when the sinister voice tells her, "The question isn't 'Who am I?' The question is *'Where am I?'"*

Going against audience expectations, Sidney bravely (perhaps naively) walks outside with her cordless phone when the killer says that he is calling from her front porch. She looks around incredulously, picks her nose, and asks the killer to tell her what she is doing. When he does not respond, she prepares to hang up. At this point, the killer tells her that she will die just like her mother. As she races inside and locks the front door, the killer lunges at her from the closet, and she is forced to follow the exact horror film rules that she ridiculed just moments earlier. Crane (2004a) points out that *Scream* and its imitators rely heavily on "a fan's familiarity with the rules of the game," increasing audience involvement in films that "are both serious—they can be very threatening—and they jest" (pp. 147–148). The audience is rewarded for its horror film knowledge as Sidney runs *up the stairs* to escape into her bedroom. Billy climbs through her bedroom window, and she embraces him until a cell phone falls from his pocket. She fears that he is the killer unmasked, and she now runs *out the front door* to find that the police have arrived. Her bedroom, despite its lacey curtains and stuffed animals, now represents a place of danger and, apparently, very easy access by uninvited intruders. Like Brier Rose, Sidney is surrounded by death, but she does not yet recognize her connection to the victims nor does she understand her role in stopping these deaths. She must become an active participant and not a passive victim-in-waiting.

STALKING THE FAIRY PRINCESS

The killer, while often invincible enough to survive for the obligatory sequel, is not invulnerable. Once the mask is donned, the killer also risks his own life, as horror film convention requires his climatic confrontation with the character defined by Clover (1992) as the Final Girl:

> She is intelligent, watchful, and levelheaded; the first character to
> sense something amiss and the only one to deduce from the accumu-
> lating evidence the pattern and extent of the threat; the only one, in
> other words, whose perspective approaches our own privileged under-
> standing of the situation. We register her horror as she stumbles on
> the corpses of her friends. Her momentary paralysis in the face of
> death duplicates those moments of the universal nightmare experi-
> ence—in which she is the undisputed "I"—on which horror frankly
> trades [p. 45].

In films from the *Halloween* and *Friday the 13th* series, the audience roots for the Final Girl as she stabs, shoots, burns, and even beheads the killer. It is important to keep in mind that, while the Final Girl may well survive the final reel, sequels to these films tend to emphasize a disturbing end for her. As the series continue, the killer emerges yet again, dispensing with her in the opening scene to make room for the next girl in the cycle. In the first minutes of *Friday the 13th, Part II* (1981), the original's lone survivor, Alice (Adrienne King), is tracked down and killed in her own home by Jason. While Jamie Lee Curtis's Laurie survives *Halloween* (1978), *Halloween II* (1981), and the Kevin-Williamson-penned *Halloween H20* (1998), in which we are led to believe that she decapitates Michael, her brother returns and kills her in *Halloween: Resurrection* (2002). For all her intelligence and vigilance, the Final Girl is taught that she cannot ever truly escape the male grasp.

In "Brier Rose," the suitors who find themselves ensnared in the protective brier of thorns surrounding their prey come across just as mechanistic as Michael and Jason. And they are just as relentless: They are all willing to risk their lives in their pursuit of the sleeping bride, a girl they have never actually seen. Reviving her becomes part of their mission, along with the male bragging rights that would accompany such an achievement. Brier Rose becomes a legend, and "a tale about her began circulating throughout the country," (p. 187) making her the Final Girl of the fairy tale, the one worthy of being chased again and again. The death of each suitor merely adds to her legend and worthiness as a potential mate. After years of pursuit and grisly deaths, the princes continue to stalk her until one—it does not matter which one—is finally allowed to reach her.

One hundred years pass from the time that Brier Rose is pricked to the time her prince arrives to greet her. He happens to be the first man to arrive at the moment when she is to awaken, and she has no idea just how many men have died trying to reach her. The *Scream* series plays with the idea of having the right man come along at exactly the right moment and inverts it in several ways. We learn throughout the original film that our Final Girl, Sidney, may be dating Billy, but her platonic friends Stu (Matthew Lilliard) and Randy both have crushes on her. And while she actually bucks the trend and survives the sequels, her suitors and protectors do not. Thus, their bodies start piling up like princes caught in the surrounding hedge. In *Scream 2* (1997), Sidney's story—like that of Brier Rose—gains popularity outside of her control as a film is released based upon what happened to her. Randy, still pining for Sidney, is brutally slaughtered, as are her boyfriend Derek (Jerry O'Connell) and the male detectives assigned to guard her. When the killer calls Sidney, he sarcastically refers to her as "girlfriend," and red herrings are left to make it appear that her new boyfriend could be the killer. As *Scream 3* (2000) opens, we learn that Sidney has isolated herself completely from the world, having changed her name and moved to a small house in the country. This film alludes to the disturbing Laurie/Michael relationship by having the killer be Sidney's long-lost, psychotic brother (Scott Foley). The lone male who can be trusted— and who lives through each of the films—is David Arquette's Deputy Dewey, a child-like innocent who serves as no sexual threat to our Final Girl.

At any moment in *Scream*, we are led to believe that brave Prince Charming could turn into psychotic Prince Harming. Using horror-movie logic, Randy argues that Billy is the likely killer all along: "There's always some stupid, bullshit reason to kill your girlfriend. That's the beauty of it all—simplicity. Besides, if it get's too complicated, you lose your target audience." Fairy tales employ a similar simplicity as well to teach their lessons. Thus, we readily accept the convenient, last-minute emergence of the hunter in "Red Riding Hood" and the appearance of the helpful dwarfs in "Snow White." One of the fascinating aspects of "Brier Rose" is that we have made her tale more complex by requiring (at least in the Disney version of the tale) a specific prince's kiss as the defining moment that awakens the young bride to her new life. According to the curse, she could simply awaken on her own at the conclusion of the one hundred years, and the prince's victory is predicated upon nothing more than happenstance and coincidence.

A number of folklore critics, most notably Bruno Bettelheim (1989) in *The Uses of Enchantment: The Meaning and Importance of Fairy Tales*, tie Brier Rose's loss of innocence to the psychosexual images of her climbing the tower, turning the rusty key, and finally getting pricked on the spindle. The pricking can be viewed as a sexual symbol that signals the start of her menstruation cycle. After this has finally occurred, she can be pursued by countless, eager men and prepare for her eventual, inevitable marriage. When Brier Rose wakes up, however, she does not really appear any wiser, nor is she particularly selective in choosing her mate. The lesson here implies that by simply waiting for the prince to arrive, the princess will be incapable of making a foolish choice.

After the initial slayings, Sidney and her friends talk through a profile of the killer. Stu argues that a man would have to be the killer, since a man's strength would be necessary "to hollow out" the victims. His girlfriend, Tatum, responds that what is really needed for such crimes is "a man's brutality." The audience knows that the killer is likely male, and we are alternately led to trust and mistrust all of the male characters, particularly the boyfriends. After Billy is arrested as a possible suspect, Sidney receives a phone call from the killer. He mocks her, stating, "An innocent guy doesn't stand a chance with you.... Looks like you fingered the wrong guy. Again." Here, the killer ironically implicates Sidney as the wrongdoer who does away with supposedly innocent men like Billy and Cotton Weary (Liev Schreiber), whom she identified as her mother's rapist and killer. Jancovich (1996) claims that most horror film killers "are presented as blank mechanistic automatons" (p. 230) along the lines of the masked Michael Myers and Jason. Any man can put on the mask and assume the role of the killer, stalking victims in anonymity and without remorse.

In contrast to Brier Rose, who remains untouched during the length of the spell, Sidney can only open her eyes following the willing loss of her virginity. Her reawakening is tied directly to the moment that she decides to sleep with Billy. She determines, "I can't keep lying to myself about who my mom was. I think I'm really scared that I'm going to turn out just like her, you know, like 'the bad seed,' or something." Yet, her trust in Billy does not grow stronger following their dangerous liaison. In keeping with the themes of "postmodern horror," Sidney discovers the root of sexual terror which Badley (1995) defines as "part of a much larger anxiety about gender, identity, mortality, power, and loss of control" (p. 14). Thus, instead of post-coital relief or pleasure following her first sexual encounter, Sidney instead reflects upon the sinister phone call that she received while Billy was in jail. She asks him whom he called with his one phone call. When he replies that he phoned his father, she responds that the sheriff did that. He leans in closely and menacingly and asks her what he must do to prove that he is not the killer. And just when Sidney seems most prepared to piece the mystery together, the killer appears and stabs Billy. In effect, Sidney's boyfriend, whose alibi she has just questioned, is immediately replaced by her stalker, whose motive she has still not yet determined. She flees into the darkness, terrified and alone with no idea who the killer truly is.

CONFRONTING PARENTAL GUILT AND COMPLICITY

In describing the basic elements of slasher and stalker films, Hutchings (2004) explains, "The whodunit structures adopted by these films involve their characters having to probe into the past—either their own past or *the past of their community*—in order to make sense of the present and then be able to act decisively on the basis of the knowledge thus acquired [emphasis added]" (p. 215). As far as we know, Brier Rose is never warned by her parents about the impending curse and how it came to be. Instead of simply telling her to stay away from spindles, her father goes to the trouble of having all of the spindles in the kingdom burned, ostensibly destroying the danger to his daughter, but also destroying the item most closely associated with his tragic error. He invited relatives, friends, and acquaintances to the celebration in addition to twelve of the wise women; thus, the exclusion of one wise woman seems particularly pointed as she is made a social outcast throughout the land and within her own group. Ultimately, the king and queen's silence, as well as that of their entire kingdom, creates an aura of guilt that pervades the story. The Grimm Brothers likely consider the parents and kingdom at least partly to blame since they (a) have the entire town fall asleep at the time Brier Rose pricks her finger and (b) allow the vindictive wise woman—as opposed to Red's wolf and Snow White's stepmother—to escape unscathed.

The final moments of the film focus on Sidney's confrontation with the killer and the truth about her (and her mother's) past. She is cornered in the kitchen where she and the audience learn that there are actually two killers: Billy, whose earlier stabbing death was staged, and his accomplice Stu. They both wore the same black, flowing costume with white ghost mask and used the same voice box to disguise their voices. When disguised as the killer, the two men are as indistinguishable as the men who pursue the sleeping Brier Rose. They even employ the identical technique of wiping the blade clean after stabbing a victim, just like two young men who share their special "moves" in the bedroom. They explain that a year has passed since they killed Sidney's mother and framed Cotton Weary, and tonight they plan on killing her in a final slaughter. When Sidney tells them that they've seen one too many scary movies, Billy quickly tells her not to blame horror films for their actions. He also reveals his motive and, for the first time to Sidney, the full extent of her mother's infidelities. Billy explains that Sidney's mother had affairs with multiple men including his father, which led to his parents' divorce and his mother leaving town. Just as Brier Rose spent years wandering around in ignorance that kept her in danger tied to a specific date (her fifteenth birthday), Sidney has suffered by not knowing the truth about her family and boyfriend until the anniversary of her mother's death. With the truth finally told, they bring out Sidney's father, gagged and bound, and tell her that they plan to frame him for all of the killings. Then they stab each other—violently but not mortally—so that they will look like victims who just barely survived his rampage.

No fairy tale is complete without a happy ending for its heroine, and *Scream* combines the final, requisite horror scares with clever details that connect the film back to fairy tale lore. Gale Weathers (Courtney Cox), a television reporter who can be viewed as one of the wise women in "Brier Rose" (she knows what is happening but cannot really stop it) arrives, declaring a bit too triumphantly, "I've got an ending for you. The reporter left for dead in the news van comes to, stumbles on you two dipshits, finds the gun, foils your plan, and saves the day." Upon hearing this, Sidney replies, "I like that ending." No one else can write an ending for her, however, and Gale is quickly knocked unconscious. As Billy and Stu prepare to kill Gale, Sidney is able to sneak away with her father.

Newitz (1995) comments that the male serial killer "kills off the 'feminine vulnerability' in himself when he kills women, and thus proves himself a man" (p. 40). In an intriguing gender reversal, Sidney calls Billy and Stu using their voice box to assume the killer's threatening tenor, asking, "Are you alone in the house? ... We're going to play a little game. It's called: Guess who just called the police and reported your sorry motherfucking ass!" When Billy threatens to kill her, she reveals that she has become an empowered Brier Rose, insulting his manliness by commanding, "You've got to find me first, you pansy-assed momma's boy!" Paralleling the attack that happened in the virginal Sidney's own home when she was forced to react according to horror film rules, Billy is now forced to play by her rules. As a video of *Halloween* plays in the background with Jamie Lee Curtis cowering in a closet with Michael hacking through the doors, Billy reaches a stalker's epiphany and heads to a closet as well.

Clover (1992) maintains, "A phenomenally popular moment in post–1974 slashers is the scene in which the victim locks herself in (a house, room, closet car) and waits with pounding heart as the killer slashes, hacks, or drills his way in" (p. 31). *Scream* subverts this idea while still operating within the rules of its genre. Taking complete command of this film's final act, the sexually aware Sidney does not curl into the fetal position clinging to a coat hanger as her only weapon. Rather, she boldly stabs Billy with an umbrella while wearing the killer costume herself. Not only does she survive the horror film's rule that non-virgins must die, she also penetrates the masculine role, literally as well as figuratively. After Billy falls to the ground, she throws the mask on top of him, having successfully assumed and rejected the role of masculine serial killer. Stu suddenly appears and attacks her, proclaiming, "I always had a thing for you, Sid." She knees him in the crotch and responds, "In your dreams," while pushing the television—still playing *Halloween*—on top of him. She is fully awake and prepared to put these two perilous princes to rest. When Randy warns her that Billy will jump up for one last scare, Sidney stands squarely over the body and waits for him to awaken. He does so on cue, and she shoots him in the center of his head, confidently concluding, "Not in my movie."

After Brier Rose wakes up, she and her prince walk downstairs to find the rest of the court awakening from their concomitant state. Likewise, now that Sidney has awakened, her father can be released along with the battered Dewey and Randy (who happily credits his virginity with saving his life), and the rest of the town can be awakened to a safer place. Gale Weathers provides the final lines to the film, speaking directly to the camera and assuring, "Several more local teens are dead, bringing to an end the harrowing mystery of the mass killing that has terrified this peaceful community like the plot of some scary movie."

SOFTENING THE SPELL, PART II

The idea of softening a spell's intensity has special meaning for a film like *Scream*, which would have likely been rated NC-17 (no children under 17 permitted) without some stylistic slashing by its director. In this brief examination of ratings and censorship, Craven can be viewed as the wise woman who casts the lethal spell in "Brier Rose." His film, like this spell, is meant to have a severe and particular effect on the viewer, representing the largely uninvolved Brier Rose herself. Working against him as the powerful wise woman who can reduce the severity of the spell is the Motion Picture Association of America (MPAA) which screens films to determine their rating (G through NC-17). The MPAA is careful to point out that filmmakers are not required to use ratings and submission to the MPAA ratings board is voluntary; however, some filmmakers respond that they are often contractually bound to deliver films at a certain rating (to ensure profitability) and that most major theater chains refuse to show films rated NC-17. Additionally, if a film is rated NC-17 or unrated, some newspapers and television outlets will not show paid advertisements for them, again limiting their exposure, and even though DVD releases allow for restored footage, some retail chains, like Blockbuster, do not stock NC-17 releases.

As described by Craven, MPAA rulings when judging film violence closely resemble discussions of fairy tale violence. In "MPAA: The Horror in *My* Life," Craven (1996) argues passionately about required edits on such films as *A Nightmare on Elm Street* (1984) and *The People under the Stairs* (1991). He asserts that the MPAA has an agenda beyond critiquing a film's content to determine its rating: "And in the case of jurors assigned to rate genre films, these agendas often have to do with ill-defined but pas-

sionately held notions of saving children from having their minds cor-
rupted by films that actually are merely threatening the MPAA viewers
rather than the kids" (p. 36). He goes on to lament, "Increasingly, the tactic used by the MPAA that really can devastate your film is judgment not
against specific content (blood, whatever), but against intensity itself!" (p.
36). The Grimm fairy tales—with depictions of birds pecking out eyes
("Cinderella"), little girls getting eaten by wolves ("Little Red Cap"), and
persistent princes being ripped apart by thorns ("Brier Rose" and "Rapunzel")—have come under similar scrutiny since they were first published.
Tatar (2003) points out that contemporary critics of the Grimms frequently
called into question the appropriateness of the tales for children and even
today, "[o]ne camp of educators and psychologists rallies to the side of
censorship, perfectly prepared to remove the *Nursery and Household
Tales*—even in its adulterated versions—from the shelves of libraries and
nurseries. The other camp ... argues for the civilizing power of the Grimms'
tales and sees in them instruments of enlightenment" (pp. 190–191).

   In both fairy tales and horror films, the danger most feared seems to
be that we will subject our youth to images that are "too real," for them
to handle. Tatar (2003) notes that, in later editions of the tales, the Grimms
"were careful to eliminate violence whenever it appeared in *too realistic*
a setting [emphasis added]" (p. 21). In the DVD commentary for *Scream*,
Craven and Williamson discuss the edits required for nearly every one of
the film's grisly murders. Craven explains that the MPAA warned him that
they feared the simple knife-wielding violence could be too easily imi-
tated, and he determines:

> I think they're really more comfortable with the sort of Rambo-ish
> murder and mayhem where people are machine-gunning and stuntmen
> are flying off of air rams, and it's always kind of unreal. But it's when
> it's so personal, intimate as this film was at so many times, especially
> in that ending scene, they feel like, 'Oh, my God, that's *too real*
> [emphasis added]! We can't show that to people, or they'll go out
> and do it.' Which I think is really a gross misunderstanding of the
> audience's intelligence and integrity.

   These heated debates lead to the question: Which is more terrifying,
fairy tales and films with masquerading wolves, witchy stepmothers, and
masked, relentless killers or the too-real stories on which they are often
based? As Zipes (1988) notes, the Grimm tales certainly reflected their
times: "The history of the family in the eighteenth and nineteenth centuries

is filled with reports about long periods of swaddling, child killing, abandonment of children, corporeal punishment, sexual abuse, rape, intense sibling rivalry," and so on (p. 121). Part of the reason these tales remain so relevant today is because these same kinds of social and filial dangers continue to exist. In his forward to the *Scream* screenplay, Williamson (1997) himself acknowledges that the story evolved, in part, from the terrifying real-life attacks on college students in Gainesville, Florida in 1994. He explains, "It was scary as hell and was really spooking me. The idea that this man was stalking and killing these college kids in this small, unsuspecting town was very frightening" (p. xi). Examining horror films based upon real-life serial killers like Ed Gein and Ted Bundy, Newitz (1995) logically concludes, "Because fictional representations of serial killers are often based on the biographies of actual killers, one might say the serial killer narrative spans both fictional and non-fictional genres" (p. 39).

Outside of the fairy tale forest, the wolf assumes the cunning form of Jeffrey Dahmer, the witch takes on the treacherous manner of child-killer John Wayne Gacy, and Brier Rose becomes vengeful Aileen Wuornos, one of the few female serial killers on record. That films about each of these killers have been released—David Jacobson's *Dahmer* (2002); Clive Saunder's *Gacy* (2003); and Patty Jenkins's *Monster* (2003) starring Oscarwinner Charlize Theron—to varying levels of critical acclaim further blurs the factual/fictional lines. One wonders if any of these films could have been deemed "too real" if they had not been based upon actual events and people.

THREE

The Hand that Hawks the Cradle

"Rapunzel" and *The Ring*

A GRIMM VIEW OF THE FAIRY TALE FREAK OF NATURE

Outside of Germany, the Brothers Grimm are primarily known for their collection of fairy tales. However, a few years after they first published the *Kinder- und Hausmärchen* in 1812, they completed an impressive collection of over 500 German legends (*Deutsche Sagen*) as well. Although fairy tales and legends are considered separate genres, with the former considered purely fictional and the latter thought to be at least partly historical, both share a strong oral tradition and a tendency to convey some type of moral or lesson to their audience. As they explain in their forward:

> The fairy tales are thus destined ... to capture the pure thoughts of a childlike world view.... The legends, by contrast, serve as a far richer diet, bearing simpler yet therefore more pronounced colors, and demanding more serious contemplations and reflection [p. 2].

The German legends also have a particular subcategory that ties nicely to the more fanciful fairy tales: changelings and killcrops.[1] In these legends (particularly those numbered 49, 60, 82, 83, 88, 90, and 91), babies and children are kidnapped by supernatural beings or even the devil, and they are replaced by their wicked, malformed spawn who typically eat without ever growing larger or being sated. This theme even arises in the fairy tale "The Elves," in which the title characters also replace a mother's child with "a changeling who had a fat head and glaring eyes and would do nothing but eat and drink" (p. 141).

One of the most compelling changeling tales in German history comes from Martin Luther in 1532. Luther describes coming into contact with a twelve-year old changeling that could have been mistaken for a "real" child by outward appearances. What distinguished it from human children, however, was that it seemed to do nothing but eat, and its emotions were the opposite of what would be expected. Whenever it was touched, it cried. Luther goes on to say that it also cried whenever anything good happened, but it laughed and was happy whenever anything bad occurred. He finally recommends that the child be drowned in the water, because it has no soul. The Brothers Grimm were likely familiar with this tale and others from Luther, as they chose to include a separate changeling tale (number 82) from Luther in their collected legends.

According to Windling (2003), Goodey and Stainton (2001), and Ashliman (1997), people believed in changelings and killcrops as a way to understand various naturally-occurring diseases and genetic disorders that afflict children, but it also allowed them to justify abusing or murdering such children as evil creatures. As Windling explains, "Children afflicted with diseases such as cystic fibrosis, cerebral palsy, and spina bifida, or by congenital problems such as Downs syndrome, could be explained away as fairy changelings, sometimes with deeply tragic results." So-called cures could be as mild as using prayer and baptizing the child; however, if the child did not improve, the cure would often lead to infanticide. Ashliman (1997) notes that "prior to the mid-nineteenth century, public opinion, religious attitudes, and legal indifference made it unlikely that such cases would be prosecuted."

We realize that the term "freak of nature" is not politically correct in our more progressive times, but the term remains appropriate for the some of the unusual characters found in these early nineteenth-century legends and fairy tales. In addition to such anthropomorphized antagonists as the

crafty wolf, enchanted frog prince, and wish-granting flounder, the fairy tales include human characters who might have been considered change-lings at the time. Many of these would have easily found their calling in carnival side shows of yore, if they survived their upbringing. In fact, several of them are treated specifically like side show attractions.

In "Thumbling" (commonly called "Tom Thumb"), a poor and lonely farmer and wife want so desperately to have a child that they declare they would love any child given to them, even if that child were no larger than a thumb. Thus, their wish is granted, and they are rewarded with a child who is clever and kind but who never grows larger than the size of a thumb. Two men stumble across the father and son one day, and they offer to buy Thumbling so that they can place him on exhibit in the city to earn money. The father is reluctant to give up his son, but Thumbling agrees and goes on a series of adventures that pit him against thieves, a cow, and a wolf. He finally returns home where his parents embrace him warmly and promise never again to sell him, even for all of the riches in the world.

In "The Stubborn Child," a brief fairy tale that is only one paragraph in length, we learn of a child who will never do what he is told by his mother. We are advised that the Lord does not look kindly upon this will-ful child, so he becomes ill and quickly dies, in spite of the doctor's efforts. His body is lowered into a grave and covered with earth.[2] Suddenly, his little arm pops out from the ground, and this happens repeatedly despite attempts to push it back into the ground. His mother is summoned, and she swats the hand with a switch. Thereafter, the hand goes back into the earth, and the child is said to be at peace.

The tale of "Iron Hans" includes imagery that is frighteningly similar to the video villainess of Gore Verbinski's *The Ring* (2003). In this story, a king fears that he lives near an enchanted forest from which none who enter return. A huntsman offers to go into the forest where he finds a deep pool along with his dog. A long arm reaches out of the water and snatches the dog, dragging it down below, so the huntsman decides to empty the pool with the help of some other men. When they finally empty the water, they discover a wild-looking man at the bottom: "His body was as brown as rusty iron, and his hair hung over his face down to his

Opposite: **After Rapunzel is locked away from the world by her adoptive mother, her hair grows wildly out of control and cannot be contained within the tower. (Illustration by E. H. Wehnert from *Household Stories Collected by the Brothers Grimm*. London: Routledge and Sons, 1880.)**

knees" (Grimm & Grimm, 2003, p. 444). The men capture the wild man and take him to the king who confines him to an iron cage in the court-yard. One day the king's son is playing, and his ball falls into the cage. The wild man agrees to return it only if he is released. The son finally agrees, but after he unlocks the cage, he worries that he will be beaten in punishment. The wild man takes the boy with him and tells him that he will offer him help whenever he comes to the forest and calls out for Iron Hans. They boy grows up, and Iron Hans helps him win a war and the heart of a king's daughter. At their wedding, Iron Hans appears trans-formed into a proud king in his own right, having been released from a magic spell.

In addition to these physically different characters, fairy tales also show us figures who can be considered "freaks" by the way they treat their children. In many fairy tales, children become a kind of currency, and they are readily bartered by greedy parents who think only of their own needs and desires. In the previously mentioned "Thumbling," the father sells his son into a fairy tale freak show, while in "Hansel and Gretel," the parents famously leave the children to starve in the forest so that they will have enough to eat. In "Rumpelstiltskin," a poor miller's daughter offers the strange title character her first born child in exchange for spinning straw into gold.

In the lesser-read "The Maiden without Hands," a miller inadvertently promises his virtuous daughter to the devil for great wealth. She is able to keep the devil from taking her by washing herself clean. When the devil insists that she be kept from water, she cries, and her clean hands again keep the devil at bay. Thus, he commands that her hands be cut off as well. When the father tells his daughter what he must do, she replies that he can do whatever he wants with her, since she is his child. After cutting off her hands, she continues to cry, bathing in her tears so that the devil cannot touch her. Eventually, she marries a kind king who has silver hands made for her, but the devil wants his revenge. When the king leaves for war, he replaces letters between them with forged ones that demand the death of his wife and child, whom he believes is a changeling due to one of the fake letters. The king's mother sends her daughter-in-law into hiding, and she is cared for in a small cottage by an angel. When the king returns and learns what has happened, he spends seven years searching for his wife and son. Once they are reunited, they hold a second wedding and live hap-pily ever after.

TRANSLATING THE OCCIDENTAL TOURIST

Since one of our purposes is to look closely at ways images from the Grimm fairy tales continue to emerge in American films, we have elected to compare "Rapunzel" to Gore Verbinski's *The Ring* (2002), although it is, in fact, an American remake of Hideo Nakata's *Ringu* (1998).[3] Despite our emphasis on the American version, we have nevertheless found that the Japanese original also shares much in common with the Grimm tale. And while we are not claiming that there is a direct link between *Ringu* and "Rapunzel," we would like to highlight the surprising popularity of the Grimm Brothers' work in Japan.

From 1987 to 1989, Japanese anime versions of the Grimm fairy tales aired under the titles *Grimm Dowa, Grimm Meisaku Gekijoo*, and *Shin Grimm Meisaku Gekijoo*, which was later translated as *Grimm Masterpiece Theater* and *Grimm's Fairy Tale Classics* for airing on the cable channel Nickelodeon/Nick, Jr. A total of 47 episodes were produced, including one that focused on the golden-haired Rapunzel. According to Tohan's Bestseller List (Japan's equivalent of the New York Times Bestseller List), *Honto ni osoroshii Grimm dowa* (*Grimm Fairytales in their Terrifying True Form*)[4] ranked number four in 1999. And in 2000, the popular Japanese singer Cocco released her third album which was entitled *Rapunzel* and featured an iconic long blonde braid on its cover.

Intriguingly, a Japanese fairy tale called "The Maiden of Unai" shares several features with European versions of "Rapunzel" as well as the film *Ringu*. In this story, a soothsayer reveals that a seven-year old girl "with her black hair loose and hanging to her shoulder" (James, 1987, p. 134) will grow up to be so beautiful that two men of great honor will die for her. Her grief-stricken parents decide to hide her in a secret chamber "where an old wise woman tended her, fed her, bathed her, combed her hair, taught her to make songs and to sing," and so on (p. 136). Where Rapunzel "grew to be the most beautiful child under the sun" with hair that "was long and radiant, as fine as spun gold" (Grimm & Grimm, 2003, p. 43), her Japanese counterpart grows more beautiful "with every season that passed," and her hair "hung down to her knees and was black as a thundercloud" (pp. 136–137). She remains completely isolated until she is fifteen, by which time word of her forbidden beauty has passed across the land. Great warriors come to the house and demand to see her, so the parents relent and bring her out on the balcony: "And all the warriors who

After Samara (Daveigh Chase) is locked away from the world by her adoptive parents in *The Ring* (Dreamworks, 2002), her powers continue to harm those around her and cannot be contained in the asylum. *The Kobal Collection, Merrick Morton*

were there looked upon her and were silent, for already they were faint with love and longing" (p. 138). When two heroes decide to fight to the death for her, she leaps into the river below, drowning herself. Her suitors jump into the river to rescue her, but they drown as well due to the weight of their armor. All three are buried together with the Maiden of Unai between them.

With regard to both *Ringu* and *The Ring*, the plotlines are essentially the same: A female reporter investigates a mysterious videotape that leads to its viewer's death seven days after watching it. Once she views it, she realizes she only has one week to find out how to lift the curse to prevent her own death, as well as that of her son who watches it accidentally. There are also some significant differences worth noting, however. The female reporter's former boyfriend—and father of her young son—plays a more dominant role in the Japanese version, and he possesses strong psychic abilities that help him understand the deadly events surrounding the videotape. In the American version, his role is reduced somewhat to support a more active female lead, and he has no psychic visions. In *Ringu*, the mysterious biological mother and daughter, here named Sadako, are both psychic, and the daughter reveals that she has the power to kill just by wishing it. The mother in *The Ring* is thought to have adopted the daughter after three miscarriages, and she ultimately appears less psychically connected to her daughter, Samara, fearing that she is burning disturbing images into her mind. Perhaps the most important change between the two films lies in the murder of the daughter by a desperate parent. In Nakata's version, the father of Samara is shown hitting his daughter over the head and pushing her into the fateful well. In Verbinski's version, the mother becomes the desperate murderer of her only child. Thus, Verbinski's retelling strengthens all of the female roles, which not only makes the tale more contemporary and American, but also allows it to have a more traditional fairy tale feel.

FIGHTING IRRESISTIBLE URGES

Both "Rapunzel" and *The Ring* reveal the cost of giving in to primal urges despite the well-known danger associated with doing so. The Grimms tell us of a husband and wife who, like Thumbling's parents, have long wished to have a child. After the wife becomes pregnant, her cravings for a salad of rampion[5] lettuce from a neighboring garden overpower her. The well-tended garden has the most beautiful flowers and herbs, but it is also protected by a high wall and guarded by a powerful sorceress who is feared throughout the land. Although it is widely, commonly known that no one should risk entering the sorceress' realm, the wife tells her husband that she will die if she does not get to eat the forbidden rampion. Playing a fairy tale Adam to his wife's desperate Eve, the husband sneaks into the garden and is caught by the sorceress. After listening to his explanation, she offers a bargain: He can take as much of the rapunzel as his wife can eat, but they must then give her the child as soon as it is born. She assures him, "You needn't fear about the child's well-being, for I shall take care of it like a mother" (p. 43). Thus, an agreement is made, and she takes away the prized child as soon as it is born, making it her own changeling daughter. The parents are not mentioned again in this tale, and we assume that they never see their daughter again, a punishment, perhaps, for their lack of control when confronted with selfish, personal desires. According

to Tatar (2003), their actions follow standard fairy tale fashion, since "ultimately the hero's parents—his progenitors and guardians—are directly
implicated in the misfortunes that besiege him" (pp. 59–60).

"Rapunzel" also shows that some uncontrollable urges can be worth
pursuing, even though they remain dangerous. When Rapunzel turns twelve
years old, the sorceress locks her away in a tall tower in the forest for
unexplained reasons. After several years have passed, a prince riding
through the forest hears Rapunzel singing, and "the song had touched his
heart so deeply that he rode out into the forest every day and listened" (p.
44). Intriguingly, his love for her differs from that of most other fairy tale
princes (particularly the princes in "Brier Rose," "Snow White," and "Cinderella") since it is not based upon her physical beauty. He falls in love at
first sound rather than love at first sight. Porter (1998) therefore asserts,
"It is the beauty of her soul that makes him want to ascend the tower" (p.
279). He eventually overhears the sorceress calling to Rapunzel, allowing
him to discover that the only way to enter the tower is by calling for Rapunzel to let down her braided hair as a ladder. Once the two finally meet,
they immediately agree to deceive the sorceress, and Rapunzel tells him
to bring skeins of silk each time he visits so that she can weave a ladder
to escape. Their adolescent longing becomes the overriding reason for
their shared duplicity.

Similarly, the characters in *The Ring* find that the most dire of consequences result when they ignore warnings as well. As the film opens,
Katie (Amber Tamblyn) and Becca (Rachael Bella), two teenaged girls,
are watching television alone in the upstairs bedroom of a large, ivy-
covered home. A commercial for a hair product is ending, and the light
from the television flickers in front of them. They are wearing private
school uniforms, suggesting their purity, like two little Rapunzels hidden
away from the world. Then they begin talking about an urban legend—our
modern-day fairy tale—that centers on a videotape, and Becca says, "You
start to play it, and it's like somebody's nightmare." She then notes that
she heard that anyone who watches it gets a phone call that says, "You will
die in seven days." Katie reveals that she saw the tape one week ago while
secretly visiting her own prince and some other friends in a cabin at the
Shelter Mountain Inn. After pretending to be afraid, Katie's fear becomes
real when a television turns on by itself when she is downstairs in the
kitchen. She hesitantly walks back upstairs alone and sees water flowing
out from under her bedroom door. Terrified, she turns the knob and enters

the room to see that television turned on. As she opens her mouth to scream, static covers the frame.

From this frightening introduction, the film shifts to its heroine, Rachel (Naomi Watts), a reporter and single mother. Her son, Aidan (David Dorfman), seems psychically connected to Katie, his cousin and regular babysitter, and he is very disturbed by her death. At her wake, Katie's mother asks Rachel to find out what really happened to her daughter, and Rachel reluctantly agrees to investigate. She soon learns the story of the deadly videotape at the cabin by talking to Katie's friends at the wake, and she becomes increasingly driven to discover the truth, confidently telling her editor that she cannot be fired due to the explosive nature of this story. Her research shows that the other teenagers who watched the tape with Katie all died that same evening. Rachel drives to the Shelter Mountain Inn, finds the unmarked videotape[6] on a shelf in the lobby, and cautiously, knowingly watches it in the same cabin where her niece had seen it. At this moment, she seems driven by her desire to help her sister learn the truth, but also by her very nature as a professional reporter after a good story.

In an interview with Holben (2002), Bohan Bazelli, the cinematographer, explains that the video created for the film was meant to elicit a certain reaction from the characters and the audience: "The images were supposed to be shocking, not [graphic], but disturbing and unsettling" (p. 57). The viewer watches the tape along with Rachel. It is a grainy, black-and-white video filled with seemingly unrelated, nightmarish images: a glowing ring, flowing water, a single chair, a woman combing her hair in a mirror, a fly, a finger being punctured on a nail, maggots, a burning tree (the only color image), a ladder, dead horses, a woman allowing herself to fall from a cliff, and a stone well in a forest. As soon as Rachel finishes watching the tape, her pupil dilates in close-up. The phone rings and a young girl's voice whispers, "Seven days." The tape—and Samara herself—fit the definition of impure, interstitial objects of art-horror described by Carroll (1990) as "categorically contradictory, incomplete, or formless" (pp. 32–33). They inspire disgust in the audience, and their origins remain unsolvable mysteries. They are frightening because something about them does not belong in our world.

Freaks, film, and photography have a bizarre connection in American pop culture. In *Sideshow U. S. A.: Freaks and the American Cultural Imagination*, Adams (2001) explains, "The freak show's ascendancy in the mid-nineteenth century coincided with the birth of photography, and sideshow promoters rapidly learned to exploit the potential of the new visual technology as a publicity tool" (p. 114). So-called freak *cartes de visite*, photographs of the sideshow freaks in everyday household settings with a biography on the back, became a popular collectable. Adams asserts, "The photography of physical and social deviance creates a visual record that aspires to contain or alleviate the problem it depicts. Whereas clinical photography serves the modern tendency to segregate and institutionalize abnormality, the freak portrait belongs to an era when a greater array of human differences were at least partially incorporated into the social fabric" (p. 120). The juxtaposition of clinical and freak photography is one of the fundamental leitmotifs of *The Ring*: On one videotape taken at a psychiatric hospital, Samara is shown sitting in a sterile, all-white room as clinicians question her ability to make images burn into film. She is completely isolated from the real world as an object to be studied. Her own tape, however, allows her to tell her story using images from her short life. The urban legend centering on the deadly power of her tape provides all the publicity of a video *cartes de visite*, allowing her to enter society again and again.

The film cleverly shows how almost imperceptibly one's self image can become altered by doing that which is forbidden. In the DVD Chapter called "Photographs," Rachel finds a film receipt for a photo mat in Katie's journal and picks up photos chronicling her trip to the Shelter Mountain Inn. In the pictures taken before they arrive to the cabin, she and her friends are shown in clear focus, smiling and laughing. In the pictures taken the day after they watched the tape, their faces have become grotesquely distorted, transforming them into models for Samara's *cartes de visite*, visual evidence that they have broken a taboo. After viewing the tape themselves, Rachel finds that her image is equally misshapen on her digital camera, while her ex-boyfriend, Noah (Martin Henderson), notices that his face is malformed on a security camera in a convenience store. In each of these cases, only the facial images of those who have seen the tape are distorted, while the image of everything surrounding them—including those who have not seen the tape—remains unchanged. Likewise, their living, non-photographed image does not change to the outside world to reveal what they have done. Thus, it is as if their very souls have been captured on tape and become irrevocably altered by their actions. In an interview with Dunkley (2002), Mark Sourian, the executive who initially brought the film to the DreamWorks studio, remarks, "It has a great central idea: If you watch this tape, you will die in seven days. But the very thing you're told not to do, you want to do. It is one of the basic premises of horror movies" (p. 87). And it is one of the basic premises of fairy tales like "Rapunzel," as well.

DISFIGURING PARENTAL FIGURES

"Rapunzel" continues the fairy tale tradition of presenting absent, ineffectual fathers and severe, self-serving mothers. Poor Snow White is forced out of her own home by a jealous stepmother who apparently controls the kingdom with no input from her husband while Hansel and Gretel are left in the forest after their stepmother convinces their father that there is not enough food for everyone. In "Rapunzel," the father sacrifices the child he and his wife have longed to have in exchange for rampion to appease his gluttonous spouse. Thus, Rapunzel never knows her parents. However, this fairy tale offers additional critiques of absent fathers and self-serving mothers. For her part, the sorceress raises Rapunzel quite alone and sheltered away from the world, keeping her as her own private property. Her reasons are never overtly stated, but the Grimms do not judge her too harshly for her actions. Bettelheim (1989) maintains, "Although selfish love is wrong and always loses out, as does the sorceress' ... one does not want some other person to enjoy that love and deprive one. To love so selfishly and foolishly is wrong, but not evil" (p. 149). Similarly, Cashdan (1999) argues, "[The sorceress's] decision to keep Rapunzel in the tower flowed not from malice but from maternal concern" (p. 160). Therefore, unlike the stepmothers in "Hansel and Gretel" and "Snow White," she is not described as wicked or evil in the tale, nor is she punished at the end of the fairy tale as one would expect if she were irredeemably villainous. In fact, the sorceress is called "cruel" only once—at the time she completely disowns Rapunzel and banishes her to a desolate land, thereby severing her role as a surrogate parent.

Sanitized versions of this tale excise the ending, which reveals a pregnant Rapunzel who has given birth to twins and which brutally transforms the prince into an absent father. After learning about their secret affair, the sorceress cuts off Rapunzel's beautiful hair and strands her in a desolate land where she eventually gives birth to twins, a boy and a girl. The betrayed sorceress then awaits the arrival of the prince, telling him, "The cat has got her, and it will also scratch out your eyes. Rapunzel is lost to you, and you will never see her again!" (p. 45). In his great despair, the prince falls from the tower into thorns that blind him. He then spends years wandering the land and mourning the loss of his forest bride. The much-anticipated happy ending is long in coming, but the prince finally hears Rapunzel's voice and wanders blindly to her. Her tears of joy fall into his eyes and restore his vision, and the whole family returns to his kingdom. Oddly, this ending does not reveal a particularly noble and ready father figure, and no mention is made of his love for the children. Bettelheim (1989) notes that the prince and Rapunzel are ready to make a good life for each other, but the story does not even hint that they are prepared to do the same for the children. As with Rapunzel's father, an emphasis is placed instead on the husband's love for his wife, not on the father's love for his offspring.

Both "Rapunzel" and *The Ring* are comprised of two primary parental couples, an older couple (Rapunzel's parents/Richard and Anna Morgan) who desperately want to have a child and must then abandon her (Rapunzel/Samara) for painful reasons after their wish is granted, and a younger couple (Rapunzel and the prince/Rachel and Noah) who have conceived perhaps too easily and accidentally in their youth. In both sets of relationships, we see that children may not be meant for those who seem to desire them most. Conversely, those who do not expect children may find themselves required to fill the parental role, however awkwardly and unexpectedly.

As Rachel and Noah research the tape, they learn that the woman combing her hair is Anna Morgan (Shannon Cochran), a pretty middle-aged woman married to a horse breeder, Richard Morgan (Brian Cox). After enduring several miscarriages, the couple had a daughter, Samara (Daveigh Chase) and they all resided on an island with a lighthouse. They also learn that Anna was eventually committed to a psychiatric hospital and that she likely killed herself. When Rachel finally locates Anna's husband, she tells him about the tape and that she thinks it is a message from his wife. He expresses no interest in seeing it, and when Rachel asks him about his daughter, he replies coldly and matter-of-factly, "I don't have a daughter." Rapunzel's father could have well responded in the same manner if asked about his daughter following the treacherous trade with the sorceress.

Rachel next visits Dr. Grasnik (Jane Alexander) on the island and discovers more about this frightful family, as the doctor tells her a tale reminiscent of those old changeling stories:

> She wanted a child more than anything, poor Anna. They tried hard for years, but sometimes it's just not meant to be. Then one winter they went away. When they came back, it was with Samara. Adopted, they said, never did say from where. Said the mother died of complications. But they had their baby, they had their horses, everything was fine. Til Anna started coming to see me. Said she was suffering visions, seeing things, horrible things, like they'd been burned inside her. And it only happened around Samara, like the girl put them there.

Returning to Richard's house, Rachel finds a different tape taken of Samara while she was in the psychiatric hospital for observation. She is wearing a hospital gown and sitting in a sterile room. Her long, dark hair is parted sharply down the middle and mostly covers her wan face. We hear a psychiatrist asking her questions and taking notes. When Samara asks flatly, "Can I see my mommy?" he replies, "No Samara, not until we understand what's wrong with you." She replies, "I love my mommy." However, when the psychiatrist reminds her, "Your daddy loves you," Samara responds to the contrary, "Daddy loves the horses. He wants me to go away.... But he doesn't know...." The screen goes fuzzy, and the tape stops.

Richard suddenly appears behind Rachel, slapping her violently to the ground. He unplugs the television, screaming, "She's never gonna whisper in my fucking ear ever again!" while carrying it upstairs. As Rachel follows him up the stairs, he yells back, "My wife was not supposed to have a child!" He plugs the television into an extension cord with a surge protector and steps into a bathtub already overflowing with water, warning Rachel, "She never sleeps," as he electrocutes himself. Rachel now understands that the message on the tape is not from Anna Morgan, but rather from her daughter, Samara.

At the beginning of *The Ring*, Rachel appears to have the limited parenting skills and short temper of the sorceress—she does not seem naturally suited to a maternal role, and she depends on the eerie maturity of her young son. When we first meet her, she is walking down an elementary school hall swearing at her editor on her cell phone, "You touch my column, and I'm coming down there and *poking your eye out* with that little red pencil you like so much [emphasis added]." She is more protective of her stories than she is of her son. She is late to pick Aidan up, and her lateness seems to be a trend. Her son has become as isolated from her as Rapunzel is from the outside world and from her own foster mother who visits but once a day. Aidan is shown to be a self-sufficient young boy who seldom speaks and shows little emotion. When he talks to his mother, Aidan calls her by her first name, Rachel, not by "mother" or "mom." Similarly, Rapunzel calls the sorceress "Mother Gothel," showing that she does not recognize the old woman her natural mother. However, the more research Rachel conducts, the more she becomes a natural, comfortable mother. In a thorough discussion behind the film's cinematic artistry, Holben (2002) comments that "Rachel's search for the truth behind the tape is frequently depicted with low-angle shots. Bazelli [the cinematographer] explains that this perspective helps connect Rachel with the clues she finds" (p. 54). These low angles also put Rachel in a position of power and authority, making her the knowing parent to the audience.

We slowly come to learn that Aidan is the result of a failed relationship between Rachel and Noah. And while Rachel sacrifices time with her son to focus on her career, Noah sacrifices his paternal time out of fear of being a bad father. He watches Aidan from afar, even taking pictures of him at school, but he plays no active part in his life, filling his fatherly role as completely as the blind, wandering prince. Both Noah and Rachel become caring parents instinctively only after Aidan watches the tape, and their goal becomes one to save him. In one of the film's quietly touching, intimate scenes, Noah and Aidan sit in a car while Rachel searches Katie's room. They talk awkwardly about Noah's absence from Aidan's life, and Noah explains, "The thing is, I don't think I'd make a good father.... Thing is, I don't want anyone else to do it, either. Be your father." When Rachel returns to the car, Aidan hands her a family picture with him, her, and Noah in it. However, the three of them are standing outside of the Morgan home, allowing for a full juxtaposition between the two families. By saving the lost child Samara, Rachel and Noah come to believe that they can save their own son and redeem themselves as parents.

As the story shifts from searching for what happened to Anna to discovering what was done to Samara, Rachel increasingly becomes a searching, surrogate mother to the deadly daughter through Aidan, who says that Samara shows him things, and through her own investigative skills. She becomes focused on learning what Samara needs to say through the images she burned into tape, and Samara provides her otherworldly clues so that she can find her. Together they play the horror-film equivalent of hide-and-seek.

ESCAPING FROM THE HIDDEN TOWER

Rapunzel and Samara share some striking similarities that tie them together as sister "freaks" in their distinct worlds. Both are changeling daughters taken from their original homes by foster mothers who believed that they wanted them more than anything in the world and who ultimately abandon their daughters when they find that they cannot control them. Rapunzel and Samara are both isolated from the outside world as they get older, and they reach out through the media of their time, whether song or video, as they try to save themselves. And, yes, their hair serves as a defining physical characteristic for each of them, from Rapunzel's golden locks to Samara's ebony tresses. In this section, we examine these shared characteristics in more depth, as each of these imprisoned daughters emerges from her solitary confinement.

As was mentioned earlier, the sorceress promises to take care of Rapunzel as if she were her own child, and the Grimms do not show her to be an unloving caretaker until she learns that Rapunzel has betrayed her. Indeed, Rapunzel and the prince carry on their affair for quite some time until Rapunzel absentmindedly asks the sorceress why she is so much heavier than her prince. At this moment, the sorceress cries out, "I thought I had made sure you had no contact with the outside world, but you've deceived me!" (p. 44). She immediately snips off Rapunzel's braids and abandons her in that desolate land of never to be heard from again.

This intense, immediate change in the sorceress upon learning of Rapunzel's deception shows that she has not simply secreted her daughter away for the girl's own protection, but rather for her maternal salvation as well. As her daughter nears puberty, the sorceress may well fear the loss associated with Rapunzel's growing up (Bettelheim, 1989; McGlathery, 1991; Cashdan, 1999). Therefore, she strategically removes her from a sexual world and locks her in a seemingly impenetrable tower that has no doors or stairs. The only means of entry is the small window at the top of the tower. Even here, however, Mother Gothel cannot keep her daughter untouched by adulthood, sexual maturity, and deception.

Compare the sorceress's sudden change to the following description of Anna by Rachel:

> *You could almost draw a line through her life.* On one side, there's this happy woman who spends her time with her husband riding horses, everything sheltered, protected, and comfortable. Her face: There's

light, there's pride. *And then one day, something happens, and she*
takes this hard corner, and the light goes out. [emphasis added]

For the sorceress, the line is drawn and the hard corner taken only after
she is deceived by her beloved, sheltered foster daughter. For Anna, the
line and corner are likewise connected to her discovery that the daughter
she always wanted is not what she ever expected. She finds that she and
all of those around her—her husband, their horses, the entire island—
become infected by Samara's burning images. When the psychiatrist in
Samara's interview tape tells his young patient, "You don't want to hurt
anyone," she replies honestly, "But I do, and I'm sorry. It won't stop." Like
Rapunzel's inevitable maturation, symbolized by her ever-growing hair,
Samara's inexplicable telepathy cannot be halted. McGlathery (1991) argues
that, even if Rapunzel's hair is at first a "gift" from the sorceress, it becomes
one which the older woman can no longer control. Similarly, Samara's
"gifts" cannot be controlled by her adoptive mother. Anna and Samara are
both linked to contrasting images of their hair, the former captured brush-
ing it carefully in front of a mirror in the cursed videotape, and the latter
typically shown with it cascading over her face. Rachel, the new mother
figure, may brush back Samara's hair in the well to reveal a seemingly
fragile young girl, but when Samara unexpectedly emerges to kill Noah,
her hair once again disguises an angry girl with the power of a pre-
pubescent Medusa.

Samara is hidden away for her parents' protection as shown in the
DVD Chapter "The Barn" and the immediately following "The Well."
Rachel and Noah discover a tiny loft room high up in the Morgan family
barn, an equestrian tower on a desolate island. A single wooden ladder
leads up to Samara's first prison where they find a child's bed, rocking
horse, and little chair facing an old, black-and-white television set. The
wallpaper is decorated with pictures of horses and conceals the image of
a tree burned into the wall. Rachel remembers seeing this image at the
Shelter Mountain Inn, and it is here—on Rachel's seventh day—that they
find Samara's final prison, a stone well that, like Rapunzel's tower, has neither door nor stairs, only a little opening high above.

Cabins have been constructed over the well, and Rachel and Noah
must first break through the floor of the cabin Katie stayed in so that they
can find it. Samara's otherworldly powers push Rachel into the well so that
she can discover what happened to her. As she searches for the body, Rachel
sweeps her hand through the watery grave into a long lock of dark hair.

In the tradition of the Grimms' "The Stubborn Child" and de Palma's *Carrie*, Samara's hand suddenly emerges and grabs Rachel's arm, transporting her back to the day of Samara's murder. Rachel sees that Anna's light was extinguished by her acceptance that the child she always wanted was purely destructive. On a bright, clear day, Anna walks up to her daughter who is standing in front of the well in an open field with horses running in the distance. A forest surrounds them. She comments on how beautiful and peaceful it is here and assures Samara, "All I ever wanted was you." She then pulls a plastic bag over her daughter's head and lets her fall headfirst into the inverted tower where she will survive for seven days, having been abandoned by the only mother she has ever known.

Although they are but young girls, both Rapunzel and Samara are quite powerful. Even though Rapunzel is a fairy tale heroine awaiting a prince, he does not really rescue her. Rapunzel is forever associated with her astounding hair—over sixty feet in length and strong enough to be climbed—but her true power lies in her voice, which captivates the prince and draws him to her. She does not scream for help while locked away in her tower; rather, she spends her time singing, her lovely voice resonating throughout the empty forest. Her famous hair then becomes his only means to enter the tower. When they finally meet, her reason for running off with him is more practical than fairy-tale romantic. She finds him handsome enough and calmly decides, "He'll certainly love me better than old Mother Gothel" (p. 44). She is in control of this situation, and she makes her choice based upon *his* good looks and her desire to be loved *better*. Rapunzel is the one who comes up with the idea to weave a ladder, and she gives him permission to take her away on his horse. When the sorceress discovers the plan, she is destroyed emotionally by her daughter's duplicity, and we do not hear from her again after she banishes Rapunzel and confronts the prince. As the blind prince wanders the world, it is once again Rapunzel's voice that brings him to her, and her tears restore his sight. Thus, it is she who ultimately rescues him. Porter (1998) infers that Rapunzel's powerful tears come from "a lifetime of sorrow" (p. 279), although the Grimms do not show her express any grief until her banishment.

After discovering that Anna killed Samara, Rachel laments, "She wanted that child more than anything in the world. How could she have done that? *She just wanted to be heard.* Sometimes children yell, or cry, or draw pictures [emphasis added]." Like Rapunzel, Samara makes herself heard from a desolate, lonely realm by appealing through an entertainment medium. Instead of acting as a singing siren, however, she employs video. That her tape appears next to other well-known films in the lobby inn reveals innate her understanding of how best to reach an accommodating audience. Early in the film, Rachel steps out onto her apartment balcony as Noah first watches the video. She quietly scans the apartments facing hers, and she notices that most of her neighbors have television sets prominently placed in their kitchens, living rooms, and bedrooms. Essentially everyone in the modern world becomes accessible through their television sets, and those who cannot resist the lure of the tape become Samara's prince, seduced by gaining entrance into her forbidding and forbidden world. The viewer's curiosity, like Rapunzel's flowing braids and Samara's climb through the television—is seemingly boundless. Rachel also discovers that Katie and her friends all died at exactly the same time but in different locations; thus, Samara can broadcast herself to separate locations at the same time as a kind of syndicated serial killer.

Having solved the mystery and survived her seventh day, Rachel believes that the curse has ended, and she returns home. Noah asks her to call him tomorrow, and the day after that, and a happy ending appears inevitable. Samara does not merely want to be heard, however, she wants her voice to be deafening. She emerges from Noah's television right on time, just like a regularly scheduled program, having been given the power to climb out of the well by his initial viewing a week earlier. He stumbles backward as she walks toward him, her waste-length, black hair covering her face, showing him no mercy in spite of his earlier assistance. After Rachel discovers his body, she realizes that she must figure out why she did not die so that she can save Aidan, whose week will soon end. As she pieces all of this mystery together, she realizes, "I made a copy." The final scene reveals Rachel as the kind of mother neither Rapunzel nor Samara could have. She decides to protect her child at the expense of others and teaches Aidan how to copy the tape. Once he has made his copy, he asks, "What about the person we show it to? What happens to them?"

RETELLING THE TALE

Perhaps the greatest power of fairy tales lies in their combined durability and mutability. They are told again and again, forever reaching a

larger audience to deliver their moral lesson. Yet, some of the most popular tales can be—and have been—told and re-told in diverse cultures, far
removed from their original source, but maintaining the essential structural elements.[7] Heiner (2003) describes 22 tales (from Greece, Italy,
France, Egypt, and Germany) that are similar to "Rapunzel," for example,
with Giambattista Basile's "Prezzemolina" (Italian for parsley) dating back
to 1637. As we discussed at the beginning of this chapter, "The Maiden of
Unai" similarly features a beautiful, long-haired girl who is locked away
from the world and raised by an elderly woman. She is released only when
men come to hear of her great beauty and seek her out, her eventual emergence leading to immense suffering for the lovers.[8] In one sense, fairy
tales can be viewed as precursors to modern film and video, recorded tales
that can be translated (such as *The Ring* from *Ringu*), copied, shared, and
enjoyed over and over again. *The Ring* carries this idea through on a frightening technological level and, as Dunkley (2002) notes, "[It] also adds a
twist to a favorite horror theme: the evils of modern technology and the
notion that images can hurt you" (90). During the very first scene of the
film, Katie and Becca are shown watching television almost catatonically,
apathetically clicking through the channels, passing time casually, because
they simply have nothing else to do. It is unclear where their parents are,
and we learn that the girls have their own Rapunzel-like secret relationships. Even though she seems to be talking without really thinking, Katie
delivers the film's early message:

> I hate television. Gives me headaches. You know, I heard there's so
> many magnetic waves traveling through the air because of TV and
> telephones, that we're losing, like ten times as many brain cells as
> we're supposed to. Like, all of the molecules in our heads are unstable.
> All the companies know about it, but they're not doing anything about
> it. It's like, a big conspiracy.

As Badley (1995) explains in her discussion of horror films, "Horror's language is somatic, communicating on a preliterate, subconscious level ...
horror descends into primal fear and desire. It is a loss of ego in cellular
chaos" (10).

     This cellular chaos is as far-reaching as a fairy tale passed down
through generations and cultures, mutating on its own to fit the mores of
its time. Eventually, the tale can become so removed from its source that
its progenitor is no longer singularly identifiable, even though the story
itself can remain largely unchanged. Similarly, Noah and Rachel discover

that their mysterious tape has no identifying source code that will allow them to track it back to its cinematic origins, nor do its subsequent copies. As he explains to Rachel, it is like being born without fingerprints. White (2005) argues that this idea creates "a new cultural logic" in which "copies of copies vary continually from an always already lost original" (p. 41). Tracing the tale to its original source—and meaning—becomes an impossible goal; thus, the context of the copies gains as much significance, however intangible and fleeting. Tatar (2003) and Blamires (2003) point out that even the Grimms' edited the tales carefully through several editions, altering them to serve as much for the moral education of children as for their entertainment. Yet a tale heard (and repeated) without reflection is like a televised program viewed without comprehension. Time passes; nothing changes. *The Ring* asserts that we are, in a sense, all willingly insulated Rapunzels, whiling away the hours in isolated towers with television serving as our little windows to a world we dare not physically enter. It cautions that Samara might just be lurking on the other side of the screen, awaiting an invitation to climb out from her dark well so that she can wake us from our slumber.

• FOUR •

The Object of My Reflection

"Little Snow White" and *The Talented Mr. Ripley*

A GRIMM VIEW OF THE FAIRY TALE VAMPIRE

In the Grimm Brothers' German dictionary, which was completed after their deaths, the vampire (*der Vampyr*) is defined simply as one of the dead who rises nightly from the grave to suck out the blood of the living. Textual citations are provided from renowned philosophical and literary greats like Johann Gottfried von Herder and Johann Wolfgang von Goethe, who notes that the vampire can even "vampirize" others from his own grave.[1] McNally and Florescu (1994) point out that stories of vampires, including the famous Dracula, were popular in Romania and Germany as early as 1463 when Michel Beheim composed *Story of a Bloodthirsty Madman Called Dracula of Wallachia*, a lengthy poem read frequently in the court of Holy Roman Emperor Frederick III as he entertained guests (p. 83). McNally and Florescu go on to explain that "[no] fewer than thirteen different fifteenth- and sixteenth-century Dracula stories have been discovered thus far in the various German states within the former empire. Printed in Nuremberg, Lübeck, Bamberg, Augsburg, Strasbourg, Hamburg, etc., many of them exist in several editions" (p. 83). Porter (1999) goes so far as to say that vampire hunts essentially replaced witch hunts of earlier centuries: "Vampirism attracted considerable attention—more than routine witch-burnings in the same period in Hungary, Poland, Austria, and Germany—since for churchmen, the notion was acutely threatening, involving as it did a blasphemous reversal of key Christian dogmas, including resurrection and the Eucharist" (p. 214).

According to Barber (1988), many books continued to be written about vampires in Europe and especially in Germany during the early eighteenth century (p. 5). Bunson (1993) explains, "The Germans also made a lasting contribution to vampirology in the numerous treatises written by 'experts' on the undead during the seventeenth and eighteenth centuries. These included the works of Michael Ranft, Johann Christopher Rohl, Johann Stock, and Johann Zopfius" (p. 107). Ramsland (2002) adds that an anonymous, scholarly treatise of vampires was published in 1810 entitled *Travels of Three English Gentlemen from Venice to Hamburg, Being the Grand Tour of Germany in the Year 1734*. In this source, the author recommends staking a vampire through the heart or burning it to ashes in order to destroy it completely.

By the time they had published their first edition of the fairy tales in 1812, the Brothers were no doubt quite familiar with some of these fascinating tales of the bloodthirsty undead. Although the Grimm fairy tales do not directly include references to vampires—particularly in the context of classic film images of the vampire, fangs bared with a flowing cape— a number of the tales include images that we have come to associate with these preying creatures of the night. Returning from the dead, falling under the spell of a mysterious stranger, and, of course, arising from that carefully prepared coffin: These are but a few of the defining vampiric elements that also have some bite in some of the fairy tales.

In "The Three Snake Leaves," a beautiful princess declares that she will marry only the man who agrees to be buried alive with her should she die first. A young man agrees to this request, and his new wife promptly becomes ill and dies. He is escorted to the royal vault, where he and his deceased bride are bolted inside. When a snake finds its way inside, he hacks it into three pieces to protect the purity of his wife. A second snake enters and places three green leaves on the severed parts of the other snake, miraculously bringing it back to life. He places the leaves over his wife's eyes and mouth, and she awakens from her death. They are released from the vault, and while his wife appears the same physically, her spirit and emotions have changed drastically. Coming back from death, she no longer feels any love for her husband. She has an affair with a captain, and they throw her sleeping husband into the sea where he drowns. Fortunately, a faithful servant rescues him by using the same three snake leaves to revive him. As punishment for her crimes, she and the captain are sent out to sea in a ship filled with holes. They sink beneath the sea never to rise up again.

In "The Glass Coffin," we encounter a poor tailor who is carried away to a desolate cliff by an enchanted stag. A voice cries out asking him to enter the cliff through a small door, and he is compelled to do so by a mysterious power. He finally comes to an area that contains two large glass chests. In one, he sees a tiny castle and its surrounding village. In the other, he sees a beautiful maiden who appears to be asleep. Her long blond hair is wrapped around her like a cloak.[2] She suddenly opens her eyes and asks him to unbolt her glass coffin to free her. Thereafter, she explains that a stranger arrived to her own castle some time ago and used a mysterious power to deprive her of speech and enter her locked bedroom at night. He asked her to be his bride, and when she denied him, he swore revenge. She explains that he transformed her dear brother into a stag and that she tried to shoot the evil stranger, but the bullet simply bounced off of his chest. He then put her into a death-like sleep and locked her in his underground cavern along with her village. The stranger took the form of a bull and was finally killed by her brother, who was able to thrust his antlers into his body. After hearing her story, the tailor helps her free her castle and village, and her brother is transformed back into a human being. The tailor and the maiden marry, bringing our tale to its expected happy ending.

"The Castle of Murder" was omitted from the Grimms' final collection of tales, but it includes truly sadistic allusions that could be traced to vampire folklore and the murderous Vlad the Impaler (Dracula).[3] A nobleman arrives to town and falls in love with the daughter of a shoemaker. He carries her off to his castle hidden away in a large forest. He gives her the keys to explore the castle, and she finds her way to the cellar where an old woman is scraping out intestines. She is horrified when the old woman says that she will be scraping out hers the next day. The readers then learn that her two other sisters were killed in this same manner. The old woman tells her that she can escape by hiding in a hay wagon, and when the nobleman returns home, the old woman says that she has already killed her. The nobleman is happy to hear that his wife is dead. In the meantime, the new bride makes her way to a nearby castle and tells her story to its lord. He holds a great feast and invites the nobleman. The new bride is disguised and asked to share her tale, causing great fear in her murderous husband as the story unfolds. When he tries to flee, the authorities apprehend him. His castle is destroyed, and all of his treasures are given to his former bride.

VAMPIRIC REFLECTIONS IN "SNOW WHITE"

Although the evil stepmother of the Grimms' "Snow White" is not specifically labeled a vampire, she shares some remarkably similar features with vampire folklore, as does the tale itself. We will examine each of these similarities in more depth a bit later in this chapter, but we briefly highlight some of these intriguing, iconic images below:

• Like the famed Count Dracula, the queen is aristocratic and rules her own castle. Although men would have typically held power at this time, she obviously controls her house and husband who does not assist his abused daughter in any way. Additionally, just as vampires keep their coffins hidden away from the world, she has her own secret chamber that she alone can enter;

• As with most vampire legends, a mirror plays an important role in revealing the queen's true nature. In some folktales, the vampire casts no reflection, while in others it actively avoids mirrors. Barber (1988) notes that the mirror is thought to reflect the soul, and vampires are thought to be soulless beings. In this case, the queen does not seem to see her own reflection either; rather, she sees that of the fairest in the land, Snow White;

• Vampires are known for sucking blood from their victims, and Snow White is essentially born of blood. After her mother pricks her finger, three droplets of blood fall to the snow, and she is so mesmerized by this image that she wishes for a child "as red as blood" (p. 181). Folklore also describes vampires who attack the heart and organs of their victims. German tales of Dracula state that he dipped bread into the blood of his victims and forced others to eat human flesh (McNally and Florescu, 1994, pp. 84–85). The queen is insistent upon eating the lung and liver of Snow White, and she greedily consumes these organs with salt after her huntsman brings them back (from a boar), as proof of her stepdaughter's death;

- In many tales, vampires appear immortal and eternally young. Bunson (1993) describes Elizabeth Bathory, a Hungarian noblewoman who "developed obsessive interests in her own beauty" and "became convinced that blood was a useful cosmetic and restorative when she hit a victim so hard that blood splashed onto the countess's face and arms" (p. 17). Thereafter, "she drank, bathed, and showered in the blood of maidens, murdering hundreds of young girls who were brought into her service" (p. 17). Our fairy tale queen is likewise obsessed with her own youth and beauty, and her belief that she can remain the fairest in the land forever is tied not merely to death of Snow White, but to the queen's consumption of her organs;

- Ramsland (2002) notes that vampires are thought to have the ability to change into various animals, dust, or a form of mist. Likewise, this queen can change shape, magically altering her image three times as she stalks Snow White;

- In many tales, the vampire must be invited into the victim's home before it can enter. Bunson (1993) suggests that "people remain safe as long as they do not provide hospitality for the undead. Once entry has been secured, however, it is difficult to be rid of the guest" (p. 254). Here, the queen has first been invited into the castle by Snow White's otherwise absent father. After Snow White finds refuge with the dwarfs, she invites the (transformed, disguised) queen into the home on three separate occasions;

- Some vampire tales require the vampire to bite its victims at least three times in order to transform them into vampires as well. Here, the queen visits Snow White three times, and the young stepdaughter finally falls victim after the third attempt with the apple;

- In order to transform a human into a fellow vampire, the siring vampire often has the human consume blood as the final step. On her third visit, the queen has Snow White consume the red portion of the apple only; thereafter, Snow White falls into her own death-like state, sleeping in a glass coffin for years without ever decaying;

The beautiful queen gazes upon her reflection in the enchanted mirror, darkness covering her jealous features in comparison to the fairer Snow White. (Illustration by E. H. Wehnert from *Household Stories Collected by the Brothers Grimm*. London: Routledge and Sons, 1880.)

- Both Barber (1988) and Bunson (1993) explain that it was commonly thought that the deceased could be stopped from rising again as a vampire if they were bound or staked. The queen uses these methods on Snow White, first binding her tightly with laces until she passes out and then "staking" her with a hair comb. Additionally, an item was often placed in the deceased's mouth to keep it from biting should it transform. In "Snow White," the heroine falls down as if dead when she eats a bite of apple, and she comes to only after the piece of apple is dislodged from her throat.

- In addition to being killed by with a stake through the heart, vampires can also be killed through sunlight and through fire. The queen is destroyed when she arrives to the wedding and red-hot iron boots are strapped to her legs, burning her to death;

- In modern vampire films (such as Neil Jordan's 1994 *Interview with the Vampire*, based upon the Anne Rice novel and starring Tom Cruise and Brad Pitt or Tony Scott's 1983 *The Hunger*, based upon Whitley Strieber's novel, with Catherine Deneuve and Susan Sarandon as lesbian vampires), a strong homoerotic theme emerges. This interpretation can be applied to the queen's obsession with Snow White, a beautiful young maiden who is not related to her through blood.

EXTENDING AN INVITATION

Young Snow White has no say regarding the invitation extended to the evil queen by her own father. Quite simply, a year following his wife's death, her royal father marries the new queen, and she assumes control of the castle and his daughter's very life. As *The Talented Mr. Ripley*[4] (1999) opens, we are introduced to Tom Ripley (Matt Damon), who charms and is charmed by the Greenleaf family. Mr. Greenleaf (James Rebhorn), we learn, is a modern-day king and the wealthy head of a shipping empire. He takes an immediate interest in Tom and, based upon one conversation, and his mistaken belief that Tom attended Princeton like his son, he asks, "Could you ever conceive of going to Italy, Tom? Persuade my son to come home? I'd pay you a thousand dollars." Tom accepts the invitation to enter the world of the younger Greenleaf, just as the evil queen is welcomed into the palace of Snow White. And in both instances, a mysterious, dangerous stranger comes into the homes of unsuspecting children at their father's behest. Ramsland's (2002) definition of a vampire suits both the queen and Tom Ripley perfectly:

> Let me repeat, then, that the vampire is a preternatural predatory creature in human form that survives by exploiting the resources of others in a way that weakens or kills them. Usually it goes for the primary resource of life—blood or energy—and often drains the victim on which it feeds to the point of death. Sometimes, the bite will transform the victim, but sometimes that transformation comes only at the behest of the vampire or by going through some kind of special initiation ritual [xiv].

We have learned that inviting a vampire into the home is fundamental to some folklore traditions, tied perhaps to the Christian notion that one should not invite the devil into one's house. In both "Snow White," and *The Talented Mr. Ripley*, the danger of such impulsive invitations is made startlingly explicit. After Snow White is rescued by the dwarfs, they warn her not to let anyone enter the cottage, especially her stepmother. Yet she does not head their repeated warnings. The first time the disguised

The everyday features and insecurities of Tom Ripley (Matt Damon) are overshadowed by the confident, vibrant Dickie Greenleaf (Jude Law) in *The Talented Mr. Ripley* (Paramount/Miramax, 1999). *The Kobal Collection, Phil Bray*

queen visits her with staylaces, Snow White foolishly decides, "I can certainly let this honest woman inside..." (p. 184). After the queen nearly crushes the life from her, she is rescued by the dwarfs who again warn her not to let anyone inside the house. Yet the queen returns with a new disguise and a poisoned comb that proves too tempting for her to resist. As Cashdan (1999) explains, "Like the queen, Snow White wants to be pretty, to be elegant, to be admired. The young child also is driven by vain impulses" (p. 53). The dwarfs manage to revive her yet again, and they beg her to be more vigilant in not answering the door for anyone. Nevertheless, she is once more fooled by the disguised queen, and she takes that fateful bite of apple that puts her into a death-like state until she is accidentally rescued by her prince.

Like the queen, Tom is dependent upon readily proffered invitations to gain entrance into his rival's world. When he pretends to bump into Dickie Greenleaf (Jude Law) and Marge Sherwood (Gwyneth Paltrow) for the first time in Italy, Marge warmly offers, "You should come and have lunch with us before you go," to which Dickie adds, "Sure, *anytime* [emphasis added]." Having gained entrance into their home, Tom now offers his own version of staylaces and pretty combs by appealing to Dickie's love of jazz. Like the evil queen, he knows that he must appeal to his rival on an emotional, primal level: Objects of vanity win the heart of Snow White while music is the key to Dickie. Tom pretends to drop some jazz records from his carrying case and declares his love of Charlie "Bird" Parker, for whom Dickie has even named his yacht. Dickie becomes so flushed with excitement, he emphatically declares, "Okay, we're going to Naples. There's a club. It's not a club, it's a cellar." Marge laughingly calls it "vile," and Dickie says that she does not have to join them. The jazz club is dark and smoky, and the sounds of horns and trumpets resonate off the low ceiling and close walls, passionate life emanating from a crypt-like club. Dickie invites Tom to perform on stage with him, kissing him warmly on the cheek at the end of one number. During a return visit, Tom even sings "My Funny Valentine" while looking longingly at his new friend. Other invitations ensue (for Tom to reside at Dickie's, for Tom to wear some of Dickie's clothes), and Tom is quickly seduced by a lifestyle that he has only witnessed before and is now allowed to experience first-hand. In an intriguing parallel to Bram Stoker's *Dracula* (1897), in which the Count forces the hero to write letters back home, assuring his impending return, Tom has Dickie write his father, implying that he, too, is close to returning: "[Tom] says he's going to haunt me until I agree to go back to New York with him."

The apple has long been considered a sexually dangerous metaphor in literature, linked inextricably to images of Eve seducing Adam to taste of the Tree of Knowledge of Good and Evil. The queen's final visit to Snow White tantalizes on multiple levels, as she has prepared a special apple that is poisoned only on its red side, the side symbolizing blood, flesh, vitality, and sexuality. She convinces Snow White to partake of the forbidden apple by assuring her, "Look, I'll cut the apple in two. You eat the red part, and I'll eat the white" (p. 186). Thus, they each bite into the same apple, Snow White having been seduced by the extraordinary beauty of the apple offered to her. Murphy (2000) compares Snow White's eating the apple to the stepmother's eating of what she believed were the young girl's organs: Both are ingesting aspects of beauty with the hope of making themselves more beautiful. Giving into this temptation leads to Snow White's final fall. This fairy tale scene parallels one of the more homoerotic scenes of *The Talented Mr. Ripley*, again centering on an invitation. Dickie is shown lounging in a drawn bath, playing chess with a fully-dressed Tom who lets his fingertips softly pierce the surface of the bath-water. In this instance, Tom issues his own invitation, asking if he can get into the tub as well. Dickie bristles at the implication, and says that Tom can get in only as he gets out. Walking naked across the room, Dickie notices Tom admiring him in a mirror, but now he seems silently flattered by the attention he has flamed, and he playfully snaps his towel at him.

The final invitation issued by Dickie to Tom results in a scene that perversely inverts their bathtub dalliance. Having tired of his poor, less-cultured friend, Dickie says that Tom really should return home to the states. In a half-hearted attempt to lessen the severity of Tom's eviction, he says that he wants to move on and casually tells Tom, "It would be great, though, if you came with me to San Remo" to help him find a new place to live. Tom accepts, of course, and the two soon appear in a small, white boat in the middle of the water. As Snow White once stumbled across the dwarfs' little home by accident, Dickie remarks that he found his res-idence in Mongi through similar happenstance, taking a boat around the bay, and declaring, "First thing I liked, I got it." The two young men are as isolated as the queen and Snow White at the forest cottage, and the set-ting is as frighteningly intimate as that of a vampire victim's bedroom. The intimacy is increased by Dickie's love of sailing. In a 2004 interview with Johanna Schneller, Jude Law claims that sailing is integral to his charac-ter, "I'll never forget the feeling of catching that first wind, the sun in my face, and thinking, 'Ohhh, this is what this guy lives for. I get this'" (p. 75). Their scene also recalls an earlier moment when Dickie made love to Marge in the cabin of his yacht while Tom listened on the deck. For Dickie, sailing represents raw sensuality, adventure, and freedom from responsi-bility. He has even named his yacht "Bird" to honor his love of jazz and Charlie "Bird" Parker. He is also very skilled at boating, and his charac-ter seems to thrive on the intense control that is required to pilot any type of watercraft. As captain, he does not like to have his authority questioned.

When Dickie tells Tom that he is going to marry Marge, Tom is incred-ulous and begins berating him for his affairs and, more importantly, for how that would affect their relationship. Tom tells him that this idea of marriage is "absurd," and he exclaims that he has been honest about how he feels. Dickie reacts angrily, comparing Tom to a true bloodsucker: "You can be *a leech*, you know that [emphasis added]." He tells Tom to quit act-ing like a little girl, and he begins slapping him repeatedly until Tom reflexively hits him with an oar. Blood drips from Dickie onto Tom's face, as he tries to choke the leech to death. Tom finally pushes him off and violently stakes him, repeatedly, through the chest with the oar handle. As the sun sets, we witness Tom cuddled up next to the lifeless Dickie, blood-drenched waters washing over them both in their sea-faring tub.

After her third strike upon Snow White, the queen proudly declares her victory: "White as snow, red as blood, black as ebony! This time the dwarfs won't be able to bring you back to life!" (p. 186). She then races home to her mirror, demanding to be told who is now the fairest in the land. Once the honest mirror replies that she is indeed the fairest in the land, the queen finds "her jealous heart was satisfied as much as a jealous heart can be satisfied" (p. 186). These same primary colors of white, red, and black become attached to Dickie as well, who is dressed in a black shirt and white slacks, both stained with his own red blood. A key difference between the queen and Tom lies in their initial level of volition. Minghella (1999a) explains that, for Tom, this first murder is "an accident which inadvertently provides Ripley with a defining opportunity. And, as so often in this story, it's an opportunity he seizes as much in shame as in calculation" (p. xiii). Following this bloody baptismal, Tom sinks Dickie in the boat, keeping his watch, jacket, and ring. He returns to the hotel, only to be mistaken immediately by the attendant for Dickie Greenleaf. Having vanquished his rival, Tom finds that his transformation to become the fairest in his land is underway.

INTERROGATING THE MIRROR

The queen, Tom Ripley, and vampires are all focused primarily on their external transformations, whether becoming young and beautiful or remaining that way for eternity. Thus, they each exhibit an obsessive fascination or fear of mirrors that reflect everything they are not. In "Snow White" and *The Talented Mr. Ripley*, the mirrors always seem to reflect and magnify their rivals' beauty to the diminishment of their own. When the queen tracks down her stepdaughter in the forest, she appears as an old hag, further diminishing her appearance in contrast to the fairest in the land (McGlathery, 1991). Likewise, when Tom is around Dickie, he wears his oversized glasses and allows his hair to fall self-consciously in his face. Whenever the queen and Tom are in the presence of their rivals, it is to the detriment of their own physical appearance. After all, Snow White and

Dickie Greenleaf are not simply beautiful, they are the *most* beautiful by their very natures. Even their names reveal their preternatural perfection, christened as they are for a natural object (snow, a leaf) coupled with its purest, freshest, and most vibrant color (white, green). Their names belie their youth and beauty, but they also reveal how they are viewed by their unwelcome rivals: For the queen, Snow White embodies an untainted beauty that reminds her daily of her own aging to the point that "her hate for the girl was so great that her heart throbbed and turned in her breast" every time she looked upon her rival (p. 182). Cashdan (1999) notes that "the dynamic that drives the story and guides it to its inexorable conclusion is vanity. Vanity is the thread that weaves itself throughout, making its presence felt soon after the king selects a new wife" (p. 43). Similarly, glowing Dickie Greenleaf brings out Tom's feelings of jealously and vanity. Moreover, he also stands for a natural connection to a respected family tree that has deep roots in highest society. As Tom is driven by Mr. Greenleaf's chauffeur to his point of departure, the driver tells him plainly that the Greenleaf name opens a lot of doors. It is therefore no surprise that he assumes it instantly when first asked his name upon arriving in Italy. In contrast, Tom Ripley's surname and personality suggest ripples like those found in water, with successive ripples becoming less and less defined as they move away from the center.

Tom's physical nature is squarely contrasted with Dickie's from the moment that they first meet on the beach. Dickie is fit and golden, shining in the afternoon sun with his equally lovely girlfriend, Marge. Tom, however, wears glasses and seems a bit awkward physically and socially. He is also as pale as a vampire, and Dickie states as honestly as a magic mirror, "You're so white. Did you ever see a guy so white, Marge? Gray, actually." Tom replies that his color is like an auto undercoating with the unstated implication being that he is ready to assume any top layer of paint. His hue fits his mutability (neither black nor white), as well, particularly with regard to his talents as he describes them to Dickie: "Forging signatures, uh, telling lies, impersonating practically anybody." He goes on to impress Dickie by doing a perfect voice impression of the elder Greenleaf. A bit later, Tom eavesdrops on Dickie and Marge and begins mimicking their voices, too, while practicing in front of a mirror.

When describing the queen versus Snow White, Seifert (1986) claims, "The fairy tale alludes specifically to blood in the snow and thus to a particular sort of polarity. If in the snow we see an image of death, then in the blood we see an image of life. *Cold and warm, hidden, and self-revealing life meet* [emphasis added]" (p. 49). Likewise, the differences between Tom and Dickie come across as cold night and warm day. After Dickie grows tired of Tom and begins paying attention to his wealthy, boorish friend, Freddie Miles (Phillip Seymour Hoffman), Marge explains, "The thing with Dickie, it's like the sun shines on you, and it's glorious. And then he forgets you, and it's very, very cold." Dickie is adverse to having any ugliness, darkness, or responsibility in his life, and despite his outer appearance, he is not an emotionally appealing character. As Bronski (2000) points out, Minghella has "coarsened" Highsmith's original character to make Tom Ripley appear more sympathetic to the audience by comparison. Dickie seems to care little for his cancer-stricken mother in the states, and he has multiple affairs while carrying on with the devoted Marge. He also refuses to help Silvana (Stefania Rocca), an Italian girl who is secretly carrying his child. After she drowns herself in town, he briefly shows some remorse, and then quickly decides to make a fresh start by moving and leaving behind the ugliness he has created.

This contrast between light and dark emerges most strongly in their personalities and sense of self-awareness. When Tom analyzes Dickie's handwriting, he says that it shows him to be vain, which Dickie proudly agrees with, and carrying a secret pain, which Dickie vacuously declares must be so secret that he does not even know about it. In contrast, when Tom describes himself to Peter Smith-Kingsley (Jack Davenport), a friend of Marge who is truly taken with him, he reveals an acute awareness of the real, secret pains that he must hide:

> Don't you just take the past and put it in a room in the basement and lock the door and never go in there? That's what I do.... And then you meet someone special and all you want to do is toss them the key and say, "Open up, step inside." But you can't, because it's dark, and there are demons, and if anybody saw how ugly it is... I keep wanting to do that—fling the door open, just let the light in and clean everything out.

Tom's description echoes the description of the queen's own hidden room, "a secret and solitary chamber where no one else ever went" (p. 186). And, in the end, the differences between Tom and Dickie seem as superficial and fleeting as those fancied between the former beauty queen and Snow White. The true difference between Tom and Dickie, a difference that Tom comes to comprehend with frightening clarity, is not that one is filled with light and the other darkness, but that they are both internally dark characters whose shadings are defined by their social status and acceptance by the world around them.

Vampire folklore suggests that vampires cannot cast a reflection because they are soulless beings. The queen and Tom both willingly sacrifice their own souls at the alter of their mirrors. The queen can find no solace as she gazes into her mirror only to be reminded that Snow White surpasses her in beauty. As Blake (2000) hypothesizes for Tom, "If he appropriates the clothes and the body, why not the soul?" (p. 19). Minghella employs mirrors and reflections in ingenious ways to reveal the image (and soul) of Dickie prominently over that of Tom. In the bathtub scene described earlier, Tom quietly takes in the full reflection of his naked rival as he towels himself dry. Tom is later embarrassed when Dickie arrives home to find Tom wearing his dress shirt and jacket while dancing giddily around Dickie's bedroom. Tom races behind a free-standing, full-length mirror with just his head and feet in view around the frame. A statue of a man's torso missing the head, arms, and legs stands on a pedestal to the right of the mirror. We see Dickie's head-to-toe reflection fully in the mirror, facing Tom in disgust. It appears as if Dickie has been consumed by Tom, and we are witnessing an x-ray to his soul. On their final trip together, Dickie appears to be asleep on the train, and his profile is reflected in the train cabin window. Tom carefully positions his head perpendicular to Dickie's profile so that half of his face joins with Dickie's to form a complete image. Dickie catches Tom—as he did in the bathroom and in front of his full-length mirror—and asks him why he always does "that thing" with his neck. In each of these instances, it seems as if Dickie's reflection has a consciousness of its own, watching Tom as Tom watches him.

Even after Dickie's death, his countenance still haunts Tom. While riding his scooter past a furniture store selling dozens of mirrors in the street, Tom imagines Dickie's reflection surrounding him, causing him to crash onto his side. When he stands up, he looks down into a cracked mirror reflecting his own broken image back at him. Throughout the remainder of the film, his reflection is shown in variably distorted ways that symbolize his vanishing self and soul. Thus, when he writes a suicide note for Dickie, having him say, "You've always understood what's at the heart of me, Tom," we witness his distorted reflection in a piano, his visage being pulled in opposite directions. In the DVD chapter "Suspicion," after Marge finds Dickie's promise ring in Tom's apartment, she asks Tom to explain how it appeared there. He has just emerged from the bath and quickly begins looking for any instrument that might be used as a weapon. As he finds a razor blade, he catches a brief glance of his face in a magnifying make-up mirror, his own fear and determination enlarged proportionately. He puts the razor in the pocket of his white bathrobe and confronts Marge, stammering, "He has so many realities, Dickie, and he believes them all." White, red, and black again take prominence as the tension steadily builds. Tom draws closer to Marge, declaring his love for her while clutching the razor in his pocket so hard that blood seeps through his pristine robe. He does not seem to notice, but Marge does. As she backs away in utter terror, Tom slowly approaches, his face masked in dark shadow. Tom's magnified, malformed image converges with his insistence on perverting reality. As the blood flows freely onto his bathrobe, we realize how quickly Tom's world, constructed as it is on coincidence and prevarication, can be shattered by even the smallest truth. Like the queen who visits Snow White only when the dwarfs are away, Tom attacks only when completely alone with his victim, and Marge is only saved by Peter's unexpected arrival.

DANCING IN THE RED-HOT SLIPPERS

Meredith Logue (Cate Blanchett), an original character created by Minghella for the film, appears only in a few brief scenes throughout the course of the film. She seems a bit frail, emotionally available, yet always on her guard. She also becomes one of the film's most compelling characters, because she is ultimately the driving force behind Tom's transformation into Dickie Greenleaf. Meredith crosses Tom's path at three primary junctures in the film. After each of these encounters, Tom's personality changes in distinct ways that parallel the deadly objects offered to Snow White by the queen on each of her three visits. Her appearance also precipitates Tom's murders of Dickie, Freddie, and Peter, since each of these men becomes a threat to the image she creates of Tom as Dickie:

• The queen first appears offering staylaces to squeeze the life force out of Snow White. Following his first meeting with Meredith when he claims to be Dickie Greenleaf, Tom quickly becomes a suffocating personality around Dickie. The film's conclusion is foreshadowed as Tom rides behind Dickie on his Vespa, with Dickie twice cautioning Tom, "You're breaking my ribs!"

• The queen next appears with a comb that appeals so much to Snow White's vanity that she lets her in to comb her hair. During Tom's second encounter with Meredith, she appeals to his vanity by helping him pick out new tailor-made suits and asking him to the opera. Freddie, who has regarded Tom with suspicion since first meeting him, even comments, "Hmm, in fact, the only thing that looks like Dickie is you."

• The queen returns a third time to tempt Snow White to eat from the same irresistible apple, signaling a sexual awakening in her stepdaughter. Tom seems fully prepared to enter into a sexual relationship with Peter when Meredith appears again. He kisses her as Dickie, effectively dooming his future with Peter.

Every vampire needs a sire to transform him completely into his altered state, and Meredith serves as Tom's from their very first meeting when the ship from America docks in Italy. In the DVD chapter "Partners in Disguise," Tom innocently looks for his luggage under "R," for Ripley, while Meredith immediately notices and appears attracted to him. He does not notice her. When they end up in line together, she questions immediately, "What's your secret?" ostensibly referring to his ability to travel with but one suitcase to her dozens. She asks probing questions, particularly when he tells her that his name is Dickie Greenleaf, and she wonders why he would be traveling under "R." When he lies that he is using his mother's maiden name to give himself privacy from the famed Greenleaf name, she reveals that she is actually doing the same to hide from her family's renowned wealth. They talk briefly and arrive "at a crossroads on the stairs.... They're going in different directions" (Minghella, 1999a, p. 10). This description is especially apt and telling, as a crossroads is considered a meeting place of evil in folklore. Vampires, in particular, are said to find the crossroads confusing, as they prefer a specific direction (Bunson, 1993, p. 57). Although Tom fails to recognize their similarities, Meredith comments, "So—partners in disguise," pointing to their shared hidden nature as they say goodbye. Around Meredith, a stranger whom he will come to know more intimately on two additional, pivotal occasions, he must repeatedly slip on the red-hot slippers and dance the dance of Dickie Greenleaf.

In the DVD chapter "New Beginning," Meredith makes her second appearance, this time in Rome, coincidentally bumping into Tom just after he has killed Dickie. Her presence again forces him into the role of shipping-heir/prince, but now he is a bit more practiced and polished. He claims to have broken up with Marge, and, revealing his increasingly vampiric nature, declares, "I feel like I've been handed a new life." In "Snow White," the dwarfs not only place their beloved in a glass coffin, they write her title of princess on it in gold letters. When the prince happens to come along, it is important that he see her comparable title as well as her incomparable beauty. Likewise, when Snow White rises from her transparent tomb, the prince proudly announces his heritage by asking her to accompany him to his father's castle where she will be his wife. So ends their curt courtship leading up to their wedding and the queen's fiery funeral. Social class and title are just as important in Meredith's world; thus, she again points to the similarities—as she sees them—between herself and her partner in disguise. She explains, "The truth is, if you've had money your entire life, even if you despise it, which we do—agreed?—you're only truly comfortable around other people who have it and despise it." On the surface, her simple comment could seem to be a flirtatious faux pas uttered under false circumstances. Tom, after all, has no money of his own, nor has he ever had any to despise. Meredith continually, almost desperately, feeds the image of Tom as Dickie, and she needs him to remain in character in order for her to feel "truly comfortable" not just with him but also with herself. Her societal constructions allow Meredith her most meaningful reactions with a living, deadly delusion.

She helps him pick out new, tailor-made jackets and escorts him to the opera *Eugene Onegin*.[5] Shakespeare's Hamlet taught the world that "the play's the thing" in order to "catch the conscience of the king," and act two of this opera serves that same purpose. A duel occurs between two friends, and as one shoots the other dead, bright red blood seeps across a snow-covered stage. A black cape is draped across the victor, again highlighting the primary colors of the queen's and Tom's jealousy and guilt. Tom naturally seems mesmerized by the performance; Meredith, however, looks straight ahead, completely unaware of its emotional effect on Tom. She remains in the dark. During an intermission, Tom excuses himself and bumps into Marge and her friend, Peter, who is, like Meredith, instantly enamored of Tom. This unexpected encounter breaks Meredith's spell temporarily, as Marge immediately notices that Tom is not wearing his glasses. Tom must also covertly take off Dickie's promise ring, a gift from Marge that Dickie swore he would never remove. He learns that Peter and Meredith know each other, and the two now become polarizing forces, one attracted to Tom and the other to his portrayal of Dickie. In order to protect his secret life, Tom rushes Meredith from the opera, breaking off their friendship by claiming she reminds him too much of Marge. As he gets ready to leave her, she asks, "Will you meet me tomorrow? Just to say goodbye in the daylight, properly? So it's not just this, it's too—you should always save pain for daylight."

In "Snow White," the new, young queen shows that she has indeed learned from her wicked stepmother. Snow White issues a final invitation to her, knowing that she will not be able to resist the offer. And while the queen initially—and wisely—hesitates, "[S]he could not calm herself until she saw the young queen" (p. 188). Snow White has not risen again as a forgiving soul, and she seems as determined as her stepmother to remain the fairest in the land. When the evil queen arrives, red-hot slippers are placed on her feet, and she is forced to dance in them until dead. No dwarfs come to this queen's rescue, and no prince happens along to revive her. In contrast to some of the other fairy tale princesses, like Brier Rose and Rapunzel, this tale does not conclude with a declaration of "happily ever after," but rather with a proclamation of vengeance that is explicit, painful, and final.

In the last DVD chapter, "A Fake Somebody, A Real Nobody," Tom accepts a final invitation of his own, this time to travel with the perfectly well-adjusted Peter on a cruise ship. He is Tom again, and he appears ready to leave his costume of Dickie behind forever. Meredith happens to be aboard the same ship, however, and she soon recognizes Tom as her rogue, Dickie, whom she'd left behind in Rome. She is surrounded by family members who would easily miss her absence, and Tom is forced to prepare an improvised, encore performance on their behalf. As Minghella (1999a) argues, his version of this work "contains an implicit cautionary tale.... [Tom's] rebirth is a temporary disguise and, worse, one that condemns the imposter to a constant fear of exposure and the humiliation which follows. To be uncovered as a sham is the very thing which prompts Ripley to sham in the first place" (p. xii). Following Meredith's third appearance, Tom naturally becomes Dickie once again, realizing to his horror that he cannot dance fast enough for Tom and Peter and Dickie and Meredith. He kisses Meredith and tells her that he will meet her later; thus, she has succeeded in staking Tom and resurrecting her image of Dickie.

In *The Psychopath in Film*, Wilson (1999) discusses film psychopaths in a manner befitting our vampiric queen and Tom:

> Character development for the psychopath does not mean becoming more benevolent and loving with age. Quite the contrary, it *can* mean that the evil personality assumes greater sophistication in learning how to tweak the opposition. The psychopath's selfish gratifications do not change, merely the process by which he or she gains those gratifications [p. 104].

As he returns to Peter's cabin, Tom seems to realize the truth about his own gratifications, and he laments, "I'm going to be stuck in the basement, aren't I, that's my, that's my—terrible and alone and dark—and I've lied about who I am, and where I am, and so nobody can ever find me.... I always thought it'd be better to be a fake somebody than a real nobody." Perversely, sadly, and selfishly, he then has Peter tell him "some good things about Tom Ripley," and Peter's list comes to serve as a eulogy for Tom. Peter offers, "Tom is talented. Tom is tender. Tom is beautiful." As Peter continues his heartfelt series of attributes, Tom climbs on top of him in bed, slowly crushing him—and the remaining vestiges of Tom Ripley—to death. Peter's final, horrified words are the realization that "Tom is crushing me."

Blake (2000) concludes, "In the company of the talented Mr. Ripley, we have experienced unadorned evil and come to realize that its emissary has no face, no identity. He is talented indeed, but empty" (p. 20). Having removed the threat of Peter, the fake somebody goes back to his cabin and sits silently on his bed. The camera pans from one side of his face, bathed in light, to the other side, covered in darkness. The cabin door to his closet opens and we see Tom's reflection in its door mirror. The door then slowly closes, cutting his reflection ever smaller until the door shuts, like a casket lid closing up after a vampire's feasting has finally come to an end.

• FIVE •

Mother of the Pride

"Cinderella" and
Aliens

A GRIMM VIEW OF MANMADE MONSTERS

Our most immediate image of a manmade monster likely derives not from the Grimm fairy tales but rather from James Whale's 1931 *Frankenstein*, starring Boris Karloff as a grunting, slow-moving monster stitched together from discarded human remains, including an abnormal brain.[1] Yet, this monster is a drastic shift from Mary Shelley's 1818 version, a nameless monster that is articulate, literate, and philosophical about its creation and fate. It is also dangerous and calculating, killing Victor Frankenstein's brother and framing Justine, a friend of the family, for the murder. The monster later kills Frankenstein's friend, Clerval, and young bride, Elizabeth, when Frankenstein fails to follow through on a promise to create a bride for him. Frankenstein fears that doing so would allow the monsters to create a race of demons to overpower humanity. He spends the remainder of his life tracking the monster in the hope of killing his creation, but he dies before accomplishing the goal. The monster learns of its creator's death and sails off on a small raft into the darkness, vowing to reduce itself to ashes on a funeral pyre.

Despite the apparent "maleness" of Shelley's *Frankenstein*, the story

100

has undeniably maternal underpinnings. Jones (2002) suggests that the novel "is rich in its accounts of anxieties surrounding childbirth, gender and sexuality and also in its account of neglectful parenthood" (p. 61), and he points out that childbirth was statistically the greatest killer of the eighteenth and nineteenth centuries. Victor Frankenstein serves as a hermaphroditic father and mother by giving life to the monster on his own. Yet once his progeny surges with life, he flees in horror, abandoning his artificial offspring to fend for itself. Jones (2002) remarks that the creature's size and power allow it to become a hyper-masculine counterpart to the feminized doctor. In both the novel and the film, the creature's violence stems primarily from its immediate and continued rejection from a "normal" outside world that is repulsed by its grotesque appearance. Thus, while it is an unusual being created through the science of Frankenstein, it is ultimately made into a monster by the perceptions of a fearful, judgmental society. Although it is made entirely of human parts, Shelley's monster finally defines itself against humanity: "There was none among the myriads of men that existed who would pity or assist me; and should I feel kindness towards my enemies? No: from that moment I declared everlasting war against the species, and, more than all, against him who had formed me, and sent me forth to this insupportable misery" (p. 162).

The Grimm Brothers do not provide us with monster tales to warn us of the dangers of modern science and technology; rather, they see monsters residing in everyday homes, maniacal, menacing (step)mothers[2] who favor their own like children over those who better fit into "normal" society. In many of the tales, the "monster" is, ironically, considered the beautiful, helpful child by a calculating maternal figure trying to protect her own interests and those of her biologically similar children. And, in most cases, she is a stepmother who has married into a family to usurp its resources for her own plans. Tatar (2003) reminds us that "given the high mortality rate for women during their childbearing years, a stepmother in the household (and a hostile one at that) came perilously close to counting as the rule rather than as the exception" (pp. 49–50). She goes on to explain that the Grimm stepmothers, in particular, emerge as villains equal in wickedness to wolves and witches, while their persecuted stepdaughters "take on the role of innocent martyrs and patient sufferers" (p. 141).

Two of the most famous stepmother monsters arise in "Hansel and Gretel" and "Snow White." In the former tale, the poor stepmother convinces the father to abandon his children in the woods where they encounter her witchy doppelgänger, while the royal stepmother of the latter tale comes to envy her stepdaughter so much that she demands that the young girl be killed and cooked for her. Regardless of their social standing, these stepmothers clearly view their stepchildren as threats to their own physical and psychological welfare. For them, the monster is not a helpless child, but rather a genuine, growing danger to her livelihood. It is therefore not surprising that each of these women is ultimately killed—burned to death in an oven and red-hot iron boots, respectively—by the child she feared most. In the Grimm fairy tale world, any judgment of the child's actions is tempered by the apparent justice delivered to the evil stepmother.

In "Mother Holle" (discussed in the Conclusion) we learn of a widow with two daughters who are polar opposites: Her stepdaughter is beautiful and works hard, while her own daughter is ugly and lazy. Naturally, she has the stepdaughter do all of the household chores, including spinning by an enchanted well. One day, she drops the spinning reel into the well and must go down to get it. Therein, she discovers the hidden world of Mother Holle, a magical woman who lets her work for her. The girl stays with her for several years and when she asks to return home, Mother Holle rewards her with gold for all of her service. Upon hearing this tale, the stepmother has her biological daughter enter Mother Holle's service, but she is too lazy to complete any of the tasks asked of her. Thus, instead of gold, she is rewarded with a covering of black pitch that sticks to her for as long as she lives.

In both "One-Eye, Two-Eyes, Three-Eyes" and "Eve's Unequal Children," the Grimms show us birth mothers who distinguish their children based upon their physical attributes. The mother and daughters One-Eye and Three-Eyes abuse and curse the noble Two-Eyes because she blends in with the rest of society, telling her that she cannot possibly belong to their family. They give her shabby clothes to wear and only leftovers to eat. A wise woman takes pity on the girl and teaches her a spell so that she can call forth a goat that will bring her food, but her family discovers the secret and they kill it. A young knight eventually comes along and marries Two-Eyes, leaving her sisters and mother behind. After several years pass, the sisters visit Two-Eyes, begging for alms. She treats them kindly, and they regret how they once treated her. The "normal" one is, naturally, given the opportunity to show largesse to her now sycophantic siblings.

Similarly, "Eve's Unequal Children," shows us a mother with both

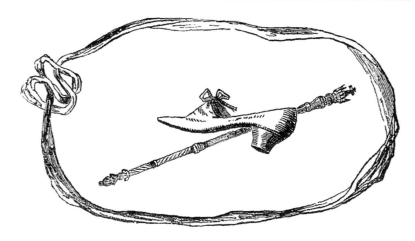

The prince identifies Cinderella despite her dirty complexion and ragged
clothing by having her try on the golden slipper provided by her mother's
spirit. (Illustration by E. H. Wehnert from *Household Stories Collected by
the Brothers Grimm*. London: Routledge and Sons, 1880.)

beautiful and ugly children; however, she fears that the Lord will only look
kindly upon her beautiful ones, so she hides the ugly offspring when He
comes to visit. She is so delighted when the Lord blesses her beautiful children—telling them that they will be knights, scholars, and princes—that
she brings forth her "misshapen" children as well. When they are blessed
as fishermen, blacksmiths, and tailors, Eve asks the Lord how he can treat
these children so unequally when bestowing his blessings. The Lord
explains to Eve that all of her children and His disparate blessings are
part of a greater plan, and no child is any less (or more) important—or
blessed—in His eyes than any other. While the moral superficially shows
the value of all individuals, regardless of their appearance and profession,
the lesson clearly indicates that the beautiful children will be favored by
their parents, society, and even the Lord throughout their lives. He still
chooses not to make even one of the ugly children a king.

In all of these tales—as well as in "Cinderella," the focus of this
chapter—there are no male figures of consequence. Hansel is rescued by
Gretel, and their father is dominated by his wife's demands; Snow White's
father never comes to her defense, and she is rescued by clumsiness (stum-
bling by servants removes the poisoned apple piece) rather than princely
action; and the (step)mothers of "Mother Holle," "One-Eye, Two-Eyes,
Three-Eyes," and "Eve's Unequal Children" each try to control their

children's destinies, albeit with little success. The monster mother in each
of these tales is manmade in the sense that her actions are determined by
standards (of beauty and prestige), circumstances (like starvation and
birthright), and options (of marriage and little else) provided to her by her
society. When she is punished or, better yet, violently destroyed, we cheer
her passing and applaud the rewards bestowed upon her beautiful, resourceful rival.

DRESSING IN RAGS, SLEEPING IN ASHES

James Cameron's *Aliens* (1986) ties into several fairy tales. As the
film opens, the camera pans to the lone survivor of Ridley Scott's *Alien*
(1979), Ripley (Sigourney Weaver), a sleeping beauty in a glass case who
is awakened from hypersleep 57 years following her first encounter with
the lethal alien being. With her dark hair, white skin, and red lips, she is
later compared directly to Snow White when first seen by one of the
marines, Vasquez (Jenette Goldstein), on their trip back to the planet to
find and destroy the aliens. And in the film's conclusion, Ripley leaves
flares to find her way out of the unfamiliar darkness, much like Hansel and
Gretel do in the forest with shiny pebbles and breadcrumbs. Yet the film's
narrative structure and themes most closely parallel those of "Cinderella,"
in which a young girl loses her family and must struggle to survive on her
own when a new mother arrives with her own threatening, self-serving
family.

As the story of "Cinderella" begins, we learn that the wife of a wealthy
man has fallen ill and died, leaving behind a good and pious daughter. The
father then marries a new bride with two lovely daughters of her own[3], but
both possessing "nasty and wicked hearts" (Grimm & Grimm, 2003, p.
79). They soon take away Cinderella's beautiful clothes, dressing her in
wooden shoes and an old gray smock, and they have her do all of the cooking and cleaning. We are also told that they remove her bed, forcing her
to sleep in the ashes next to the kitchen hearth. From this point on, they
insultingly refer to her as Cinderella, and we never learn her birth name.
We do not know anything about the stepsisters' past, including what happened to their biological father. Interestingly, it is Cinderella's father who
comes across as truly despicable, for he does nothing to assist her in this
abusive environment, in essence leaving her completely orphaned.

Aliens provides us with two female characters who have lost all of the family and standing that they once cherished. When she set off on her original mission in Ridley Scott's *Alien* (1979), Ripley was a respected pilot with, we learn in James Cameron's extended edition of this sequel, a daughter left behind on earth. After being awakened, she discovers that her life has completely changed. She faces a stern review board and has her flight license revoked for blowing up the company's mothership, the Nostromo.[4] Thereafter, she ends up working on the cargo loading docks. Since she has no evidence of the alien creature, she is ordered to undergo monthly psychiatric check-ups. She also suffers from regular nightmares in which the alien bursts forth from her stomach. Far worse, however, she learns that the daughter she left behind has since lived an entire life and passed away, childless. Ripley has been orphaned in reverse, and her immediate stepfamily is now comprised of the conniving Burke (Paul Reiser), a company yes-man who convinces Ripley that she can get her license and life back if she will help them track the creature, and some gung-ho marines who do not take her seriously. She agrees to return under one genocidal condition: "Just tell me one thing, Burke. You're going out there to destroy them, right? Not to study, not to bring back? But to wipe them out." Ripley is purely interested in the survival of the human race, particularly after she learns that families and children have been sent to colonize and "terraform" this alien planet, sarcastically referred to as a "shake-and-bake" colony. It will not have much original flavor, but it will in a darkly comic way provide basic nutrients to the quickly breeding aliens.

When we first see Newt (Carrie Henn), she is a pretty little girl with silky blond hair. She and her brother are shown briefly along with her mother and father on their way to inspect the alien spacecraft that arrived before their colony had been shaken and baked. Her life at this moment is happy and normal, clean and content. Like Cinderella, however, she soon loses her entire family to the invasion of the new mother and her voracious alien children. When Ripley and the troop of marines finally arrive and discover her on the seemingly deserted planet, she has survived by living in a dirty little airway room that is accessible only by crawling through a series of narrow shafts and air vents. Her hair and face are filthy, and her clothes are torn and gray. Schickel (1986) describes her as "a Dickensian waif ... living an almost rodent-like existence" (p. 55). At first the traumatized girl is completely mute, having been reduced to a feral state by the traumas she has endured. Her muteness ties her even more closely to

In *Aliens* (20th Century–Fox, 1986), Ripley (Sigourney Weaver) reveals her maternal qualities, finding a pretty little girl underneath the grimy, psychologically wounded appearance of Newt (Carrie Henn). *The Kobal Collection*

the Grimm heroine who, according to Bottigheimer (1987), makes the fewest direct statements in their final version of the tale, eclipsed by all of the other characters, including her domineering stepmother.

Cinderella and Newt both go by nicknames rather than their given, "human" birth names, and each is linked to a dangerous world through that nickname. In her extensive study of the etymology of Cinderella's name, Rooth (1980) finds that its earliest meanings in Greek and Italian tie it directly to the name "hearth cat" with the Italian name being "La Gatta Cenerentola" (pp. 111–113). Although Cinderella is not compared directly to a cat in the Grimm version, she is said to be as nimble as a squirrel as she makes her escape into the trees following the ball, and her humanity has largely been stripped from her. Most intriguingly, although the nickname is given to her by the wicked stepsisters and thereafter used by her stepmother and father, it remains with her even after she marries the prince, and she does not connect any sense of shame or humiliation to the name.

Through just a few degrees of separation, the character of Newt can also trace her origins back to a cat from another author's version of a similar tale. In *Alien*, Ripley risks her life to rescue Jonesey, a cat that lives on in the sequel. Ripley leaves the cat safely on earth for her subsequent battle with the aliens, and Newt comes to serve, in Cameron's own words, as "a surrogate cat ... to have an emotional center to the film" (Goldberg, et. al., 1995). Bundtzen (1987) goes so far as to argue that Newt (another name for a salamander) hints at a reptilian animalism that ties the young girl to the alien queen. In this instance, her former life as Rebecca—we learn her name when Ripley finds a labeled picture of her showing that she won a citizenship award—is destroyed by a maternal force that is as strong as Cinderella's stepfamily. When Ripley first calls her "Rebecca," Newt carefully corrects her, having adopted this nickname as fully as her fairy tale cousin adopted her own. On a very human level, Newt and Ripley share the pain of loss and the instinctive skills that help them survive when attacked.

PROTECTING THE MATERNAL BLOODLINE

Although *Aliens* has sparked numerous interpretations regarding feminist heroes and fears of technology, critics agree that the mother-daughter relationship is the central controlling theme of *Aliens* (Bundtzen, 1987; Schickel, 1986). This theme is also the driving force within the Grimm Brothers' "Cinderella." Before she passes away, Cinderella's mother calls her to her bedside and asks her to live a good and pious life, promising her eternal love and protection: "I shall look down from heaven and take care of you" (p. 79). Cinderella later plants a twig in her mother's grave and waters it with her tears until it grows into a beautiful tree. Her mother's spirit takes the form of a little white bird that stays in the tree and brings Cinderella anything that she wishes for, most famously the three dresses and slippers for the ball. Throughout the tale, Cinderella is helped by heavenly little birds, including two white pigeons that reveal her stepsisters' deceptive footwear and that vengefully peck out their eyes at her wedding.

Like Cinderella, Newt's birth mother is first replaced by an alien queen who uses Newt's biological father to further her own family's needs (by impregnating him with an alien embryo). Ripley enters her world as gently as Cinderella's little white bird to become a protective, spiritual mother. She descends from the heavens and immediately bonds with the little girl, wiping grime from her face and saying gently, "Hard to believe there's a

little girl under all this. And a pretty one too. I don't know how you managed to stay alive, but you're one brave kid, Rebecca." At this time, her
new charge reveals that she goes by the nickname Newt, no doubt because
she is small and moves around as quickly as this small lizard. Like Cinderella, her birth name is no longer associated with her being. They are
both renamed for circumstances outside of their control, and those names
come to symbolize their greatest strengths, whether rising from the ashes
in triumph or avoiding capture by crawling through tight spaces.

In the DVD Chapter "A Mother's Love," one of the film's few quiet
scenes plays out like a gentle bedtime story. Ripley tries to get Newt to
take a nap in the medical lab, but the clever girl fears her nightmares just
like Ripley. Newt explains, "My mommy always said there are no monsters, no real ones, but there are. Why do they tell little kids that?" Ripley responds simply and directly, "Most of the time it's true." She puts a
locator bracelet on Newt and goes on to make a promise that is almost identical to that given by Cinderella's mother: "Newt, I'm going to be right in
the next room. And you see that camera right up there? I can see you right
through that camera all the time to see if you're safe. *I'm not going to leave
you, Newt. I mean that. That's a promise* [emphasis added]." With the camera and the locator bracelet, she can watch over her even when she is not
physically with her.

As they talk, Newt compares the aliens' means of gestating inside a
living human host to her child's idea of giving actual birth: "Isn't that how
babies come? I mean, people babies? They grow inside you." Ripley
assures her that the processes are different, but *Aliens* clearly plays into
very real fears about childbirth and questions about the meaning of family. The alien birth process consists of several steps. First, a spider-like
creature hatches from an egg. It moves quickly and attaches itself to the
face of the first available human host, male or female. Next it impregnates
its host with a parasitic creature that gestates inside far removed from its
mother. The spider-like creature becomes a shell that falls off, and the host
continues living unaware that it is serving as nourishment for a growing
alien. When it finally matures, the creature busts violently out of its host
to capture other humans and continue the process. As Glassy (2001) points
out, "the Alien has the ability to find the best genes it can in the 'species
du jour' and incorporate these genes into its own genome and life cycle"
(p. 252).

This process is not much unlike what transpires in Cinderella's home following her mother's death. Her father is a wealthy man, and he invites a new woman and her offspring into the home. Like the alien queen, these parasites have found the most suitable hosts for their immediate needs. They are also outwardly appealing, disguising their wicked inner natures like an alien within its host. They subsist and thrive through the father's financial health, particularly the stepdaughters who hope to leave behind these shells after marrying the prince. They have no concern for their human hosts, and the father and prince seem completely unaware of their voracious natures. The stepdaughters even reach a point when their physical bodies seem to serve as hosts for a purely selfish core; thus, when their mother encourages them to cut off their toe and heel, respectively, to fit into the golden shoe, each does so willingly.

The maternal bonds in "Cinderella" are clear. The birth mother wants her children in power. And while the stepmother looks out for her own daughters, it is important to keep in mind that Cinderella's mother continues to look out for her as well. The nature of such filial bonds emerges again in *Aliens* with Ripley determined to save the human child who reminds her of her own daughter. Newt, in turn, literally clings to Ripley as the sole maternal figure among a group of primarily male marines. With aliens looming all around — and, sometimes, even inside oneself or one's loved ones — their connection as a common species evolves quickly into a natural relationship of mother to daughter. This relationship is further realized during the scene in which the marines find a barely conscious, cocooned survivor, Newt's mother, who begs them to kill her before an alien bursts from her body. Ripley watches from the tank monitor (not knowing who the woman is) in horror and empathy as the woman dies, a mother "who identifies with the victim's plight and pain" (Urbano, 2004, p. 32). Newt's mother, looking into the monitor stationed near her daughter, transfers her maternal responsibilities directly to Ripley, the protective bird sent from the heavens.

"Cinderella" shows what any mixed family might fear, that those who are naturally related will side with one another and try to destroy the outsider. That the "outsider" may well have been present first in the household becomes irrelevant. Thus, we are especially disturbed that Cinderella suffers so greatly at the hands of her stepmother and stepsisters in her own father's home. Where is her father, we are forced to ask, as she faces continued abuse. Tatar (2003) asserts that the father's culpability is essentially eliminated in the tales of remarriage, while "the foul deeds of his wife come to occupy center stage" (p. 150). In *Aliens*, the father, complicit through his complacency, is represented by the callow, conniving Burke, who aligns himself with the aliens over his human relations. Following the first attack by the aliens, for example, Ripley suggests blowing up the entire planet to eradicate all of the creatures. Burke, however, counters, "This is clearly, clearly an important species we're dealing with, and I don't think that you or I or anybody has the right to arbitrarily exterminate them.... Look, I'm not *blind* to what's going on, but I cannot authorize that kind of action [emphasis added]." Yet he is as blind as the father and even the prince who twice carries off brides with bleeding feet oozing through their shoes. He does not care about placing other humans and families in danger, and he cannot foresee that his survival is dependent upon their shared welfare.

Cinderella's two stepsisters receive better treatment from the father than Cinderella herself. Likewise, Burke allies himself fully with the aliens, orchestrating a plan to release the two living spider-like creatures in the med lab with a dozing Ripley and Newt. He removes Ripley's gun, turns off the surveillance camera, and locks them in with his alien stepdaughters. After she and Newt survive the attack by setting off a fire alarm to alert the marines, Ripley confronts Burke, explaining, "He figured he could get an alien back through quarantine if one of us was impregnated, whatever you call it, and then frozen for the trip home. Nobody would know about the embryos we were carrying, me and Newt." She addresses Burke in disgust, declaring, "You know, Burke, I don't know which species is worse. You don't see them fucking each other for a goddamn percentage."

The female monsters in "Cinderella" can be understood on some level, because they are looking out for their own welfare and for the welfare of their immediate family. The choices of these women are extremely limited, and their only hope of bettering themselves socially lies in marrying a man with greater standing. The lovely, single, sure-footed Cinderella is, in fact, as much a threat to their livelihood as Ripley and Newt are to the alien queen and her offspring. The stepsisters are frightening, because they cannot readily be identified from their outward appearance, but their selfish actions are comprehensible. As Casdan (1999) explains, "Though they are self-absorbed and mean-spirited, they nevertheless are real children, born of a real mother" (p. 101). The father and Burke are considerably more horrifying monsters, however. They are trusted not just on the basis of their appearance, but due to their natural affiliation with Cinderella, as the biological daughter, and with Ripley and Newt, as fellow human beings. Burke's speech concerning the importance of a species that should not be arbitrarily exterminated is not simply disingenuous, it is also grossly ironic, given that this character, played by Jewish actor Paul Reiser, rattles off an argument against a Final Solution[5] without a single moment of reflection.

DRESSING FOR THE BALL

When Cinderella asks to attend the ball along with her sisters and all the other eligible, beautiful girls in the land, her stepmother reminds her that she has no clothes to wear and she does not know how to dance, and she warns that everyone would laugh at her and she would bring shame to the family. If "Cinderella" teaches us one great lesson, it may well be that clothes do indeed make the princess. Each time she arrives at the ball in a gown from her avian mother, she goes unrecognized by her stepmother and stepsisters who think she must be from a foreign land. Even her own father fails to recognize her, although he has his suspicions. And the prince is so enchanted by her beauty that he dances exclusively with her until each evening's end.

In *Aliens*, our princes, the marines, actually approach the planet and their mission as if they are going to a ballistic ball of some kind. Sergeant Apone (Al Matthews) awakens his team, announcing, "Every meal's a banquet, every paycheck a fortune, every formation a parade." When asked about their mission, he laughingly says, "There's some juicy colonists' daughters we have to rescue from their virginity." Their ball gowns consist of flamethrowers, assault rifles, and grenade launchers, and both Ripley and Newt are at first underdressed. Hicks (Michael Biehn) finally outfits Ripley in an oddly endearing and romantic scene, explaining, "This is an M-41 pulse rifle, 10-millimeter with an over-and-under, 30-millimeter, pump-action grenade launcher. Feel the weight." He also gives her a locator bracelet that she, in turn, gives to Newt. This object becomes the film's golden slipper.

At the conclusion of each evening's festivities, Cinderella races out of the palace and hurries home. In order to avoid detection, she leaps into a pigeon house and climbs a pear tree "as nimbly as a squirrel" (p. 82) on her way back home. On the third evening, the prince has tar poured on the steps to slow her escape, and he manages to get her fabled, identifying slipper. When the aliens commence their final invasion, Ripley and the others find themselves depending on the nimble Newt whose knowledge of the air ducts can lead them to safety. She scurries ahead too quickly, however, and falls down one of the chutes and into a water-filled drainage area. As she stands waist-deep in water, an alien rises from the water behind her, and we hear her scream. When Ripley arrives, she finds only the head of Newt's doll floating in the still water.[6] Ripley is able to trace Newt down the stairs and into the bowels of the planet's reactor by following a signal from the locator bracelet, until she discovers that it has come loose and stuck in alien slime.

The prince twice chooses the wrong bride and only becomes aware of his mistake when Cinderella's heavenly pigeons sing out to him to look more closely at the ill-fitting, bloody shoe being worn by the girl he too-quickly whisked away. When he finally demands to see the third daughter, the father declares that she is "deformed," while the stepmother firmly declares that she is too dirty to be seen by the prince. Cinderella thus remains caught between warring maternal instincts with the birds' tell-tale song echoing against the stepmother's declarations. We know that the slipper can save her if the prince can just reach her untouched, hidden feet. Like the persistent pigeons, Ripley must likewise continue on her mission until she finds Newt. If she arrives too late, Newt could become impregnated by one of the queen's hatchlings. If this were to happen, Ripley knows that Newt would temporarily appear "normal" and unharmed with the alien growing within her like a golden slipper that cannot hold back the flow of bad blood.

This possible scenario parallels Burke's original plan to smuggle the aliens back to Earth inside of a comatose Ripley and Newt, but it also mirrors the plan of Cinderella's stepsisters to fool the prince by hiding their true natures, and bloody feet, through the mask of a slipper. The mother convinces her daughters to cut off a heel and toe, respectively, rationalizing that they will not have to walk again if they can just become queen. In the filmed version of *Aliens*, we are led to believe that the conniving Burke dies in a face-to-face confrontation with an alien. In Cameron's 1985 draft script, however, Burke is captured by an alien drone and then impregnated by one of the aliens. Ripley stumbles upon him while tracking Newt, and he cries out, "I can feel it... inside. Oh, God... it's moving!" Thus, like the wounded stepsisters, he was to have become a deformed pawn for the queen's own larger plans.

As Ripley is about to give up all hope, Newt awakens to find an egg breaking open in front of her. Her screams alert Ripley, who arrives just in time to destroy the emerging alien before it can implant an embryo within Newt. Like Cinderella, her lost object brings her rescuer close to her, but not directly to her. Her young life and body are nearly assumed by an alien "sister" that eagerly hopes to take over her being for its own carnivorous growth. She is found only by unleashing a primal scream that jolts Ripley into action like the pigeons' song to the prince.

CONFRONTING THE ROYAL RIVAL

Having proven herself the true princess, Cinderella wins the heart of the prince, humiliating and infuriating her stepmother and stepsisters. The protective pigeons land on Cinderella's shoulders and continue to guard her, even on her wedding day when the stepsisters arrive "to ingratiate themselves and to share in [her] good fortune" (p. 84). As punishment for "*their wickedness and malice* [emphasis added]," the stepsisters have their eyes pecked out by the pigeons, and they must live the rest of their lives in blindness. Thus, by the tale's conclusion, the stepmother has lost all hope of continuing her bloodline through her daughters, both of whom are blind and deformed due to their earlier self-mutilation.

The conclusion of "Cinderella" ties strikingly to Shelley's *Frankenstein*, which in turn ties even more strikingly to the conclusion of *Aliens*. Shelley's monster confronts its creator and demands that Frankenstein make a similarly horrific mate. The fearful Frankenstein reluctantly agrees, but he fears that "a race of devils would be propagated upon the earth, who might make the very existence of the species of man a condition precarious and full of terror" (204). Thus, he destroys the potential mother, tearing it to pieces, and promising the monster in words that mirror those said of the stepsisters, "[N]ever will I create another like yourself, equal in *deformity and wickedness* [emphasis added]" (p. 206). In both "Cinderella" and *Frankenstein*, the competing bloodline is ultimately stopped by a powerful, watchful creator.[7]

Although she is not seen until the film's conclusion, the alien queen is more than an impressive, expressive monster. In an interview about the making of *Aliens*, Cameron is careful to explain that she should be thought of "as a character, rather than as a thing or an animal" (Goldberg, et. al.,

p. 10). Like Cinderella's stepmother, she is clearly present, but her offspring tend to create the most obvious danger. And as with both the stepmother and Frankenstein, we cannot determine a paternal relationship regarding their offspring. We do not know anything about the stepdaughters' father, and we know that Frankenstein can "give birth" without following the laws of human reproduction. Likewise, we do not know what—if anything— impregnated the alien queen. She stands as a solitary, powerful mother. Earlier in the film, the marines try to determine what could be laying the eggs for these creatures, and Hudson (Bill Paxton) correctly predicts, "There's like one female that runs the whole show.... Yeah, the mama. She's badass, man. I mean big." Indeed, she is. After Ripley rescues Newt, she ends up running directly into the queen's birthing chamber where both she and the audience first view the queen. As Ripley looks up, the queen has laid another egg. Ripley's eyes follow a filled, glowing egg sack up to the angry queen. She slowly raises her head and faces Ripley. Her black skull has the shape of a royal cowl, and she has a smaller set of mandibles that can jut forward beyond her primary razor-sharp teeth. She hisses a royal command, calling two of her offspring from the shadows.

As mothers, the queen and Ripley fully understand one another, and they communicate through threats to their respective offspring. In order to strike an immediate bargain, Ripley uses her flamethrower to destroy a few of the eggs. The queen has her two guards back away so that Ripley and Newt can exit. As they are about to leave, however, one of the eggs hatches, and Ripley realizes that she must abort all of the queen's eggs for Newt and humanity. Using her flamethrower, grenades, and rifle, she dec-imates all of the potential offspring, and the explosions eventually rip the queen from her egg sack.

Ripley and Newt flee with the enraged queen in pursuit. She manages to attach herself to their rescue ship, piloted by the android Bishop, and emerges from the ship's underside to take her revenge. After they land, she rips Bishop in half and signals that she intends to destroy Newt as ret-ribution for her own lost young. Ripley tells Newt to run, and she draws the queen's ire directly to her. As the queen charges after her, Ripley runs into a cargo bay and shuts a heavy metal door behind her. The queen then hunts for Newt, who manages to stay just out of her grasp until Ripley re-appears, appropriately dressed for a final confrontation. Initially, Cinderella becomes a suitable rival to her beautiful stepsisters only after she dons her ethereal regalia. Outfitted by her mother's spiritual tailor, she easily outshines her stepsisters at the ball. Likewise, Ripley requires the right outfit to outwit the monster.

As the door to the cargo bay opens, Ripley emerges in a robotic loading suit that resembles an enormous, metal exoskeleton. She looks at the queen and issues a direct, audience-pleasing command: "Get away from her, you bitch!" The two engage in bitter hand-to-hand combat with Ripley slapping the alien queen to the ground. She drags the queen to a cargo bay that opens into space, and as she drops her into it, the queen grabs onto Ripley's suit and pulls her down with her. Ripley climbs out of her robotic shell, opens the bay doors into space, and ascends the ladder in the cargo bay. Like the stepsisters forced to live in blindness, the alien queen is flushed into dark, empty space. Free of her heavy costume, Ripley pulls herself out of the cargo bay, and is greeted by Newt who recognizes and rewards Ripley's inner nature by hugging her and calling out, "Mommy!"

In *Cinderella: A Folklore Casebook*, Dundes (1982) reminds us that the Cinderella story "is *not* a story of rags to riches, but riches recovered; *not* poor girl into princess but rather rich girl (or princess) rescued from improper or wicked enslavement" (p. 296). When Cinderella's mother dies, she promises that she will take care of her from heaven, and, indeed, her security is assured through the presence of the two watchful pigeons that remain on her shoulders by the tale's conclusion. The spirit of her mother remains an ever-present—and dangerous—force that protects her. Newt realizes that she has this same security through Ripley, telling her, "I knew you'd come," after Ripley risks her life to rescue her. Once they have defeated the rival queen, Ripley and Newt prepare to dream in hypersleep. As the camera pans out, Newt sleeps in the foreground with Ripley resting at shoulder-level in the same frame.

EMPHASIZING THE MORAL

Sanitized retellings of the Grimm fairy tales tend to excise the more violent endings, replacing them with less satisfying, more generalized conclusions that have our hero/heroine riding off into a utopian world that is apparently absent of wanton wolves, voracious witches, and self-serving stepmothers. The moral in such versions suggests that, if children can survive just one great trial, they will be rewarded with a lifetime free of danger and adversity.

Tatar (2003) reminds us that the Grimms rewrote and revised the tales in several editions, highlighting "cultural codes and rules of conduct" (p. 48). In contrast to other versions of these tales, the multiple endings to the Grimm tales offer a more practical reminder that supposedly vanquished villains often make a not-so-surprising return. At the conclusion of "Little Red Cap," for example, the Grimm heroine fills the wolf's stomach with stones that cause him to fall over dead. Rather than simply end the tale here, the Grimms include a brief follow-up to show that she has truly learned her lesson: On a return trip to her grandmother's house, she encounters another wolf (for there will always be dangerous wolves lurking in those dark woods); however, rather than chat with him, she races immediately to her grandmother's house, and the two of them plot to kill the second wolf soon after he arrives. Similarly, Snow White could easily go off to enjoy her life happily ever after with the prince—a reward for being such a good, beautiful girl—but the moral requires that the wicked stepmother be confronted and destroyed. Thus, she is invited to the wedding and forced to dance in red-hot slippers until she falls over dead. Like her red-cloaked counterpart, this heroine has learned that protection does not exist through passivity.

In this regard, modern horror films mirror the structure of the Grimm fairy tales. The Jasons, Michaels, and Freddies can be stopped temporarily, but they always return to torment a new batch of clueless, helpless teenagers. As Randy (Jamie Kennedy) points out during the conclusion of Wes Craven's knowing slasher-parody *Scream* (1996), "Careful: This is the moment when the supposedly dead killer comes back to life for one last scare." Even our female attackers—Sissy Spacek's uncontrollable Carrie White seems to be attacking the lone prom survivor (Amy Irving) from the grave; Glenn Close's obsessive Alex improbably rises up after being "drowned" in the bathtub in *Fatal Attraction* (1987)—are capable of rising up from the dead to attack us.

Structurally, "Cinderella" and *Aliens* share comparatively similar double endings that force the heroine into a confrontation with her nemesis following an apparent escape. In the Grimm tale, Cinderella's stepmother hides her away while encouraging the prince to carry away her own daughters. The tension of this scene is maintained by having the possibility exist that Cinderella just might not get away. If the prince is fooled, then we know that she will continue sleeping in the ashes while evil is rewarded. She is ultimately saved by the white pigeons who alert the prince to the deception. He is then free to carry her away on his horse. In *Aliens*, time is also of the essence. The planet is about to explode, and the alien queen is fast approaching Ripley and Newt. At the moment that Ripley accepts that they are about to die, Bishop arrives in the rescue plane, hovering at her shoulder-level like a protective fairy tale pigeon. They fly away, while the planet—along with, they believe, the alien queen and her young—explodes behind them. In both of these conclusions, we are led to believe that our heroine just might not be rescued in time from her dangerous environment by the man with the physical means of escape.

Both "Cinderella" and *Aliens* temper this earlier male rescue, however, by showing that the female rival has not been so easily destroyed. Despite their earlier actions, Cinderella's stepsisters invite themselves to her wedding in the hope of feeding off her new-found wealth. Thus, even on her wedding day and in her own court, Cinderella is not spared their possibly dangerous intrusion. In their final confrontation, Cinderella is armed with knowledge of their wickedness and with appropriate weaponry to stop them. Thus her pigeons peck out their eyes, one at a time as the bridal couple enter and then exit the church. Cinderella's prince does nothing. The story ends not with the expected, "And they lived happily ever after," but rather with the very stern warning that living wickedly and maliciously can lead to a lifetime of justified blindness. Likewise, *Aliens* allows Ripley and Newt a very brief moment of relief. But just as they—and we—believe that they have reached a safe haven free from menacing monsters, the queen emerges, having shared in their good fortune by attaching herself to their rescue ship. Bishop is ripped immediately in half, while our other male prince, Hicks, lies unconscious on the ship. Like Cinderella, Ripley is able to discern the queen's vengeful motives, and her available weaponry allows her to fight the queen handily, releasing her into infinite darkness. In life, as in fairy tale kingdoms and outer space odysseys, we learn that parasites are always ready to attach themselves to a thriving host.

• Six •

The Devil in the Details

"Rumpelstiltskin" and *Rosemary's Baby*

A Grimm View of the Fairy Tale Devil

Ever since Satan slithered out of the biblical Garden of Eden, having tempted Adam and Eve out of their dull, blissful paradise, the devil has played a key role in literature. His cunning, shape-shifting ability, and desire to play with man for the sheer sport of it make him the archetypal villain. In the Grimm Brothers' politically and religiously fractious Germany, the devil makes himself at home quite easily in the deep, dark forest where "the Devil was an active force and magic and sorcery were possible forms of intervention to change the world" (Scribner, 1992, p. 167). Germany, after all, was the birthplace of the Protestant Reformation, a movement that challenged the seemingly omnipotent papal authority in the Holy Roman Empire of the German Nation. Most significantly, the role of the Church and its clergy as mediators profiting off of the sale of indulgences came under scrutiny when a monk named Martin Luther nailed 95 theses on a church door in Wittenberg in 1517.

The Church maintained a large part of its authority by cloaking itself in mystery: Church services and the Bible were provided in Latin, a language only a few exceptionally learned members could understand, and one that was completely foreign to the mostly illiterate populace attending German mass. Additionally, holy relics and artifacts were employed as marketing tools, transforming some churches and towns into areas of pilgrimage. Fulbrook (2004) explains that Martin Luther's own prince maintained a particularly well-stocked collection that reportedly included "parts of the holy cradle, bits of swaddling clothes, and remains of infants slaughtered by Herod" (p. 37). Thus, Wittenberg was able to draw large crowds looking to buy salvation for themselves and family members already serving time in purgatory. Luther's primary complaint against the Church lay here, in the commercialization of salvation, and his reforms "dismissed not only the theological foundation for the sale of indulgences, the traffic in human souls, and the established church's abuse of its authority but also the clerical monopoly on mediation between God and humankind" (Schulze, 1998, p. 52). Luther also translated the New Testament into everyday German that the people could understand, giving them the authority to comprehend the Bible without a holy interpreter. By removing the Church and its clergy as necessary mediators between man, God, and Hell, Luther created a theological system in which man gained possession of his own soul.[1]

Allowing individuals possession of their souls also meant that they could attempt to sell their ethereal commodity, and no figure could be a more dedicated buyer than the devil himself. One of the most famous German tales to feature a dealing devil prominently as a character is the legend of Dr. Faust. According to Ashliman (2005), *Historia von D. Johann Fausten,* a chapbook published by Johann Spies in 1587, tells the story of a scholar educated in the Holy Scriptures, math, science, and areas of sorcery and necromancy. One day, he decides to enter into a contract, signed in his own blood, with the devil. In exchange for his body and soul, Faustus has the devil promise to serve him and grant his every request for a period of 24 years. He also mandates that the devil never lie to him. He uses the devil's powers to secure wine, food, and women, including Helen of Troy. Although he lives 24 years of earthly pleasure, he is brutally ripped limb from limb at the end of his contract, and his body parts are found all over his room and in a pile of manure. His students learn quite clearly to reject the temptations of the devil and to guard their souls above all else.

The Faust legend also serves as the basis for two very different retellings in English and German: Christopher Marlowe's *The Tragicall History of D. Faustus* (1604) and Johann Wolfgang von Goethe's *Faust: eine Tragödie* (1808). The former follows the storyline of the original legend closely, keeping the 24-year contract signed in Faust's own blood as well as the time wasted on practical jokes, but Marlowe adds the character of Mephistopheles, a servant to the devil, and an unholy mediator between Faust and Satan. Marlowe's drama epitomizes the dangers of the Renaissance man who strives for omnipotence only to be sentenced to eternal damnation for his hubris. In contrast to Marlowe's version, Goethe's Faust emerges as a tragic figure of Germany's Romantic period, torn between his emotions, reason, and spirituality. Rather than sentence his conflicted hero to the torments of hell, Goethe allows his Faust to flee with Mephistopheles to experience other adventures at the conclusion of the dramatic poem.

The Grimm fairy tales provide us with several versions of the devil, and surprisingly, not all of them make him out to be unilaterally wicked. When he makes deals with people, he follows through on his end of those bargains, and he seems determined to obtain solely those figures who have gravely sinned. Far from being an all-knowing figure, he can also be tricked out of his treasures and agreements. In "The Devil with the Three Golden Hairs," for example, an evil king tells a lad that he can marry his daughter if he travels to hell and returns with three golden hairs of the devil. With the aid of the devil's grandmother, he is able to collect the hairs and learn the answers to several riddles that allow him to trick the king into becoming a ferryman for the devil.[2]

"The Devil's Grandmother," again works against her grandson who has lined up the souls of three starving soldiers who have deserted their posts and king. The soldiers agree to give the devil—who first appears to them as a talking dragon—their lives following a period of seven years, during which time they are given a magic whip that produces as much money as they need. The devil has them sign their names into his book and tells them he will return at the end of their contract. He also tells them that they will be allowed to go free if they are able to solve a riddle at that time. Just before their time has expired, the soldiers go to the devil's grandmother for help, and she allows one of them to hide in her house as she tricks the devil into telling her the riddle. When the devil comes for payment, they solve the riddle and are allowed to live their lives in wealth and peace.

Clever Germans do not need the devil's grandmother to help them in all instances. In "The Peasant and the Devil," for example, a crafty peasant comes across a devil sitting on a treasure. He agrees to share his crops with the devil over a period of two years in exchange for the gold and silver. During the first year, the peasant offers the devil all that grows above the earth, while he will keep all that grows below it. The devil accepts the offer, only to find that the peasant has planted nothing but turnips. For the second year, the devil demands that they reverse their crop shares, with the devil now getting all that is grown below the earth. This time, however, the peasant decides to grow wheat, again leaving the devil with nothing. Despite his having been fooled twice by the peasant, the devil keeps his word and lets him keep the treasure.

In two contrasting tales, "Brother Lustig" and "Gambling Hans," the Grimm Brothers give us characters who not only try to fool the devil but St. Peter and the Lord as well. Brother Lustig (whose name can mean "jolly" and "lazy") is a discharged soldier who offers a disguised St. Peter part of his money and food. As the pair travel around looking for income, St. Peter performs miracles, and Brother Lustig tries to secure rewards for the good deeds. When St. Peter can no longer tolerate Brother Lustig's greed, he severs their ties, leaving him with a magic knapsack that can be filled with anything he desires. Brother Lustig uses the knapsack to capture devils in a possessed castle. He kills eight of the nine devils, and the last one escapes back to hell. When Brother Lustig feels that his time has come to die, he asks a wise hermit about the paths to heaven and hell. He is told that the path to hell is easiest and most pleasant, so that is the one he chooses. The surviving devil guards the gates of hell, however, and will not admit him. When he goes to heaven, St. Peter will not admit him either. The clever Brother Lustig returns the knapsack to its former owner on the other side of heaven's gates and then wishes himself into it, securing his place inside.

St. Peter makes a return visit in "Gambling Hans," appearing with the Lord at Hans' house when the man has lost everything. The Lord offers Hans three wishes, assuming that Hans will request that his soul be allowed into heaven; however, Hans is so consumed with gambling that he instead requests dice and cards that will always favor him, and he asks for a tree that will imprison anyone who climbs it. St. Peter and the Lord send Death to stop Hans from gaining control of the world through his gambling, but he tricks Death into climbing his enchanted tree. When the Lord demands that Death be freed, Death kills Hans who is subsequently denied entrance into both heaven and purgatory. In hell, he manages to win Lucifer's army of devils, and he uses these to battle heaven. Even after he is allowed into heaven, he continues to gamble, and the Lord is forced to shatter his soul to pieces. These pieces inhabit others all over earth, leading them to gamble as well.

In "The Devil's Sooty Brother" and "The Three Journeymen," the devil again keeps his word, lavishly rewarding those who choose to serve him. In the former tale, Hans, a discharged soldier with no money, agrees to serve the devil in hell for seven years. He is not allowed to wash during that period, nor can he groom himself in any way, allowing his hair, beard, and nails to grow uncut. His primary job is to keep the fires blazing under kettles boiling away damned souls while the devil travels the earth. Even though the devil has told him not to peek into the kettles, Hans cannot resist, and when he does so, he finds his sergeant, lieutenant, and general literally serving eternity as soul food. Since they treated him badly in life, he gladly stokes the fires under their kettles. At the end of seven years, the devil lets Hans leave, explaining that he will not punish Hans for disobeying him since he added to the fires even after peeking. He rewards him with bags of dirt that become gold outside of hell. Further, after Hans is robbed by an innkeeper, the devil personally cleans and grooms Hans and has the innkeeper return the stolen gold to him. Wealthy Hans gets to marry the king's youngest daughter, impressing the king with music he learned from the devil, and they live the traditional fairy tale ending.

Like poor Hans in the tale above, "The Three Journeymen" also enter into a deal with the devil when they find no other means of employment. The devil tells them that they can answer questions asked of them with only one reply each time: the first must say, "All three of us"; the second, "For money"; and the third, "That's all right." The three stay with a murderous innkeeper who decides to kill a wealthy merchant and frame the journeymen by having them answer questions with their unchanging replies. His plan works initially, and the journeymen are arrested for murder and placed on trial. They tell the judge, in order, that they all killed the merchant for money and are content with having done so. As they are about to be executed, however, the devil arrives in a magnificent coach, giving them permission to say what truly happened. The innkeeper is found guilty, the devil gets the wicked man's soul, and the journeymen are provided ample money for the rest of their days.

In all of these tales, the Grimm Brothers give us several images of the devil, indicating that he can change his appearance quite drastically and at will. In one tale, he has golden hair for plucking, while another has him first appear as a man with a horse's hoof and a human foot and later as a dapper, wealthy gentleman ("The Three Journeymen"). He can appear as a flying dragon large enough to carry three men in his claws ("The Devil and His Grandmother"), and he can appear as a harmless little man ("The Devil's Sooty Brother"). And in "The Animals of the Lord and the Devil," we learn that an angry devil bit off the tales of his goats when they became caught in his brier plants and then poked out their eyes and replaced them with his own after the Lord tricked him out of compensation. We are told that he likes to appear in their shape at the end of this tale.

DEALING WITH THE DEVILISH CREATURES

The Grimm Brothers do not tell us exactly who or what Rumpelstiltskin is, nor do they let us know his purpose in wanting a child: Is he a baby-bartering sorcerer akin to Mother Gothel in "Rapunzel," wanting to raise a child as his own? Is he akin to a male witch hoping to bake up a kinder-casserole as in "Hansel and Gretel"? Is he a magical gnome or helpful dwarf whose temper suddenly rages out of control when his secret name is discovered? He is described simply as "the little man" throughout most of the tale. The queen's messenger who spies him in the forest calls him "ridiculous," the only adjective used to describe him in the tale, and even then by an observer who has no interactions with him. Like a number of the Grimm devils, Rumpelstiltskin is not called evil or wicked at any point, and he appears to be an accepted member of the fairy tale realm.[3] Fink (1988) suggests that he is a "little demon" who is ultimately "chased off as a cheated devil" (p. 151), and his role is indeed very similar to those previously described devils. He and other devils barter with the poor, desperate, and hopeless, be they unemployed soldiers or young girls being threatened with execution. Knowing that their clients are in no position to bargain, these fairy tale demons require an extraordinary payment to be made in the future, whether their clients' eternal souls or their firstborn child. A magical being like Rumpelstiltskin is able to appear undetected within a locked room, and he can spin hay into gold without hesitation. Despite his abilities, he chooses to exploit the girl's circumstances for his own gain rather than simply set her free.

The strange little man stamps his foot into the ground in anger when the
queen learns his name and is allowed to keep her baby. (Illustration by E.
H. Wehnert from *Household Stories Collected by the Brothers Grimm*. London: Routledge and Sons, 1880.)

Like the Grimm devils mentioned earlier, Rumpelstiltskin is shown
to be a careful negotiator, appearing exactly at the right time to make the
trapped girl an offer she truly cannot refuse. Although he has amazing
powers, he can still be outwitted, and, like all of the Grimm devils, he stays
true to his word even when outraged. These kinds of tales also seems to
take their guiding theme from the Faust legend, as both stories center on
a deal made with a supernatural figure whose intervention provides the
hero/ine with financial, personal gain. Both Faust and the miller's daughter become so involved in their lives after the deal has been made that they
momentarily seem to forget that payment will be due for the magical services rendered. In the Faust stories, the character spends much of his time
and power playing pranks and having fun, while the miller's daughter
entirely forgets that she has promised the little man her firstborn upon
becoming queen. Like Mephistopheles, Rumpelstiltskin himself is likewise
a mysterious character of curious origin. The messenger reports to the
queen that he has seen a ridiculous little man dancing around a fire, hop-
ping on one leg, and singing a chant about his secretive name. Otherwise,
we essentially know nothing about him and his motivations.

The plot of "Rumpelstiltskin" is primarily based upon false contracts and broken promises in the name of personal greed and self-preservation. Tatar (2003) explains, "At the heart of all versions of [the tale] is a contract made between an innocent young girl and a devilish creature" (p. 126). As the tale begins, a poor miller tries to impress the avaricious king by assuring him that his daughter can spin straw into gold. Upon hearing this, the king demands that the beautiful girl demonstrate her talents to him. Oddly, he does not care to learn how she does this amazing task. Rather than observe and practice her technique, he personally locks her alone in a room filled with straw and tells her that she will be killed if she does not fill it with gold by morning. Knowing that she cannot fulfill her father's lie, the girl begins to weep until a strange little man appears and offers to do the spinning for her. In exchange for his work, she offers him her necklace. The next day, the greedy king is so pleased with her work that he locks her in a larger room filled with more straw. The nameless little man returns and again does her spinning, this time in exchange for a ring. Again, the king is pleased with the results, and again he leads her to an even larger room filled with yet more straw. Upon completion of this final task, he promises that he will make her his queen. When the little man makes his third entrance, she has nothing left to offer him for his work. At this point, he reveals that he knows what the king has promised her, and he asks for her first child when she becomes queen. Feeling completely helpless, she agrees to his demands, and he completes the task to the king's satisfaction.

Of all the Grimm tales, this one is filled with the least likable and laudable characters. For all he knows, the father has essentially sentenced his daughter to death, offering her to the king for no other reason than to sound impressive. The king feels no actual love for the girl and is shown to be among the greediest of fairy tale heroes. He does not choose his bride for her fame ("Brier Rose"), voice ("Rapunzel"), beauty ("Snow White"), or fashionable footwear ("Cinderella"); rather, his marriage is based solely upon the financial reward he believes she can provide him. She is merely the mechanism through which he can solidify his own success. As Tatar (2003) notes, "Few tales in the Grimms' collection are so crass as 'Rumpelstiltskin' in depicting purely economic motives for marriage" (p. 124). The king is not mentioned again after they marry, and he appears to have no interest in his wife or newborn child, his own namesake. By the end of the tale, the lying father and greedy king have not been punished for their vices, and, if anything, the king has been rewarded for his actions.

The daughter/queen emerges as one of the Grimm Brothers' most interesting and complex characters. Unlike the heroines rescued by a handsome prince who helps them vanquish their foes and competition, this young girl has nothing of personal worth to entice the king. She cannot, after all, spin straw into gold, and her life is dependent upon her making her own deals with the odd little man and then keeping those separate exchanges a secret. When told that her first-born child can serve as final payment for his services, she does not question Rumpelstiltskin's motives or try to come up with an alternate solution. Instead, she shortsightedly wonders, "Who knows whether it will ever come to that," and then promptly agrees to the deal (Grimm and Grimm, 2003, p. 195). The little man returns for his compensation when the new queen gives birth, and she stalls him with tears until he offers to let her keep the child if she can guess his name within three days time. At this point, we see a change in her character, for she now uses all of her resources to take advantage of this new loophole. After the queen spends two days incorrectly guessing increasingly outlandish names, her messenger finally spies the little man dancing and singing around his cottage in the woods, gleefully screeching his name. The queen then uses this intelligence to save her child and herself. Rather than confront the little man who saved her life three times, however, she teases him by guessing several false names. Then she reveals his name, infuriating him so much that he splits himself in two while throwing an angry tantrum. Without breaking her word, she gets to keep her baby and her secret. An element of true danger remains for the daughter/queen, however, as we wonder what will happen to her should the king's treasury ever be in need of replenishment.

SPINNING STRAW INTO GOLD

Rosemary's Baby (1968), adapted from Ira Levin's 1967 best-selling novel of the same name by director Roman Polanski, deals with similar kinds of bartering and betrayal as characters attempt to secure their most selfish desires. From the very beginning, we are introduced to Rosemary and Guy Woodhouse (Mia Farrow and John Cassavetes), a couple so determined to live in the Bramford ("The Bram")[4], a prestigious New York apartment building, that they break their current lease when a unit suddenly becomes available. As the opening credits roll, the camera pans

Rosemary (Mia Farrow) feels the gaze of her odd little neighbor, Minnie (Ruth Gordon), who keeps a close watch on the young mother-to-be in *Rosemary's Baby* (Paramount, 1968). *The Kobal Collection*

across a New York skyline of modern high-rise apartments and skyscrapers before scanning downward to the ominous old building which could pass for a cathedral or castle with its prominent spires and turrets. Rosemary's innocence is suggested by her simple, crisp white dress with matching white gloves, purse, and shoes. Although the building clearly requires

some renovations—the interior has chipped paint and broken floor tiles—
Rosemary is captivated by the possibilities of transformation. As she and
Guy survey the apartment, she cannot hide her enthusiasm, and she begs
him, "Oh, Guy, let's take it, please? That living room could be—oh, please,
let's take it!"

After severing their other lease, a fatherly friend of theirs, Hutch
(Maurice Evans), warns them, half-jokingly, half-seriously, about a number of unsettling tales associated with the infamous building. He explains
that a dead infant was once found wrapped in newspaper in the building's
basement and that the Bramford was "where the Trench sisters conducted
their little dietary experiments.... They cooked and ate several young children, including a niece." He also reveals what will become a central plot
point, noting that the Bramford was home to a notorious witch named
Adrian Marcato: "He made quite a splash in the nineties by announcing
that he'd conjured up the living devil. Apparently, people believed him, so
they attacked and nearly killed him in the lobby of the Bramford."[5] In spite
of his concerns, the confident couple decides to move into the gothic complex, and Rosemary begins spinning rooms of hay into gold. A remodel-
ing montage focuses on walls being painted and wall-papered and new
furniture being delivered. Rosemary proudly supervises the process while
hanging drapes and applying contact paper to shelves on her own.

In spite of her initial joy and success within the confines of the apartment, Farrow's pale, waspish Rosemary comes across as vulnerably naïve
as the poor miller's daughter. Her apartment is merely a thin gold-plating,
barely covering the mysteries that reside around her. From their bedroom,
she and Guy cannot help but to overhear their neighbors, Roman and Minnie Castevet (Sidney Blackmer and Ruth Gordon), performing some kind
of ritual chanting, indicating that the young couple is not as alone and private as they would hope. We also learn that a closet blocked by the previous tenant has a hidden entrance from and into the Castevet's apartment,
a secret entrance that Rosemary does not discover until the conclusion of
the film. She becomes an unknowing hostage in the apartment, seldom
leaving on her own while her neighbors appear at increasingly controlling
intervals. As embodied by Oscar-winning Ruth Gordon, Minnie especially
resembles a Rumpelstiltskin-like figure, a little (mini) woman who appears
a bit strange but friendly and helpful. Inviting herself into Rosemary's
apartment for the first time, she gives herself a tour, questions how much
a chair costs, and invites them over for dinner. When Rosemary tries to

put her off, saying that she will have to check with Guy first, Minnie insists, "Listen, you tell him I won't take no for an answer." And although Guy wisely intuits, "We get friendly with an old couple like that, and we'll never get rid of them," Rosemary convinces him to keep the invitation.

As the couples get to know each other, Roman reveals that he sees religion as little more than a hypocritical show, particularly with regard to Catholicism and the Pope. When pressed, an uncomfortable Rosemary admits to being raised Catholic, yet she also says she does not really know what she is now. Throughout the film, she has dreams of nuns and priests, and she seems genuinely excited to hear that the Pope will be visiting. In contrast, Roman argues, "No Pope ever visits a city where the newspapers are on strike.... All the costumes are rituals, all religions." He goes on to tell Rosemary, "Well, now you don't need to have respect for [the Pope] because he pretends that he's holy." Roman also sees Guy's ambition and realizes that he can leverage his acting dreams to further his own agenda. Guy has enjoyed limited success as a television and commercial actor, but he longs for greater recognition and respect. His most notable theatrical role is, ironically, as a character in *Luther*, and Guy seems primed to sell not just his own soul, but the right to be father of his firstborn as well. Giving Guy a combined compliment and warning, Roman suggests, "You have a most interesting inner quality, Guy. It appears in your television work, too. It should take you a long way indeed, provided, of course, that you get those initial breaks." After dinner, Minnie distracts Rosemary by having them wash dishes while Roman and Guy share a private conversation over a couple of cigars in the living room. Thereafter, Guy says that he wants to go back to hear more of Roman's stories, assuring Rosemary, "You don't have to come along if you don't want to. You can stay here." Like the father and king in "Rumpelstiltskin," the men develop a contract without seeking input from the young woman being bartered, and she becomes as isolated as the miller's daughter.

Both Bottigheimer (1987) and Tatar (2004) point out that the spinning was a common household task reserved almost exclusively for women during the Grimm Brothers' era. Tatar maintains that the act itself "goes hand in hand with industry and achievement, but it is also associated with physical oppression and enslavement" of women (p. 123). She points out that the miller's daughter in "Rumpelstiltskin" ends up gaining social status without actually sitting down at the spinning wheel herself, while she and her child are still viewed as property. *Rosemary's Baby* came along at an interesting time with regard to the rights of women in the United States. The women's movement gained considerable momentum during the 1960s, and the National Organization for Women (NOW) was founded in 1966 while affirmative action was extended to women by executive order in 1967. The National Abortion Rights Action League was formed the following year, and the Supreme Court would uphold Roe versus Wade in 1973.[6]

Rosemary comes across as a typical American housewife who is still trapped by circumstances around her. Although she is fairly strong-willed, she is far from a feminist and is perfectly content to take care of the apartment, prepare meals for Guy, and become a mother. Polanski stages a humorous, telling scene that hews remarkably close to the miller's daughter being trapped in a room with a death-dealing spinning wheel and that strange little man who longs for her baby. As Rosemary prepares for a quiet moment alone with her records and a book, Minnie arrives with her dear friend, Laura-Louise (Patsy Kelly), and they invite themselves in. Rosemary explains that it is the first day of her period, yet they continue to make themselves at home, sitting down on the couch and taking out their knitting and crocheting. Minnie and Laura-Louise continue with their sewing, subtly inviting Rosemary to join them in similar work by inquiring about her own unfinished cushions lying in a window seat. Rosemary stops her preferred spinning, turning off the record player, and Minnie presents with a charm necklace filled with tannis root to prepare her, literally, for her date with the devil. Thus, her biological worth as a woman for the coven is tied explicitly to traditional female activities like spinning. Rosemary exists like the miller's daughter, whose "only quality lies within her capacity to reproduce the species. She is reduced to reproduction and placed at the mercy of men" (Zipes, 1993, p. 68).

In one sense, Guy is also like the miller's daughter, particularly when it comes to bargaining. She gains power and prestige not through the false promises made by her father but by the deals she secretly makes herself. While she cannot spin the straw into gold, she takes credit for the bountiful bouillon, and becomes queen based upon the abilities of another. And, ultimately, she alone decides to sell her own child to protect and promote her interests. The payments offered by the miller's daughter in the beginning are certainly small in comparison to the services received. Her necklace and ring have little actual worth, certainly less than the gold spun by the little man. Similarly, Guy seems to want a showing of "good faith" on the coven's part before committing fully to the deal. He is disillusioned when he loses a part in an exciting new play to Donald Baumgart (voiced by Tony Curtis). When Donald mysteriously goes blind, Guy gets the lead. A proud Rosemary declares, "It's a fascinating part. He'll really be noticed this time.... He's suddenly very hot." Immediately thereafter, Guy tells Rosemary that he wants them to have a baby.

Having secured his first level of success, Guy agrees to a supernatural contract centering on Rosemary's reproductive abilities, but she is not party to the authoring of that deal. As far as the coven and Guy are concerned, Rosemary may as well be a mound of hay herself, waiting for them to spin her womb into their treasured son of the devil. A good portion of the film revolves around the subtle ways they work to transform her into an appropriate and acceptable mother for the devil's son. Rumpelstiltskin cleverly accepts the smaller, worthless tokens from the miller's daughter for his services before suggesting that she give him her first child. He builds a relationship of sorts with her, never indicating that his ultimate goal is her offspring. Likewise, Roman and Minnie carefully insinuate themselves into Rosemary's life with Guy's assistance. First, they give Rosemary a necklace filled with an odorous (fictional) herb called tannis root. When she decides to put the necklace away, Guy admonishes her, "Well, if you took it, you ought to wear it." As she and Guy prepare for a romantic dinner to be followed by a night of lovemaking, the doorbell rings with an offering of chocolate mousse from Minnie. When Rosemary indicates that she does not want to finish it after a couple of bites due to its "chalky undertaste," Guy again chides her until she relents. However, she is able to hide most of the contents in her napkin when he walks away to turn the record over on the record player. In contrast to the white dress worn by Rosemary at the start of the film, she is now wearing a low-cut, completely red outfit with red shoes, signaling her acceptance into the building's demonic trappings.

Having eaten part of the mousse, Rosemary collapses into a dream-like state, weaving in and out of consciousness. She feels like she is on a boat and then finds herself surrounded by members of the coven, naked and chanting. Her clothes have been removed, and she is lying on top of a bare mattress. Roman anoints her body with red paint and numbers. Guy climbs forward and appears to be making love to her, but he suddenly takes on the countenance of the devil with yellow, animal-like eyes and enormous scaled hands. As Rosemary cries out, "This is no dream—This is really happening!" her head is covered and she sees the Pope, asking him,

"Am I forgiven, father?" When she awakens the next day, she is disturbed to see deep scrapes along her arms and back, and she tells Guy, "I dreamed someone was raping me. I don't know, someone inhuman." In "Rumpelstiltskin," the miller's daughter is locked in the room alone, theoretically locking out others as well. Only a being with supernatural abilities can enter the room, and the little man does so of his own will and whenever he chooses. She has no apparent choice but to accept his offers, and his multiple entrances can be seen as a violation made on his own terms. The end result, as far as he is concerned, is a baby that he could not have otherwise had on his own.

Following her rape, Rosemary confronts Guy who attempts to cover by saying he did not want to miss "baby night," and he explains that he thought they had fun "in a necrophile sort of way." She tells him that she is concerned that he has not been looking at her, and it appears that he is momentarily shamed by his actions. The king, too, keeps his distance from the miller's daughter following her encounters with the little man. He is so focused on the prospect of unparalleled wealth that he does not question her abilities, preferring to lock her alone in increasingly larger rooms to produce his greatest desire. The fact that another man is required to fulfill his goals remains blissfully outside of his realm of knowledge. Guy and the king willingly sacrifice their brides to other men in order to attain their success, encouraging their literal and metaphorical rape and abandoning any hope of a marriage based on love. In both instances, the human male ego is nevertheless protected, since the successful rape can only be carried out by a masculine being endowed with supernatural abilities.

DELIVERING A FINE, HEALTHY BABY

The steps to becoming queen and mother are painful and increasingly difficult. The king locks the miller's daughter into progressively larger rooms filled with straw, warning her each time that she will be killed if she does not spin it into gold by the following morning. His offer to marry her seems less like a fairy tale reward and more like a life sentence to the kingdom's most self-involved, demanding, and powerful man. Even after he offers to make her his wife, he is mildly disappointed that she is just a poor miller's daughter; however, he comforts himself by noting, "I'll never find a richer woman anywhere in the world" (Grimm and Grimm, 2003,

p. 195). Giving birth to the devil's son is fraught with similarly painful, seemingly life-threatening ordeals for Rosemary as well. From the moment she becomes pregnant, she faces immediate physical and emotional deterioration. For both of these women, escalating fears about their immediate physical well-being give way to momentary feelings of elation that are then crushed beneath the realization that an even greater danger awaits their firstborn.

When Rosemary learns that she is pregnant, Guy rushes next door to tell Minnie and Roman, who immediately come over and convince Rosemary to switch doctors, even though she is perfectly satisfied with her own Dr. Hill (Charles Grodin), who happens to be as young and handsome as a fairy tale prince. One of her friends even refers to him as "a dream boy." Minnie declares, "Listen, I won't let you go to no Dr. Hill nobody ever heard of. The best is what you're going to have, young lady!" After Minnie sets up an appointment with their renowned Dr. Sapirstein (Ralph Bellamy), Rosemary says that she does not know how to thank them. In return, Minnie makes the same offer as Rumpelstiltskin, "Just have a fine, healthy baby, that's all." During their first appointment, Dr. Sapirstein appears as the older, demanding king. He has gray hair and a well-trimmed beard, wears glasses, and a suit, and warns Rosemary sternly not to read medical books or listen to friends, since "no two pregnancies are ever alike." Like the miller's daughter who never learns the secret of spinning straw into gold, Rosemary is kept ignorant of the events going on around—and inside of—her. When she feels sharp, continuous pains, she tells Dr. Sapirstein that she feared she might be having an ectopic pregnancy; he responds harshly, "I thought you weren't going to read books, Rosemary. ... Will you go home and throw it away please?" The new doctor also forbids her from taking vitamin pills, instead prescribing an herbal drink concocted by Minnie from her herbarium, one "that'll be fresher, safer, and more vitamin-rich than any pills on the market."

As her pregnancy progresses, she grows paler and thinner. Jones (2005) remarks that "her health and mental stability plummet" in inverse proportion to Guy's escalating acting career (p. 141). A surprised Hutch cannot believe that she is expecting, telling her, "Oh, Rubbish! Pregnant women gain weight, they don't lose it." Although he expresses great concern, he is relieved to hear that she is seeing Dr. Sapirstein who also delivered two of his own grandchildren. He assures her, "Well, we must assume Dr. Sapirstein knows whereof he speaks." In this moment, Hutch assumes the role of the miller, a father-figure who is momentarily overwhelmed by the reputation of the powerful man. However, he remains inquisitive, especially after meeting Roman and learning that they are including tannis root in her vitamin drink. When he asks Rosemary what she thinks of Roman and Minnie, she responds, "Sometimes I think they're too friendly and helpful." Before their conversation can progress, however, Guy suddenly appears, ostensibly due to a delay with rehearsal, but in fact to keep Rosemary from having dangerous outside contact.

Rosemary agrees to meet Hutch for lunch downtown and is worried when he misses their date. When she calls his home, she learns that he has lapsed into a deep coma, and her single fatherly influence has been removed from her life, leaving her as alone as the miller's daughter. As she makes her way home, she is drawn to a Christmas store display of the Virgin Mary holding a Baby Jesus. Her eyes refocus on her own reflection in the window, and she is horrified by her sickly appearance and the dark circles under her eyes. Even walking around in a large, bustling city, she feels alone and anonymous. However, her little friend, Minnie, magically happens upon her just in time to take her back home to rest. Worried about her continued and growing pains, Rosemary tells Dr. Sapirstein, "It's like a wire inside me getting tighter and tighter," but he continues to assure her that the pain is natural and will abate in due time. He concurs completely when she tells him that she should not go out in the world anymore.

As she gets ready to prepare a chicken dinner, Rosemary subconsciously removes the organs and begins nibbling at them. She glances at her reflection in the toaster and realizes that her cravings have become uncontrollable and abnormal. In a futile attempt to reach out to her former life, she decides to hold a party, telling Guy, "It's going to be a very special party. You have to be under 60 to get in." She also decides to pour Minnie's special drink down the drain in another showing of limited but resurgent independence. Surrounded by friends and young women who have all given birth, Rosemary finally breaks down, crying, "It hurts so much, I'm afraid the baby's gonna die." As they beg her to visit Dr. Hill again, she states another fear, declaring firmly, "I won't have an abortion." After the party, she and Guy argue about her getting a second opinion, yet all of her resolve and determination vanish as the pain miraculously stops. An overjoyed Rosemary tells Guy, "It's alive! Guy, it's moving! It's alive! It's all right!" He jerks his hand away when she places it on her stomach, and she laughs, "Don't be scared, it won't bite you."

Like the miller's daughter who has survived a series of ordeals before becoming queen, Rosemary immediately forgets the past and happily moves forward with her pregnancy, retreating completely into ignorance and denial. If the pain has subsided, then all of Dr. Sapirstein's assurances must have been correct, and her own instincts—as well as those of her girl-friends—must have been wrong. A rejuvenated Rosemary is now shown giddily standing next to Minnie, obediently gulping her herbal mixture as they look over a newly wall-papered nursery. A white, wicker crib and cradle are brought in, and Rosemary starts gaining weight. When she learns that her dear friend Hutch has died, she suddenly realizes, "I feel awful. All this time, I didn't even think of him." His final gift to her is a book called *All of Them Witches*, a gift that shocks her as much as the queen with the return of that strange little man demanding his final installment. Both women must now solve a final mystery that threatens their home, happiness, and child.

PLAYING WITH NAMES

In his oft-referenced 1898 study of tales similar to and including "Rumpelstiltskin," *Tom Tit Tot: An Essay on Savage Philosophy in Folk-Tale*, Clodd explains the significance of personal names to our souls going back to "barbaric" man: "He further believes that to know the name is to put its owner, whether he be deity, ghost, or mortal, in the power of another, involving risk of harm or destruction to the named. He therefore takes all kinds of precautions to conceal his name, often from his friend, and always from his foe" (pp. 53–54). In a subsequent study, Clodd (1920) returns to this idea, claiming that the power ascribed to names "lies at the root of fetishism and idolatry, of witchcraft, shamanism, and all other instruments which are as keys to the invisible company of the dreaded and unknown" (p. 37). The supposedly savage and barbaric power inherent in naming the villain serves as the focal point for "Rumpelstiltskin" and *Rosemary's Baby*. When the as-yet-unnamed Rumpelstiltskin makes his surprise reappearance, the queen cries and pleads with the little man to let her keep her child. Possibly feeling some sympathy for the new mother, possibly offering up what he considers an impossible task, he tells the queen that he will leave without the child if she can guess his name within three days time. She tries names that are common and bizarre, and she sends out her servants and messenger to help her create a list of possibilities. The answer is finally revealed by none other than a careless Rumpelstiltskin himself, who dances around a fire outside of his cottage chanting his name. When the messenger spies this strange scene, he reports back to the queen who is overjoyed to have the puzzle solved. On the third day, she reveals the secret, and the named little man becomes so enraged that he rips his body in two. According to Zipes (1993), "To name is to know, to recognize, to become secure through knowledge so that one can protect oneself. In this regard, the naming is the appropriate ending for the spinner, who has come to know herself and identify her enemies" (p. 51). It is significant that we never learn the names of any other characters in this tale, including the queen, king, and their royal offspring. They all remain protected, their souls shrouded in nameless secrecy.

Names play an important role in both the novel and film of *Rosemary's Baby*. In Levin's novel, we learn that Guy's birth name was actually Sherman Peden before he changed it to the more mainstream Guy Woodhouse to help further his acting career. The new name removes much of his natural humanity, linking together three generic nouns. It also appears to symbolize his decreased masculinity, having gone from a confident ("sure") man to a plain guy who resides in a stable but not indestructible house. Symbolically, the sexual double-entendre of "guy wood" also comes into question as he allows Satan to impregnate his wife. His main competition for his dream play in both the novel and film is Donald Baumgart, whose last name comes from the German for orchard-grower (literally "tree-gardener"). Guy's satanic agreement blinds the most qualified actor for the part, and it also physically handicaps a man whose name is tied to bountiful growth and harvest. And of course the name of our heroine, Rosemary, ties the conflicted Catholic girl to the Virgin Mary as well as a fragrant and powerful herb often used in recipes. She is, in fact, the key ingredient of the witches' spell.

Rosemary and Guy are shown playing Scrabble during a rainy evening, and as she gets up we can see some of the words played, hinting at the subconscious feelings of both Guy and Rosemary: atone, debit, waned, and sever(s) with a blank could refer to Guy's shameful indebtedness to the coven while ward, cot, and begin seem to reveal Rosemary's focus on the baby. In the DVD Chapter "The Name is an Anagram," Rosemary's skills as a Scrabble player come into play, as she shifts letters around in the hope of figuring out Hutch's dying clue within the book he left behind:

All of the Them Witches which discusses one of the Bram's earliest residents, Adrian Marcato. At first she tries to form new words using the title of the book. When those attempts yield no logical results, she then flips open the book and notices the name of Adrian's son, Steven, has been double-underlined by Hutch, her fairy tale messenger who shares the truth, so she tries that puzzle instead. She intuitively rearranges those letters into her neighbor, Roman Castevet.

Not having yet figured out Guy's involvement with the coven, Rosemary alerts him to her fears and tells him what she has found in the book: "They use blood in their rituals, and the blood that has the most power is baby's blood. And they don't just use the blood, they use the flesh, too." Guy feigns being worried about her and takes the book away, placing it on their bookshelf, ironically above the Kinsey studies *Sexual Behavior in the Human Male and Female* and next to a self-help book called *Yes I Can.* When he throws the book away, she buys more books about witchcraft and learns that covens often use personal items of the victims to cast their spells. She remembers Hutch's lost glove before his coma. She also calls Donald Baumgart and discovers that he and Guy switched ties on the day before he went blind, convincing her that her husband has, in fact, entered into a deal with the coven. As in "Rumpelstiltskin," seemingly nominal tokens (a necklace and a ring; a glove and a necktie) precede the heroine's realization that her baby will be the ultimate prize.

The last few scenes of the film move quickly as she learns that Dr. Sapirstein is also in the coven and as she tries to convince a skeptical Dr. Hill of all that has occurred. She pleads with him, "They're very clever people. They planned everything right from the beginning. They probably made some sort of deal with Guy. They gave him success, and he promised them our baby to use in their rituals." Although he appears sympathetic, he nevertheless has Guy and Dr. Sapirstein come to retrieve her from the supposed safety of his office. They assure her that no one will hurt her or the baby, and, having lost all hope for rescue, she quietly exits with them. When they arrive back at the apartment, Rosemary manages to lock herself up in the apartment where she tries to call friends; however, she is as protected as the miller's daughter, and the coven appears as suddenly as the little man, calmly saying, "We're your friends, Rosemary," even as Dr. Sapirstein approaches her with a sedative. As she passes out, she cries out, "Oh, Andy, Andy or Jenny, I'm sorry, my little darling. Forgive me." It is important for her to name her child, male or female, offering it a mother's love and protection and giving it a tangibility that she can hold on to even as it is being taken from her womb.

When she awakens, she's told that her baby died due to complications; however, she hears crying next door and notices that the coven is keeping her breast milk. She takes a large knife from the kitchen and uncovers the hidden passageway to the Castevet's apartment. At first, no one notices her. When they tell her to go back to bed and rest, she continues determinedly towards the black cradle with an upside-down cross hanging over it as a perverse mobile. She peers in and asks the film's famous line, "What have you done to it? What have you done to its eyes?" Roman replies, "Satan is his father, not Guy. He came up from hell and begat a son of mortal woman. Satan is his father, and his name is Adrian."[7]

Here the film takes a strong turn from the novel. Where both versions of Rosemary come to realize that they can somehow care for their new son, Levin's mother corrects Roman, telling him that the child's name is Andrew, not Adrian: "I understand why you'd like to call him that, but I'm sorry; you can't. His name is Andrew John. He's my child, not yours, and this is one point that I'm not even going to argue about" (p. 217). The film's Rosemary does not question the name Adrian as she accepts her responsibilities as his mother, and the camera pans out of the Bram and over the skyline of an unsuspecting city.

LEAVING THE AUDIENCE GUESSING

Stylistically, "Rumpelstiltskin" differs from the other tales included in this text in a number of ways. With her white complexion, ebony-colored hair, and blood-red lips, Snow White is one of the few Grimm heroines to be described physically in much detail. However, the other heroines are famously named for what they wear (Little Red Cap), what protects them (Brier Rose), what their birth mothers craved (Rapunzel), and where they are forced to sleep (Cinderella). Rather than name this tale after their heroine, "The Miller's Daughter," for example, or "The Beautiful Spinner," the Grimms award the title to the little man. In addition to solving the central mystery for the reader/listener from the outset, the Grimms set us up to believe we will likely be encountering a hero with an unusual name. The heroine remains an unnamed abstraction, apparently capable of doing nothing distinctive to alter her situation. Knowing his name in advance gives us a power that we cannot use, and we are forced to suffer along with the queen without being able to assist her with our knowledge. *Rosemary's Baby* is similarly straightforward in this regard, pointing out quite clearly that the baby is not *The Woodhouse's Baby*. Guy and his surname are purposefully absent, and the audience is primed to question the baby's parentage from the moment we meet the young couple. We also know that the film is ultimately not about Rosemary, but rather her baby, a character that never actually appears in the film.

Whereas all of the other tales include the villain's point of view as well as the hero/ine's, this tale does not. We race with the hungry wolf to beat Little Red Cap to grandmother's house and plot with the jealous, aging queen as she fumes about Snow White's beauty. We struggle along with desperate princes through the brier hedge to reach the sleeping maiden, and we eavesdrop on Cinderella's stepmother as she coerces her daughters into mutilating their feet. We observe Mother Gothel as she banishes Rapunzel and blinds the prince, and we salivate with the wicked witch as she plans her feast of Hansel and Gretel. In "Rumpelstiltskin," however, the Grimm Brothers never award us this same intimacy with the little man. His supernatural encounters with the miller's daughter are a private affair, unknown to her father and the king, and his personal motives remain nebulous. He is not noticeably hungry, vain, love-struck, or power-hungry. And while he may share much in common with lonely Mother Gothel, we do not learn exactly what his intentions are with the child. This tale revels in questions without explicit answers. Does he plan to raise it or use it in a ritual sacrifice? We only know what he tells the queen when she offers him any other form of payment: "No, something living is more important to me than all the treasures in the world" (Grimm and Grimm, 2003, p. 195). His intentions remain a mystery, however.

Polanski stages *Rosemary's Baby* carefully to keep his audience questioning reality and the intentions of others as well. According to Schreck (2001), "[Polanski] preferred to leave the possibility open that the seemingly supernatural events were nothing more than delusions of her fevered imagination. To establish this basic uncertainty about Rosemary's sanity, he decided to film the entire drama through her point of view alone" (p. 136). Throughout most of the film, we must trust Rosemary's interpretation of events, and Polanski takes steps to keep her growing paranoia questionable. We never see or hear Guy make the initial deal with the Castevets, and his first seemingly too-intimate encounter with Roman occurs out of sight in their smoke-filled living room while Rosemary looks on from the kitchen. After Hutch falls comatose and dies, Rosemary does her best to figure out the motives of those surrounding her, but her reliability remains an issue as she tries to uncover the horrible truth without any concrete proof. As Dirks (2006) notes in his review of the film, Polanski "plays upon the fears and anxieties of most pregnant young women as they approach childbirth and experience hormonal changes" (par. 27).

Polanski also sets up Rosemary's nightmarish religious dreams early on, showing her dozing off while the Castevets argue in the room opposite her bedroom. In her first dream, Minnie's rantings come from a nun, and Rosemary nonsensically tells a janitor, "I told Sister Veronica about the windows, and she withdrew the school from the competition." During the dream-rape sequence, Rosemary seems to be hallucinating: She sees herself aboard a yacht with Hutch as a captain; she seems to float through a church decorated with Michelango's paintings; and she walks naked to a bare mattress and lies down surrounded by naked, chanting members of the coven with Adrian Marcato standing to the side. Brottman (1999) asserts that Polanski "pays particular attention to the changes of form, the absence of solidity, the feeling of continuity and the impression of drowning" that he encountered while experimenting with LSD. The audience is not sure exactly what to believe when she finally looks into the devil's eyes and screams, "This is really happening!" Rosemary has her final dream after she believes that she has escaped to the sanctuary of Dr. Hill's office. Calling them all "monsters," she closes her eyes briefly and envisions herself holding a healthy baby while surrounded by her own friends. Her dream is interrupted by the arrival of Guy and Dr. Sapirstein who tells her sternly, "Come with us quietly Rosemary. Don't argue or make a scene, because if you say anything more about witches or witchcraft, we're going to be forced to take you to a mental hospital." When Guy tells her that she has been suffering from "the pre-partum crazies," we are not absolutely certain that he is mistaken. Polanski has staged a film in which the audience has no real evidence that Rosemary is not actually having delusions, and *Rosemary's Baby* emerges as "a challenge to realism, locating the ordinary world of plausible social interaction within a wider and more primitive universe of magic, sorcery, and supernatural forces" (Brottman, p. 40).[8]

The ending of "Rumpelstiltskin" stands as one of the least satisfying resolutions of all the Grimm fairy tales. The best-known tales tend to conclude in a happy marriage with vengeance taken out against a clearly defined, evil villain. In contrast, this tale concludes abruptly with a terrific and brutal act of self-mutilation. The queen, undeniably powerful and wealthy, does not have the little man latched into red-hot iron shoes or brutally attacked by watchful birds, for example, while the little man himself does not use his powers simply to track down another desperate maiden once his secret name has been revealed. Instead, he swears that the devil must have told her his name, stamps his feet, and rips his body in two. The moral of this tale remains remarkably unclear: The punishment (self-inflicted at that) seems too severe for the deed, and the heroine, while married to the king, remains in jeopardy should she ever be ordered to spin more gold. She has won her baby, but she has lost the supernatural helper who is really responsible for her success. Lacking a promise of "happily ever after," this tale may well be the most honest of the Grimms' collection.

Likewise, *Rosemary's Baby* concludes with few answers and without a clear victory for the heroine, even though she gets to keep her baby. Roman preaches, "He shall overthrow the might and lay waste their temples. He shall redeem the despised and wreak vengeance in the name of the burned and the tortured! ... God is dead! Satan lives! The year is one!" Yet his enthusiasm is tempered as Rosemary walks back to the cradle to rock her son to sleep. He quits crying while she looks lovingly at him, a slight smile coming across her face. Like the miller's daughter who becomes queen, her safety remains a genuine concern. The coven has its golden child, and her maternal services, while undoubtedly desired by the coven, are of limited value. A hypnotic lullaby (sung by an uncredited Mia Farrow) plays over the closing credits, a demonic denouement that leaves the audience hoping for a resolution that never arrives.[9]

SEVEN

Off the Eaten Path

"Hansel and Gretel" and
What Lies Beneath

A GRIMM VIEW OF THE FAIRY TALE WITCH

Witches and witch-hunts have a long history in Germany which stands out "as the central area both of witch persecutions and of ideological development. Here most of the executions [within Europe] took place, and here the bulk of demonological literature was produced, distributed and incorporated into the learned tradition in both law and theology" (Ankarloo, 2002, p. 76). Certainly the most famous work dealing with witches and witch hunts was *The Malleus Malleficarum* (1486), often translated as *The Witches' Hammer* or *The Hexenhammer*, a handbook compiled in Germany by Heinrich Kramer and Jacob Sprenger. Although the text was labeled illegal and unethical by the faculty of theology at the University of Cologne, and the Catholic Church placed it on its Index of Forbidden Works, it nonetheless became a best-selling and popular guide for witch-hunters. The work is divided into three distinct parts: Part I proves the existence of witchcraft and discusses how women fall victim to it more easily than men; Part II describes forms of witchcraft and spells and explains how to fight them; Part III details ways of detecting and trying witches and "gives great latitude to judges to elicit confessions by means of torture" (Levack, 2004, p. 123). According to Broedel, the immediate and extensive popularity of this particular work "created a certain uniformity of discourse in subsequent witchcraft debate" and served as the authoritative starting point for almost all other late-medieval texts on the subject.

Johann Weyer, also known as John Wierus, (1516–1588), was a Dutch-German demonologist and physician and one of the first defenders of witches, having authored a 1563 rebuttal to *The Malleus Malleficarum, De Praestigiis Daemonum et incantationibus ac veneficiis (On the Illusion of Demons and Spells and Witches)*. Levack (2004) notes that Weyer argued against the idea that witches consciously made a pact with the devil and that they were, in fact, "vulnerable to demonic deception because they were afflicted by melancholy or because they were of weak faith" (p. 277). According to Pavlac (2006), Weyer's claims were attacked for decades thereafter, most notably in King James I's own *Daemonologie* (1597), which vilifies Weyer specifically for his "public apology" of witches and "craft-folk." James' work argues that witches exist in league with the devil, and he promotes strict guidelines for both trial and punishment of these wicked beings.

Monter (2002) claims that Germany served as the center of so-called witch "superhunts" that occurred between 1586 and 1639 in such cities as Mainz, Cologne, Würzburg-Bamberg, and Baden. These hunts resulted in about one-forth of all executions for witchcraft in Europe, and, according to Monter, occurred in both the Protestant and Catholic-ruled states. In his extensively researched *Witchcraft Persecutions in Bavaria*, Behringer (1997) estimates that nearly 5,000 witches were burned in southern German states between 1562 and 1775, when the last known execution for witchcraft occurred in Bavaria. Bavaria's 40-page *Regulations against Superstition, Sorcery, Witchcraft and Other Punishable Diabolical Acts* (1611) was among the most severe and comprehensive legal codes against practicing witchcraft.

In most of the small German towns, practicing magic was not specifically considered evil by virtue of its simply being otherworldly. A neighbor's spell might bring famine and plague, but it could also result in bountiful crops and new-found love. According to Gijswijt-Hofstra (1999), Germans came to define magic in distinct terms that distinguished clearly demonic magic from neutral magic:

The term *Hexerei* [witchcraft] is reserved for diabolism, because the devil is invariably involved in it: there is a pact with the devil, sex with the devil, the witches sabbath and the accompanying flight, and usually also *maleficium* (inflicted harm).... With *Zauberei* [sorcery] it is more a question of ritual actions in order to achieve harmful or beneficial objectives [p. 162].

Thus, there were essentially three categories of magic as far as the common folk were concerned: witchcraft, which was always evil, since its practitioners were aligned with the devil; good sorcery used to assist; and bad sorcery used to injure. Behringer (1997) agrees that "reason and belief in magical relationships or supernatural phenomena were not opposed to each other, and that sorcery was not regarded as morally reprehensible or 'wicked' by people, but as neutral" (p. 84). Behringer, Levack (1999), and Clark (2002) compellingly argue that the witch hunts gained momentum during the 16th and 17th centuries not so much for religious and ethical concerns of the people and rulers, but rather primarily due to the incredible social and economic changes that ravaged Europe and Germany in particular. As Levack explains:

Over-population, an unprecedented rise in prices, a decline in real wages among the poor, chronic famine and dearth, especially during years of climatic severity, periodic outbreaks of the plague, extraordinarily high levels of infant mortality, migration of the poor from the countryside to the town, pestilence among men and beasts, and the social dislocations that resulted from widespread domestic and international warfare often lay at the root of those personal conflicts hat found expression in witchcraft accusations [pp. 44–45].

The first volume of the Grimm Brothers' fairy tales was published in 1812, with images of neighborhood sorcerers, witches, and witch trials still fresh in their societal memory. Within the tales, the Grimms provide examples of good and neutral sorcery (*Zauberei*) as well as images of purely evil *Hexerei*. For example, Mother Gothel, the sorceress who demands a child in exchange for rampion lettuce in "Rapunzel" (discussed in Chapter 3), is never called wicked or evil, and no revenge is exacted upon her at the end of the tale. The worst declaration made against her by the Grimms is that she is cruel for abandoning Rapunzel in a desert for deceiving her. In "Brier Rose" (discussed in Chapter 2), we encounter twelve magical wise women who bestow gifts of beauty and virtue upon the newborn princess. A thirteenth wise woman who is not invited to the ceremony sentences Brier Rose to death on her fifteenth birthday, but another wise woman is able to lessen the severity of her spell. In these tales, we see figures capable of human emotion and suffering. They act out of passion when they are injured and can be as generous as they are vengeful. In the most extreme example, "Eve's Unequal Children," even the Lord is shown to deliver unequal blessings, marking her beautiful children to become knights and noblemen while awarding her misshapen children with roles as shoemakers and tailors.

Of all the fairy tale villains, perhaps none is more vilified that the wicked witch (*die böse Hexe*), a figure that is almost always in league with the devil. Most commonly, she appears as a cruel stepmother in the tales, a woman who has supplanted the natural mother and who thrives on making her new children's lives intolerable. In "Brother and Sister," the stepmother beats the children so savagely that they run away. Their leaving alone does not placate her, however, and she follows them through the forest, cursing all of the springs throughout the forest. When the brother accidentally drinks from one of bewitched springs, he is turned into a fawn. His sister protects him from the king's huntsmen, and the king naturally falls in love with her. After they marry, the stepmother and her own envious daughter suffocate the new queen and have her daughter assume her appearance. When the queen's ghost appears at night to nurse her newborn son and feed her fawn, the king realizes what has happened, and she comes back to life. The stepmother is burned to death, and her daughter is devoured by wild beasts in the forest. The queen's brother assumes his human form again, and all live happily ever after.

A similar spousal switch occurs in "The White Bride and the Black Bride," as an evil stepmother/witch uses her powers to have her ugly daughter replace the beautiful stepdaughter whose portrait has entranced the local widower king. The devious duo push the rightful fiancé into a river where she is transformed into a white duck, and the stepmother casts a spell making her own daughter appear attractive to the king. After they marry, the talking white duck swims up the kitchen drain and learns what has happened through the kitchen boy who then tells the king of his magical encounter. When the duck next appears, the king cuts off her head, turning her instantly back into the beautiful bride. The witch and her daughter are sentenced to one of the Grimm Brothers' most violent deaths and are stripped naked and dragged behind a horse in a barrel studded with nails.

In "The Little Lamb and the Little Fish," a stepmother who grows annoyed at the noisy antics of her stepdaughter and stepson turns them into a lamb and a fish respectively. She then tells the cook to slaughter the lamb so that she can serve the girl as dinner to her guests. When the cook realizes that the lamb and fish are actually the children of the house, she slaughters another animal and secretly carries them to the house of a kindly wise woman. A blessing from the wise woman transforms them back to human form, and they live contentedly on their own in a little cottage in the forest. We do not learn what happens to their stepmother and can only assume that she spends her life happily milling about her castle in peace and quiet.

Intriguingly, witches are not always condemned to death in the tales of the Brothers Grimm. In addition to the stepmother/witch of "The Little Lamb and the Little Fish," several other witches manage to escape their tales unharmed as long as the focus of the tale is on teaching girls to be obedient and true to their word. The witches in these tales serve as a warning that evil figures are always nearby and do not always get caught. "Mother Trudy" gives us an old woman who lives in a strange house and is widely known to be wicked. A stubborn young girl tells her parents that she wants to go see the woman since she has heard so much about her, and even though they warn her and expressly forbid it, she sneaks off on her own. After Mother Trudy catches the girl spying through her window, she transforms her into a block of wood and tosses the disobedient girl into a roaring fire.

The witches of "The Frog King, or Iron Heinrich" and "The Iron Stove" do not even appear in those tales. Rather, they have moved on to other enchanted forests, leaving behind cursed princes and princesses. In the former, a princess loses her prized golden ball in a well and promises a frog that she will let him be her companion if he retrieves it for her. However, she breaks her word and leaves the frog once he gives her back her ball. The next day, the frog arrives at her castle, demanding to be let in. The princess tells her father what she promised, and he demands that she do as she offered. When the frog asks to sleep in her bed, she angrily throws him against a wall, and he is magically transformed into a handsome and worthy prince. He then explains that a wicked witch cast a spell upon him, and he had to wait for the princess to free him.

In a similar set-up, the unseen witch of the "Iron Stove" has bewitched a prince and already left the story from its beginning. A prince who has been imprisoned in an iron stove offers directions to a lost princess if she agrees to marry him. When she returns home, however, her father does not encourage her to keep her promise; rather, he sends other maidens in her place. The prince is not fooled by these imposters, a miller's daughter and a swineherd's daughter, respectively, and he demands that she return or her kingdom will be destroyed. She returns to the stove and cuts a hole in it so that the prince can escape. The prince returns home, and she agrees to marry him after saying goodbye to her father. She gets lost on her way back to the prince and comes across a cottage filled with toads—bewitched princes and princesses—who give her the resources to find her intended. After the two finally unite, they return to the cottage, releasing the toads from the witch's spell and transforming the cottage into a large castle.

In addition to featuring the best-known fairy tale siblings, "Hansel and Gretel" gives us the most indelible impression of the stepmother-as-witch.[1] During a period of famine, the self-centered stepmother coerces her weak-willed husband that they can only survive by abandoning the children deep in the forest. The children overhear the plan, however, and clever Hansel leaves a trail of shiny stones for him and Gretel to follow home under the moonlight. The family survives this period of hunger but soon encounters another period of famine. Again the stepmother convinces her husband to leave the children in the forest, and again the children overhear the plan and plot how best to mark their path. The stepmother blocks Hansel from gathering any more stones, however, so he marks their trail with breadcrumbs on this second journey. Birds devour the trail, preventing the children from finding their way home.

Tatar (2003) explains, "Once Hansel and Gretel enter the forest, they find themselves in a world that not only admits the supernatural, but also takes it completely for granted" (p. 51). Thus, neither the children nor the audience is completely surprised when they come across a house made of bread with a cake roof and sugar windows. The home proves too tempting for the starving children to resist, and they soon fall into the clutches of a witch who acts friendly and maternal at first only to reveal herself as a *kinder*-cannibal. She cages Hansel and tries to fatten him up while forcing Gretel into servitude. When the time finally comes to roast the young boy, Gretel tricks the witch into climbing into her own oven, and she is roasted in her own juices. Having vanquished the witch, the children journey home with her hidden riches. They complete one final task, crossing a river with the help of a duck, and are united with their father. The stepmother has, not-so-coincidentally, passed away during their absence, and the natural family lives happily ever after.

ENCHANTING OUR IMAGE OF WITCHES

In the frothy romantic comedy *Bell, Book, and Candle* (1958), stunning Kim Novak entrances James Stewart using her potions and incantations. The popular television series *Bewitched* (1964–1972) would continue with this idea a few years later as Samantha Stevens (Elizabeth Montgomery) entered into a mortal marriage with that dullard Darren (Dick York, 1964–1969; Dick Sargent, 1969–1972), an advertising executive who insisted his wife try to run her home in "the everyday mortal way." Films like *The Witches of Eastwick* (1987), starring Cher, Susan Sarandon, and Michelle Pfeiffer as a coven of witches around "horny devil" Jack Nicholson, and *The Craft* (1996), featuring four lovely teenage girls abusing their powers to avenge themselves against cruel classmates, cemented the Hollywood ideal of witches as young, beautiful women. The long-running series *Charmed* (1998–2006) enjoyed a campy tone of self-parody, dressing its version of *Macbeth*'s powerful "Weird Sisters" in revealing outfits as they fought off demons and protected the innocent with their "power of three."[2]

The most indelible image of a witch in popular culture, however, contrasts all of these comely representations: Margaret Hamilton as Miss Gulch, the crone determined to destroy Dorothy's dog, Toto, and her alter-ego, the Wicked Witch of the West in *The Wizard of Oz* (1939). Evil is quite easy to spot in the Land of Oz, as Glinda, the Good Witch of the North (Billie Burke) explains to Dorothy that only bad witches are ugly. Dressed in black with green skin, bony fingers, a terrifying stare, and a horrifying cackle, Hamilton's witch popularized all of the accoutrement associated with witches. She even flies on a broom and stirs a steaming cauldron while plotting the demise of young Dorothy.

Like the twister that spins Dorothy out of black-and-white Kansas and into multi-hued Munchkin Land, *The Wizard of Oz* can serve as our link between "Hansel and Gretel" and *What Lies Beneath*. Dorothy (Judy Garland) is basically a lost Gretel: Forced to leave a home where she feels unappreciated, she enters a supernatural world with talking trees and wicked witches. She must confront—and kill—the witch before she can

Gretel can return home only after vanquishing the witch and communicating with a miraculous duck that can carry her from the supernatural world back to the real world. (Illustration by E. H. Wehnert from *Household Stories Collected by the Brothers Grimm*. London: Routledge and Sons, 1880.)

return home using the ruby slippers, a magical means that Glinda tells her she had to figure out for herself. Once she returns home, Dorothy is able to see the ambiguity of life, recognizing the farm hands as her colorful companions through Oz, the Scarecrow, the Tin Man, and the Cowardly Lion. Like the evil stepmother who dies along with the roasted witch in "Hansel and Gretel," Miss Gulch appears to have vanished along with her melted metaphorical self as well.

The Wizard of Oz also ties in to the supernatural thriller *What Lies Beneath*: Michelle Pfeiffer's Claire steps into Dorothy's ruby slippers and is transported from her own seemingly black-and-white world with a "perfect" husband and marriage and into the supernatural, multi-faceted world of ghosts. Like Dorothy, Claire must help another mystical being (her Scarecrow takes on the form of a young woman's ghost) who existed in the real world of the living as well. Once she enters this other world, Claire follows her own yellow brick road of clues that leads her to the realization that her doctor-husband, Harrison Ford's Norman is not quite as he appears. While holding Dorothy captive in her sprawling castle, the Wicked Witch cannot resist teasing her hostage, showing her an image of a distraught Auntie Em (Clara Blandick) that gives way to the cackling crone mocking Dorothy's cries to go home. Taking on the role of the Wicked Witch, Norman unveils his own evil nature and uses his powers to try to stop Claire from revealing his murderous past. In *The Wizard of Oz*, the Wicked Witch casts a spell using poppies to make Dorothy go to sleep before she reaches the Wizard. The cunning doctor uses a special drug to paralyze his wife before attempting to drown her in the bathtub of their own castle-like home. And once she has been drugged, he teases her as well, forcing a kiss and hinting that he might become much closer to her daughter once she is gone. In both cases, supernatural intervention (Glinda and the ghost) allows our heroine to recover so that she can complete her journey. The witch will stop at nothing to get the ruby slippers, and he will resort to any tactic to protect his career and reputation.

For both the Wicked Witch and Norman, water serves as their ultimate undoing and, conversely, as their victims' life-saving force. In *The Wizard of Oz*, Dorothy and her friends have been cornered in one of the castle turrets when the witch approaches. Feeling assured of victory, she lights the Scarecrow on fire; however, Dorothy instinctively grabs a nearby bucket of water and throws it on him, also hitting the witch. Screeching uncontrollably, the witch begins melting away, crying out that her beautiful wickedness should never have been so easily destroyed by a good little girl. In *What Lies Beneath*, water also leads to Norman's demise, as he and Claire drive off a bridge and into a lake, landing just above the car of the girl he murdered and abandoned there a year ago. He, too, seems sure of his victory, as he hushes Claire and begins to push her head underwater. Emerging as a *deus ex aqua*, the girl's ghost rises up, pulling Norman beneath the water and allowing Claire to escape.

SATISFYING HUNGER PAINS

What Lies Beneath (2000), directed by Robert Zemeckis, includes a number of shots that could have been inspired by some of the most popular Grimm fairy tales. Michelle Pfeiffer's Claire, a lonely wife whose daughter has gone off to college, occupies her time with a garden of beautiful rose bushes that surround the fence on her property. As in "Brier Rose," the hedge seems ideally suited not just to keep intruders out, but to isolate her within her sprawling home. She even awakens her daughter, Caitlin (Katharine Towne), on her last morning at home by gently announc-

Claire (Michelle Pfeiffer) can face the truth about her adulterous, murderous husband only by communicating with the ghost haunting her house and bathroom in *What Lies Beneath* (Image Movers/Dreamworks/Amblin Entertainment, 2000). *The Kobal Collection, François Duhamel*

ing, "Good morning, beauty." As the film progresses and Claire comes to suspect that her neighbor has killed his wife, she snoops around his house and finds a woman's single shoe that appears stained with blood at the toe. In the Grimm version of "Cinderella," the prince has the title heroine's stepsisters try on the left-behind slipper. Their mother encourages them to cut off their heel and toe in order to assure a good fit, and the prince carries each of the daughters off after she has forced her mangled foot into the single shoe. Helpful birds alert the prince to the bloody shoe, preventing him from marrying the false bride. Finally, Claire finds a small chest with a keyhole that can be opened only by a tiny key she discovers in her husband's office. In the last of the Grimm tales, "The Golden Key," a young boy prepares to open a similarly mysterious chest that he has found in the woods. We are led to believe that the chest contains wonderful things, although we never learn the contents. Opening the chest in the film leads the less-fortunate Claire into a painful confrontation with her husband about his relationship with her house ghost.

With regard to its main structure and most prominent themes and images, *What Lies Beneath* shares its most fundamental connections with "Hansel and Gretel," a cautionary tale of starvation and filial betrayal at its most primal level. This suspense film may begin as a hybrid of evolving genres (first an empty-nest drama, then a detective story, and finally a traditional ghost story), but it is ultimately a tale of deeply personal, human hungers left unchecked. The story also hinges upon Claire's ability to follow clues and look beyond the surface in her seemingly perfect marriage. As she ventures into a dangerous supernatural realm of her own, she becomes a middle-aged version of the Grimm Gretel who must fend for herself against the wicked witch while her brother lies helpless in the kitchen cage. And like the children's slow-witted father, she must also come to see that her spouse has constructed a double life that does not include her or her daughter.

As the film opens, we are introduced to Claire and the dashing Dr. Norman Spencer (Harrison Ford), a seemingly perfect couple who are preparing to send her daughter, his stepdaughter, off to college. The standard Grimm role of the witch-stepmother is reversed with Claire as the natural, caring parent and Norman as the stepfather who may not be as wonderful as he seems. Unlike Claire, he is eager for the daughter to go, giving the couple privacy and, he hopes, a renewed intimacy. For her part, Claire also seems ready to focus on her home and freedom. She assures Norman, "I'm excited.... Get my life back. Have some time for myself, some time for us," as he agrees, "It's just us now." Like the parents in "Hansel and Gretel," the two can focus completely on their most neglected needs once their home is empty. The clear implication is that the daughter has been consuming parts of their privacy and time, and Norman, at least, feels that his marriage has been malnourished. Caitlin's departure signals a crucial stage in their relationship and in Claire's personal growth. It is time for the parents to feast.

In "Hansel and Gretel," the famine can be viewed realistically and representative of the time it was transcribed, emblematic of what Tatar (1999) calls "the harsh social realties of an earlier age" (p. 180), but it can also be interpreted metaphorically. In addition to the children, the parental figures hunger for something in particular, and this hunger feeds their actions and motivations throughout the story. The father, the natural parent gives in, twice, to the demands of his wife, even though he has witnessed famine as a periodic event that can pass. Although he is overjoyed when his children find their way home the first time, he nevertheless escorts them back into the forest upon the next wave of famine. His traditional role within the family is that of bread-winner, yet he has essentially failed in that regard. He relinquishes his position as provider to his children at the bidding of his wife, even though he acknowledges that wild beasts could devour the children when they are deserted in the wilderness. Ultimately, he is defined by his desire—and choice—to be a loyal, satisfied husband instead of an unsuccessful provider. Outside of these two roles, he has no clear identity of his own within the tale. His hunger to succeed in at least one of these roles pushes him to abandon his children and satisfy his wife's demands.

Like the fairy tale father, Claire confronts the same competing roles of parent and spouse. We know that she once had a promising career as a cellist, but she abandoned that opportunity, and an important part of herself, for her family. While dining with friends, an old girlfriend of Claire's comments, "I would sit onstage during Claire's solo, and I mean, truly, I had tears streaming down my face. I mean, she's fabulous." Before she married Norman, Claire was educated at Julliard and performed at Carnegie Hall. She did not give up her career for her child, and she was, in fact, quite successful while touring as a single mother. Rather, she feels that she gave up her career to be the so-called perfect wife for Norman. When asked why she stopped playing, she offers an answer right out of a fairy tale: "I met a dashing, handsome, genius scientist, and three months later, I was married." While Claire sees her choice to marry Norman as one that benefited him and helped further his career, Norman believes that Claire has come to resent him for giving up her professional aspirations. When Claire finally remembers that Norman had an affair, following a year-long period of amnesia due to a car crash, their opposing views surface. Claire swears, "I gave up everything.... My life, my music! ... You had to topple perfect daddy—That meant perfect wife, perfect family!" Trying to explain the resentment that led to his affair, Norman responds, "You were a single mother touring with a baby, and when I came along, you were only too happy to give it up. And when you did, you hated me for it, so you gave it all to her!" In both "Hansel and Gretel" and *What Lies Beneath*, we see that hunger is an ever-present fear and trying to sate one appetite ironically leads to new and more intense cravings.

The father's sexual appetite for his wife is subtly hinted at as the wife coerces her husband to abandon the children primarily when they are in bed together. We are also aware that the children can plainly hear their parents' nightly discussions and, therefore, their moments of physical intimacy as well. This lack of parental privacy emerges as an initial motivator in *What Lies Beneath* as well. On the morning of Caitlin's last day at home, Norman tries to initiate sex with Claire, only to be reminded that their daughter is awake. When he suggests that they can be quick and quiet, Claire responds, "I don't want to be either." We further see Claire's desire for sexual freedom after Caitlin has left, and she and Norman get to enjoy their first night alone. Wearing a silk, white negligee, Claire crawls into bed next to Norman who is doing some research. She playfully grabs his medical book and reads, "Ooh, a couple of Swedish sailor cells just gang-divided a virginal cheerleader cell." He saves his document, and they begin to make love when they overhear their neighbors engaging in vocally vigorous intercourse. As Norman begins to shut their bedroom window, Claire mischievously commands, "Leave it open" and insists that they can outdo them. Claire is most comfortable expressing her sexual needs and desires only after her daughter has gone. Yet, like the father in "Hansel and Gretel," who "had not had a single happy hour" (Grimm and Grimm, 2003, p. 58) since leaving his children in the forest, she continues to miss her daughter greatly. The scene immediately following her night of competitive love-making with Norman shows her folding clothes in her daughter's room and then nostalgically looking through a scrapbook and being overcome with tears.

A key element within "Hansel and Gretel" requires the natural parent to be saddened by the loss of the children while the stepparent reinforces its necessity, and *What Lies Beneath* firmly adheres to this formula. When Claire denies Norman's sexual advances, he tersely responds, "When's she outta here?" He then sulks off, sighing, "All right, I can't take the rejection—I'm going for a run." In both the fairy tale and the film, the jealous, self-serving villains force their spouses to choose between their parental and marital relationships. Hansel and Gretel's stepmother is a wicked replacement for the natural mother and the previous wife, and it is clear that she places her needs above those of the children and, most likely, her husband. She knows that the husband's acquiescence and complicity are necessary, however, in order to implement her plans to rid them of the children. Her power in the real world is limited, and she cannot act alone in his house. Once the lost siblings have found the witch's house, however, the witch-stepmother assumes full control and can reveal herself as a cannibalistic crone who captures children for her own consumption.

Her sugary shelter hides the danger lurking within and attracts the starving children to her tasty trap. She is obsessed with devouring her young competition, taking them into herself as a final means of showing her power and control over the husband. That she cages Hansel, the lone male figure, and forces him to gorge on her finest food to fatten him up for slaughter shows her primary desire to consume the masculine representation of her husband. Although she is clever and a master of disguise, she is also so assured of achieving her gastronomic goals that Gretel easily fools her into climbing into her own oven where she burns to death.

As the unfaithful spouse and villainous stepparent, Harrison Ford's Norman fulfills the deceptive witch-stepmother role in the film quite effectively. In the director's commentary track to the DVD, Zemeckis notes that Ford was his first choice for this particular role, as his screen persona would create "a misdirect" away from his wicked character. His character's name even implies a nebulous, mysterious identity that is neither beast "nor man." Like the witch-stepmother, Norman is a fill-in for Claire's first spouse (a fellow musician) and Caitlin's natural father. He is also acting as a replacement for his own father: They are living in his father's house, and he is teaching at his father's school, in his father's old position. Norman even jokes that his father is the ghost that Claire has been hearing. He hungers for success and for his own identity, but that seems just out of his reach.

In describing the parents in "Hansel and Gretel," Bettelheim (1989) argues that "poverty and deprivation do not improve man's character, but rather make him more selfish, less sensitive to the suffering of others, and thus prone to embark on evil deeds" (p. 160). This same interpretation could describe Norman. In this marriage, Claire sacrifices part of her life for her husband, but it is not enough to stave off his selfish need to control her. When Claire first believes she is being visited by a ghost, Norman sends her to a Dr. Drayton (Joe Morton), a psychiatrist who inquires whose idea it was for her to visit him. She replies honestly, "Mine. His. We both thought—I didn't want to come here." She half-jokingly continues, "I'm sure he's hoping you'll pack me full of Prozac or lithium or something so he can live out his life in peace." When Dr. Drayton tries to probe deeper into the complexities of her marriage, she acknowledges, "I mean, sure, he can be obsessed with his work, and sometimes it's like, um, that he doesn't see me. Or, you know, like I'm, that there's something wrong with me.... But my marriage is fine."

His affair initially seems an odd turn, and his excuse that he turned to another woman due to Claire's focus on her daughter appears mostly unsubstantiated. Rather, like the witch-stepmother, he emerges as a villain consumed entirely by his passion to control those around him. His affair is with a student, Madison Frank (Amber Valletta), who looks like a younger Claire, essentially a version he believes he can mold. When Madison makes demands that jeopardize his control, however, he admits to a stunned Claire, "Should I have sacrificed everything? Our marriage? My work, which I spent my whole life on? ... She was going to go to the dean. She would have ruined us. Did she think I was just going to sit there and watch it happen?" He has fully rationalized drowning Madison and hiding her body in the nearby lake, as much as the witch-stepmother was able to justify abandoning the children for her own sake. After Claire finally learns that Norman is the girl's killer, he emerges as a true witch-like figure, using an almost magical medicine to paralyze her while keeping her awake to witness her own death by drowning. While she is in this state, he shares all of his secrets and even hints provocatively that he will also take care of Caitlin: "I'm sure, in some tragic way, your suicide is gonna help bring Caitlin and I closer together. And every time I look at her, I'll see you." For Norman, these women are interchangeable commodities, each one as dispensable as the next when they start to feed too much on his time and priorities.

FOLLOWING THE PATH BACK HOME

A hallmark of "Hansel and Gretel" is the creation of distinct, parallel worlds in which the realistic and the fantastic co-exist and eventually converge. The children must venture into the supernatural realm to confront and overcome the true horror of their stepmother. Although they are able to mark the path clearly—with stones that shine in the moonlight—on their first trek into the wilderness, their second attempt to do so is thwarted when they leave a trail of breadcrumbs that are eaten by birds. As the lost children wander deeper into the forest, they are drawn to the witch's house which at first promises them all that they have been missing: the house itself is made of bread and sugar, and the witch speaks kindly to them and offers them a delicious meal of pancakes and milk. When she reveals her true nature, the children, Gretel in particular, must outwit and destroy her before they can finally return to their home in the real world. Their reward for accomplishing this goal does not merely consist of the treasure they find in the witch's home, but rather it includes the death of the witch's parallel personality, the equally wicked stepmother, who has simultaneously died in their absence. They return richer, happier, and safer.

Like the wanting, wandering children in the Grimm forest, Claire must leave the real world and complete a journey through the supernatural realm to solve her personal crises. Claire has two dilemmas that drive the story, one far more extreme than the other: As the story begins, she feels the typical loss associated with a newly empty nest; concurrently, however, she lives with the repressed knowledge that her husband has cheated on her. Claire's ideal of a flawless, genius husband is a mere memory away from shattering. With her daughter gone, Claire must first face the intense emotional void in her life. As she packs the car with Caitlin's clothes and boxes, Claire half-heartedly assures her daughter that her life will remain quite full: "I have Norman, and the garden, and the new house. You really don't have to worry." Alone in the house, Claire now assumes the role of the undernourished Hansel and Gretel who could, in fact, starve to death if they remain in their impoverished home. Their desire to return immediately to a home where they are not wanted—and, concretely, where there is no real security or reliable source of food—is understandable, but it is also hinders their growth and maturation. They are clinging to an impossible and unrealistic hope that they will missed enough to be seen as an integral part of their witch-stepmother's house. Their innate worth as members of the household remains in question as long as she is in control.

According to Bettelheim (1989), the children's first return home "tells about the debilitating consequences of trying to deal with life's problems by means of regression and denial, which reduce one's ability to solve problems" (p. 160). For the past year, Claire has also been living a life of regression and denial about her husband's affair. At a party at the dean's house, the dean's wife (Sloane Shelton) reminds Claire that she was so upset at last year's party that she dropped a wine glass: "You went completely pale; you couldn't catch your breath. It was as if you had seen a ghost." Like the children, we learn that Claire returned home unexpectedly as well, surprising Norman. She followed these first clues back to her home, having seen Madison at the party, and realizing the connection between her and Norman. Finding Norman and Madison together in his study, she fled and ended up in a terrible car accident. When she awoke, she had amnesia and resumed her life as if nothing had happened. The house still needed some work, her daughter was still at home, and her garden still needed tending. In "Hansel and Gretel," the children return home and are at first welcomed back; however, their second journey even deeper into the forest comes when a second wave of famine arrives. Likewise, Claire's second journey, also deeper into the unknown, is necessitated by her sudden famine. The house has been completely restored, her daughter is gone, and her garden is in full bloom. And for this journey, her clues will be largely intangible, supernatural ones, as hard to follow as a trail of leftover bread crumbs. For Hansel, Gretel, and Claire, their journey into the deepest part of the magical woods and their direct confrontation with the villain in their home is essential to their development and independence.

Claire's journey into the unknown arises from her desire to feel useful and needed, yet her misinterpretation of events at first creates a detour that prevents her from addressing her past and seeing the growing peril in her own house. The mystery surrounding her neighbors, Warren and Mary Feur (James Remar and Miranda Otto), initially takes the place of her daughter and gives Claire's life continued meaning. The couple also serves as an emotional counterpart for Norman and Claire in much the same way that the witch serves as the stepmother for Hansel and Gretel. Like Norman, Warren is a professor at the same New England college, Mary is his dutiful wife, and they have no children at home. Initially, they appear as volatile as Norman and Claire seem composed, embodying fully their name which connotes images of "fire" (*Feuer*) and "fiery" (*feurig*) in German. Norman and Claire's interactions coincide closely with the Feur's on several occasions, on the one hand foreshadowing and warning Claire about her own troubled marriage, while drawing Claire's attention away from her most pressing goal, remembering Norman's affair, on the other. In the opening scene, they hear the Feurs arguing as Norman tries unsuccessfully to initiate sex with Claire. The largely unspoken tension between Norman and Claire ironically signals greater jeopardy than the Feur's passionate argument. After Caitlin has left and they prepare for an intimate night, they overhear the Feurs loudly making love and try to compete with them. And when Claire tearfully runs out to her garden while thinking of her daughter, she is interrupted by Mary's sobs on the other side of the fence. When

Claire approaches her, seeing just a sliver of her face and a green eye through the fence posts, Mary admits that she is terrified "that one day I'll just, just disappear."

The DVD Chapter "Spying on Mr. Feur" serves as a clear homage to Alfred Hitchcock's classic *Rear Window* (1954)[3], starring Jimmy Stewart as an injured photographer who suspects his neighbor of murdering his wife. Following her conversation with a terrified Mary Feur, Claire begins spying even more closely on her neighbors. After she sees Warren packing a suspiciously large bag into the trunk of his car, she picks up her own pair of binoculars and begins watching him at night. When she reports to her friend, Jody (Diana Scarwind), that he's eating dinner alone, Jody jokingly responds with a line that ties him to the Grimm Brothers' cannibalistic witch, "Listen, call me back if he starts in on some serial killer dessert, like lady fingers." Most significantly, this chapter shows the danger of getting so lost on a journey that one cannot see the peril standing directly in one's path. When Hansel and Gretel arrive at the witch's house, they are so hungry that they do not stop eating even when the witch calls out to ask who is nibbling on her house. Instead, they reply that it is only the wind, "and they did not bother to stop eating or let themselves be distracted" (Grimm and Grimm, p. 56). When the witch opens the door, the children are frightened until she assures them that they will be safe in her home, and they are easily tricked by the promise of food and security. In this scene, a distracted Claire loses track of Warren for a moment, and the camera pans her desperate attempt to find where he has gone. She always seems just a moment behind him, spotting his front screen door slam shut, seeing a rustle in the bushes, hearing her dog bark, and then noticing a line of wet footprints leading up to her front door. As she backs away from the window, believing that a possible killer has come to her house, she turns around only to face Norman who has just arrived home. She screams but is immediately relieved, unaware that she is, in fact, staring directly at the killer. Like the Grimm children, she allows the appearance of safety to allay and misdirect her fears.

NIBBLING AT THE HOUSE

In both "Hansel and Gretel" and *What Lies Beneath*, the illusion of security and idealized domesticity is symbolized by an extraordinary house with a supernatural resident and a haunted past. Bettelheim (1989) remarks, "The gingerbread house is an image nobody forgets: how incredibly appealing and tempting a picture this is, and how terrible the risk one runs if one gives in to the temptation" (p. 161). This same warning could easily be applied to Claire, who has allowed the image of security, symbolized by her own restored home, to block her knowledge of past events. In the DVD documentary *Constructing the Perfect Thriller*, Zemeckis notes that their house "had to work on two layers. It had to be what looks like a perfect dream house when you see it in the sunlight in the perfect angle. But then if you start to make the shadows long and turn the light a different way and drop the camera to a lower angle, it can look ominous and scary in a way." In a way, Claire is also a guest in this house in the same way that the children are visitors in the witch's home. We know that the house was Norman's childhood home, and they have returned to it for his professional advancement. He has his own professional study while the symbol of Claire's profession, her beloved cello, has been stored in the attic for years. Her daughter has left for college, replaced by the female ghost of Norman's student lover. The ghost even begins opening the front door for Claire, signaling her transition from homeowner to guest in the supernatural world. The two will be paired as closely as Hansel and Gretel for the remainder of their journey.

Just as nibbling on bread and sugar windows can momentarily sate the children's hunger without providing any true nourishment, dining on red herrings can only stave off Claire's—and the audience's—craving for the truth for so long. Following an unsuccessful attempt with Jody to contact the ghost through a Ouija board, the ghost reveals that she will only communicate with Claire. After Jody leaves, the bathroom steams up mysteriously and the tub fills with water. When Claire cries out, "What do you want?" the ghost replies with the words "You Know" written on the fogged mirror. Claire flees the bathroom only to see the initials MEF repeating across the computer screen in Norman's study. Claire is convinced that Mary Feur's ghost is in her house, especially when the words "You Know" appear on her steamy bathroom mirror. She confronts Warren publicly at the college and is humiliated when Mary appears happily next to him. The following day, Mary stops by to talk with Claire, and the two discuss why she seemed so terrified when they briefly met by the fence. Mary asks Claire if she understands how desperate emotions can completely devour a person: "Have you ever felt so consumed by a feeling for someone that you couldn't breathe? Thought your time together was so passionate and consuming that you felt physical pain when they would leave?" This conversation, which Claire could have had with Madison about her relationship with Norman, ends Claire's dependence on false clues and helps her begin the final stage of her journey into the supernatural world.

Jody sends Claire a book titled *Witchcraft, Ghosts, and Alchemy*[4] that details ways she might be able to contact her ghost; however, she still needs some concrete clues to lead her down the correct path. While fixing a framed news clipping about Norman that keeps falling in his study (with help from her house ghost), Claire discovers a story about a missing girl on the back. She conducts an online search and learns that a student at Norman's school with the initials MEF, Madison Elizabeth Frank, has been missing for about a year. When Claire contacts the police, she is told that they believe Madison was a wild party-girl who simply ran away, and they have ceased actively searching for her. Finally, Claire decides to visit Madison's home. The mother lets her into Madison's room where Claire finds and takes a small lock of the girl's blonde hair. She returns home and performs a ritual to conjure the dead from the book Jody gave her, allowing herself to become possessed by Madison's spirit just as Norman arrives home. As Claire looks into the bathroom mirror, her eyes have changed to a haunting green hue.

This story of hunger and sacrifice comes full circle in the DVD Chapter "Forbidden Fruit," as Claire and Madison join forces to confront Norman. As the unfaithful husband takes an apple from the refrigerator, he is surprised by the sudden appearance and frank sexuality of his wife. She prevents him from biting into the apple, taking it for herself and saying, "Forbidden fruit. You got a problem with that?" She has him follow her into his study where she pushes the apple into his mouth, bites his lip violently, and finally straddles him atop the desk. When he starts to question her, she commands, "Shut up, professor." She then looks backwards at the hallway mirror which reveals both the front door and the study, and the possessed Claire smiles knowingly. She then confronts a confused Norman, saying, "I think she's starting to suspect something—your wife." As Norman throws Claire to the floor in horror, she regains her own spirit and memory of his affair. Like Hansel and Gretel, she now sees that the protection offered by the enchanted house and its primary owner has been nothing more than a ruse to ensnare its victim.

As the story draws to its conclusion, Claire remains an enslaved

Gretel, aware of the danger around her but unsure exactly how to combat
it. Although she has regained her memory of the affair, Claire still has no
evidence that Norman has murdered Madison. He claims that Madison
killed herself, and Claire initially believes that her ghost must be seeking
revenge. He even feigns a possible attack by Madison, pretending to have
been nearly electrocuted in the bathtub while Claire stayed the night with
Jody. He begs her forgiveness, and the two seem ready to move on with
their lives. With Madison's ghostly guidance, however, Claire is able to
remain skeptical and open to following otherworldly clues. She is drawn
to the pier behind her house. Clinging to the lock of Madison's hair, she
dives into the water and reaches what appears to be a strange box when
Norman pulls her out and convinces her that they must burn the hair as a
kind of exorcism by fire. After learning that Norman and Madison met
secretly in a nearby town, Claire investigates more on her own and finds
the store that sells necklaces like the one worn by Madison in her missing-
persons photo. The store also sells hand-made boxes with little gold keys
like the one she found earlier in Norman's study. Claire returns home and
dives back into the water to retrieve the box. She opens it while kneeling
on her hallway floor, finding Madison's necklace and realizing that Norman did kill her.

        In "Hansel and Gretel," Hansel is able to keep the poor-sighted witch
from cooking him for quite some time by having her feel a bone instead
of his finger to test his plumpness. She will only wait so long, however,
and preparation for the meal is inevitable. Up until this point, Claire's
amnesia and gullibility (when she asks Norman, "Do you think I'm stupid?" the audience is likely to nod in agreement by this point) have served
as her own bony finger to keep the real Norman from attacking her all this
time. With nothing left to lose, the hungry witch-stepmother decides that
it is time to prepare a last supper. Norman drugs Claire and places her into
a tub of rapidly rising water. As she lies motionless, Norman plans out her
"suicide," while the audience awaits a final supernatural intervention.

BAKING THE WITCH IN HER OWN OVEN

        A number of the Grimm Brothers' best-known tales make certain that
the villain meets a justifiably ironic fate. According to Ellis (1983), the
Grimms even "increased the level of violence and brutality when, for exam-

ple, those in the tales who suffered it deserved it according to their moral outlook" (p. 79). The jealous stepsisters in "Cinderella" have their eyes plucked out at her wedding to the handsome prince, while Snow White's envious stepmother has red-hot iron boots strapped to her legs for the wedding ball. After she is rescued from the belly of the gluttonous wolf, little Red Cap sews heavy stones into his stomach, giving him a deadly last meal. It is not enough that our heroine be rescued and delivered to a happy ending; rather, her nemesis must be destroyed in a manner befitting her wickedness and cruelty. The brutal ending for Hansel and Gretel's captor is among the best-known of all the Grimm fairy tales, balanced perfectly with equal parts irony and simplicity.

As mentioned earlier, Hansel is able to buy some time due to the witch's poor eyesight. Whenever she asks him to stick his finger out of his cage to gauge how fat he has become, he instead puts out a bone. She is puzzled by this and after a month grows so impatient that she decides to cook him anyway. Likewise, Norman seems remarkably blind to the tricks also going on around him. He tells the drugged Claire, "I can't figure out how you put it all together. At first, I though you knew, that you created the whole ghost thing as some kind of elaborate trap. Then I realized you believed it. It's a passive-aggressive masterpiece." It is an elaborate trap, of course, but one set by forces outside of his control. A true passive-aggressive masterpiece is devised by Gretel when she realizes that the witch intends on cooking her and Hansel. Feigning stupidity at being able to get inside the oven to check its temperature, she is able to trick the witch into crawling inside instead. Gretel then pushes her in, bolts the door, and runs away with Hansel while the wicked witch broils in the same oven she has used to cook countless other children.

In *What Lies Beneath*, the bathtub and water serve as Norman's oven, his murderous means to rid himself of the women threatening his control. Zemeckis notes in his commentary that critics felt the kitchen would be a more dangerous room, but he defends his choice, asserting, "Bathrooms have the same hard surfaces as a morgue." The kitchen/oven and bathroom/tub serve each of these tales perfectly, highlighting rooms that symbolize each of their villains. The witch is as hot-tempered as Norman is hard, sterile, and cold. He admits to Claire, "You have no idea what it was like to hold her underwater, watch her life slip away. But she gave me no choice. And neither have you." The witch's undoing derives from her confidence and belief that she is in total control. Her plan has worked on other children in the past, and she has no reason to doubt that it will continue to work on these children as well. Her hubris leads to her final, foolish mistake. Similarly, Norman appears fully confident that he will get away with murdering Claire just as he murdered Madison. Despite all Claire has shared, this man of science still does not believe in her ghost story. As the bathwater continues to rise, Norman leans in for a final kiss. He notices that Claire is wearing Madison's necklace, and as he tries to remove this last bit of hard evidence, Claire's face suddenly takes on the visage of the drowned girl. As powerful as Gretel's pushing of the witch, this image so shocks Norman that he stumbles backward forcefully, breaking a mirror and knocking himself unconscious next to Claire.[5]

A lesser-known aspect of the conclusion to "Hansel and Gretel" is that the two do not simply return home following the witch's demise. As they leave the witch's forest, they come to a large river with no apparent means to cross. Gretel spies a little white duck and, showing the supernatural element still present in the forest, is able to communicate with it. She has it carry her and Hansel across the water separately, and the children are then able to find their way home. As Bettelheim (1989) points out, the children have remained together throughout the tale, and this separation marks the end of their dependence upon one another and the beginning of their period of self-reliance. Similarly, Claire's journey with Madison does not end with Norman's being knocked out. As the paralyzing drug begins to wear off, she is able to kick the stopper from the drain and crawl out of the tub. She finds a still-unconscious Norman who has managed to get to the downstairs hallway before passing out again, and she manages to grab the cellular phone and truck keys to make her escape. We know from an earlier scene that the phone only receives service from the center of the bridge, however. In an elaborately choreographed conclusion involving mirrors, shadows, and a shoe dropping from the back of a truck, Zemeckis reveals that nefarious Norman has made it onto the truck bed.

When Claire stops the truck to dial 911, Norman attacks from behind, and Claire stomps on the gas pedal, steering through Madison's ghost to land the truck directly above her watery grave. As the boat sinks, Norman holds tightly onto Claire, who is still wearing Madison's necklace, and begins to push her underwater. Madison's corpse floats up from her submerged car, however, startling Norman into releasing Claire and then gripping onto him with her skeletal hand. As Claire reaches the surface, a now lifeless Norman floats between his earlier and intended victims. A smile comes across Madison's face as she releases Norman's corpse and returns to the depths. Having vanquished their common foe, she and Claire no longer depend upon each other for salvation and protection. In the film's final shot, Claire is shown leaving a rose on Madison's grave. Having ensured Madison's return home, Claire leaves the cemetery alone to face her own life outside of the supernatural forest.[6]

CASTING A SPELL ON THE AUDIENCE

When *What Lies Beneath* premiered, the reviews varied greatly. However, even when the critics disagreed about the cinematic worth of the film, most of them took equal offence at the film's trailer. *Newsweek's* Jeff Giles (2000) points out that the film's marketing campaign "renders the first hour of the movie pointless," while *The Wall Street Journal's* Joe Morgenstern (2000) declares, "If I were to list plot points and supposed surprises given away in the publicity for this film, readers would rise up in justifiable wrath." The most vociferous attack comes from the *Chicago Sun-Times'* Roger Ebert, who angrily assails the trailer in the final paragraph of his review: "The trailer of this movie thoroughly demolishes the surprises; if you've seen the trailer, you know what the movie is about, and all of the suspense of the first hour is superfluous for you, including major character revelations. Don't directors get annoyed when they create suspense and the marketing sabotages their efforts?"

The trailer undeniably gives away a good deal of this film's plot, but it also sets up a story that leads its potential audience down a separate path. Like the witch-stepmother, it is not necessarily as it appears. Claire and Norman are established as a happy couple sending their daughter away to school. The major spoiler that Norman has had an affair does not reveal him to be a murderer, however. In fact, the primary lines used in the trailer lead us to believe that he could become the ghost's victim: Claire calmly announces, "You had an affair with a girl who killed herself, and now she's trying to hurt you," while the tag line appears, "He was the perfect husband until his one mistake followed them home." The trailer misdirects our focus to sympathize with Norman and to prepare ourselves for a vengeful ghost that could possess Claire and lead her to act on its behalf.[7] The trailer serves as our tasty little house in the woods, giving us a bit to snack on while we cautiously wonder about the nature of the grandmotherly figure inviting us inside.

In *Constructing the Perfect Thriller* (2000), Robert Zemeckis reveals, "I was fascinated by the illusion of movies before anything else," and it is really this illusion of films, accepted and expected by the audience, that ties them so closely to the fairy tale world in which we accept magic and the supernatural at face value. Zemeckis is known for his ability to incorporate special effects into his stories without disrupting their emotional flow. In *Who Framed Roger Rabbit?* (1988), for example, we are treated to a world in which "toons" and humans interact on a regular basis. Even his more serious, critically acclaimed films, like *Forrest Gump* (1994), winner of Best Picture, Actor, and Director, and *Cast Away* (2000), bridge reality and fantasy through special effects wizardry. Tom Hanks' Forrest is believably inserted into actual news footage with Presidents Kennedy and Johnson, while his Fed Ex worker endures a horrifying plane crash in this updating of the Robinson Crusoe legacy.

In *What Lies Beneath*, Zemeckis again illustrates his dexterity when dealing with special effects and camera angles, many of which are so subtle that the audience remains unaware of them. The bathroom in which so many of the film's crucial scenes are staged symbolizes a film that is literally and figuratively filled with smoke and mirrors. For example, Zemeckis describes the real-time scene in which Claire exits the bathroom into her bedroom, straightens a few items, and continues walking into the hallway outside of the bathroom. With no cut-away shots, she now sees steam coming from under the bathroom door and opens it to find fogged mirrors and a fully filled bathtub. Zemeckis asserts, "It might work on a subconscious level [for the audience], but I mean to put a cut in here would have definitely been a major cheat" that could have broken the tension of that moment. In another, much smaller scene, Norman and Claire are shown driving to dinner, and we see both sets of their eyes in the rear-view and passenger mirrors respectively. Zemeckis remarks, "This is one of those moments that I don't think the audience realizes that they're seeing something that physically is not possible.... It's so wonderful to see the eyes of both of your actors at the same time in a car shot. You would never see that." The magic of this shot draws in the audience and makes us privy to a world that is as make-believe as the one where witches lure children to their edible houses. In describing these kinds of scenes, Robert Legato, the visual-effects supervisor for *What Lies Beneath* explains, "Today, you can design any shot that tells your story best without fear that mechanically you won't be able to get it," even if it would otherwise be a physical impossibility (Wolff, 2000, p. 56).

In the closing moments of the film, Zemeckis acknowledges that the scenes become more contrived and the characters act in traditionally established rules of suspense and horror. He admits freely, "And this is where we use all the audience convention. The audience just, you know, they've seen this stuff a million times. They just know exactly what's being done to them, and it's all just part of the convention in a movie like this." Like a fairy tale read over and over, the characters act out patterns that serve their plots and reward their audience with an omniscient feeling of what is to come. Zemeckis realizes that it upsets and even angers the audience when the heroine walks backwards and barefoot down the flight of stairs even though her husband could be, and is, *right behind her*. He gleefully asserts, "This is really the ultimate torture test on the audience. They can't understand why she would stop" the truck on the bridge to make a call. When Claire then drops the phone, the audience is prepared for the final jolt of having Norman appear, again, right behind her. And yet, we still jump at the scene, hungrily devouring fallen bits of popcorn left by the director along the genre's path.

• CONCLUSION •

The Writing on the Wall

"Mother Holle" and *Misery*

A GRIMM VIEW OF THE FAIRY TALE READER AND WRITER

Throughout their fairy tale collection, the Grimm Brothers' heroes and heroines confront and overcome foes at once common (stepmothers and starvation, wolves and wilderness) and extraordinary (witches' spells and devils' curses). The tales can be interpreted from any number of psychological, historical, economic, sociological, and theological perspectives. In this chapter, I argue that a number of the tales—including, the iconic ones examined earlier in this text—should also be considered metaphorically as the Grimms faced their own greatest challenges: the tortuous processes of satisfying a paying public of readers. In the forward to their 1819 edition of the tales, the Grimms lament how easily creations of the past have vanished as they claim, "It was perhaps already time to hold fast to these fairy tales, as those [storytellers] who have been obliged to preserve them become increasingly scarce" (p. 9).[1] Yet the Grimms did far

168

more than simply collect tales. Zipes (2003) explains that their primary accomplishment "was to create an ideal type for the literary fairy tale, one that sought to be as close to the oral tradition as possible, while incorporating stylistic, formal, and substantial thematic changes to appeal to a growing middle-class audience" (p. xxx).

In "Rumpelstiltskin," the Grimms introduced us to a young woman with no discernible talents. She was pretty, as all fairy tale heroines must be, but lacked the specific skill promised the king by her father, spinning straw into gold. The real skill that kept her alive was that of spinning someone else's tales as her own, and she readily assumed credit for the strange little man's work. Personally, she produced nothing but the image desired by the greedy king, her number one fan. She was not even responsible for learning the little man's name, the loophole that let her keep her child, yet she was the one to confront him with it. Ultimately, she used the work of others for her own ends, and she did this quite successfully. The Grimms spent years recording tales spun to them by storytellers, notably Dorothea Viehmann, Dorothea Wild, and Marie Hassenpflug among others. Their initial goal was primarily patriotic, "an idealistic effort to capture German folk traditions in print before they died out and to make a modest contribution to the history of German poetry" (Tatar, 2003, p. 11). However, the Grimms also added their own golden sheen to the tales, editing and revising them through several editions.

According to Zipes (1997), "By the time the last edition of *Kinder- und Hausmärchen* was printed in 1857, Wilhelm had made so many changes in style and theme that the tale [of "Hansel and Gretel"] was twice as long as the original manuscript" (p. 44). After their parents first left them behind in the forest, Hansel and Gretel easily made their way back home by following a trail of shiny stones in the moonlight. On their next trip, however, their trail of bread crumbs was devoured by birds, forcing them deeper into the forest towards the witch's irresistible home. Intriguingly, after destroying the witch, they found their way back home without the aid of crumbs or stones to mark their trail. For the Grimms, the process of researching their tales must have often seemed like a treacherous trip down a dark forest path. Sometimes, they followed clues as surely marked as Hansel's stone path back to an original source, while much of time, their clues seemed as reliable as crumbs pecked up into a bird's gullet. They never seemed deterred from believing that their versions of the tales would always lead back to a uniquely German home, however, even if that journey demanded their own edits to the original texts, such as changing the birth mother in "Hansel and Gretel" to a stepmother to protect young minds.

The tales, of course, were not inherently or, at times, even primarily German in origin. In the case of tales told to them by French-speaking Marie Hassenpflug, for example, the Grimms recognized a strong French influence. The patriotic brothers had endured a French-occupied Germany, and the well-educated brothers were admittedly familiar with Perrault's popular collection of similar French tales published in the late seventeenth century. The Grimm tale of Cinderella addressed the tenuous relationship among disparate sources nicely, as the poor, hard-working girl found herself suddenly linked to beautiful but vicious stepsisters willing to mutilate themselves for the chance of marrying a prince. The Grimms blended sources when necessary, but polished the tales in a way to have them fit the archetypal golden shoe for their own audience. In some ways, they may have hoped to blind their audience to other non-German sources, much as Cinderella's doves blinded her stepsisters. In the preface to their 1815 edition of the tales, the Grimms "insisted still more strongly that the stories were native to the German-speaking lands" and were not borrowed from any other countries (McGlathery, 1993, p. 32). Yet, in their 1819 preface they acknowledged that they did remove tales which may have had foreign beginnings.

In "Snow White" we encountered the on-going process of editing and revising texts, as the beautiful, aging queen glanced in her mirror only to be told that her stepdaughter had assumed the title of fairest in the land. As the most recent edition, Snow White was the one with whom dwarfs and princes could immediately fall in love. At her wedding, she revealed that she was not too far removed from her stepmother's deadly teachings, however, as her rival was forced to dance to death in red-hot iron boots. Like a burned-up book, the old queen fell to the floor, a pile of ashes to be discarded in favor of the newest edition of the royal text. From 1812 and 1857, the Grimms published ten editions of the tales, refining them "to make the tales more proper and prudent for bourgeois audiences" (Zipes, 2003, p. xxxi). In some instances, the Grimms published abbreviated collections containing only those tales that they considered "appropriate for children" (McGlathery, 1993, p. 37).

The Grimms admitted in their 1819 preface to the collection that they reworked a number of the tales to make them simpler and purer ("einfacher und reiner") for their audience. The tale of long-haired "Rapunzel" showed us yet another symbolic aspect of editing and research, centering on the beautiful maiden locked away in a tower in a futile attempt to preserve her from the outside world. Her golden tresses grew wildly out of control, allowing not just Mother Gothel to climb up to her, but an enamored prince as well. Despite her apparent love for the girl, a betrayed Mother Gothel sheared her now-pregnant foster daughter and sent her into a desolate land where she and her children were united by chance with her prince. Throughout the various editions, the Grimms both added and deleted tales, and by the final version, they had omitted twenty-eight of the original tales. Like Mother Gothel, they also discovered that there was no sure way to keep a tale secure and unaffected by the influence of an enchanted outside world.

In their 1819 preface to the tales, the Grimm Brothers explained their goal to protect the bare essence ("bloßes Dasein") of the fairy tales, fearing that nothing would remain of these stories that "bloomed in an earlier time" (p. 9).[2] By writing the tales down, they hoped to keep them secure and unchanged, excepting their own editing, of course. Perhaps no tale symbolized this hope better than "Brier Rose." In this remarkable tale, the Grimms gave us a beautiful, caring, and gifted princess who was to be kept from all spinning wheels, the most basic symbol of telling—and subsequently transforming—a story. Once she reached maturity, she fulfilled her destiny by coming upon an old woman spinning. Sitting at the wheel herself, she pricked her finger, thus sending her and the entire kingdom into a hundred years of slumber. She remained undisturbed despite the efforts of numerous princes to reach her through a deadly brier, awakening only when the time was right. For the Grimms, Brier Rose could represent their ideal fairy tale, one that they protected from other storytellers when they sealed her in writing. Or perhaps they viewed themselves as the prince who finally arrived to save her at the right moment, beating out other authors and researchers hoping to find the original, unaltered source.

It is only fitting to work our way back to the tale that began this journey. "Little Red Cap" gave us a heroine who did not quite understand the complexity of her trip to grandmother's house at first. She naively engaged the wolf in conversation and let herself become distracted by his suggestion that she pick flowers. Arriving a bit late to her grandmother's home, she was soon gobbled up, joining her grandmother on a gastronomical journey and awaiting rescue by the woodsman. Once freed from the wolf, a vengeful Little Red Cap killed the predator by sewing stones into his stomach. More importantly, she learned a lesson and avoided being eaten by a second wolf during a return trip to her grandmother, staying steadfast on the path. The Grimms were prolific authors and researchers, having collected not just fairy tales, but German legends, a grammar book, and the beginnings of the first comprehensive German dictionary. The fairy tales remained their passion, however, an ongoing project to which they returned again and again. Like Little Red Cap, they took on the project somewhat naively themselves, not quite recognizing its scope at first, as they attempted to trace the tales to original sources (the tales' metaphorical grandmother). In an 1809 letter to Jacob, Wilhelm optimistically and naively explained that he had come to believe that "the circle [of tales] is not very large and that we know most of them, but these are universally wide-spread" (p. 141).[3] Their continued research would reveal the vast scope of the tales and sources, a hungry wolf devouring time under a grandmotherly storyteller's night cap.

With each revision and new edition, the real-life equivalent of returning to grandmother's house, the Grimms showed that they had learned a lesson, too, marketing a collection that would appeal to the widest readership possible. Prior to the publication of the second edition, Wilhelm wrote to their friend Rasmus Nyerup, a professor and librarian, that he would find this new edition much improved and completely reworked.[4] Commenting on changes made to the collection throughout the years, Tatar (2003) remarks that Wilhelm Grimm's "nervous sensitivity about moral objections to the tales in the collection reflects a growing desire to write for children rather than to collect for scholars" (p. 19). In an effort to transform the tales into a more popular "educational" book for children, Tatar also notes that the Grimms actually increased the violent episodes, doling out the severest of punishments to their villains, while toning down erotic elements.[5] What the Grimms could not have envisioned was the lasting influence the tales would have in all aspects of popular culture, including works by the master of horror himself, Stephen King.

AN AUTHOR'S VIEW OF FAIRY TALE HORROR

In *Danse Macabre* (1981), Stephen King examines the popularity and impact of horror films and horror fiction in our society. In the opening chapter, King determines that allegory is the defining element of horror which acts as "an invitation to indulge in deviant, antisocial behavior by proxy—to commit gratuitous acts of violence, indulge our puerile dreams of power, to give in to our most craven fears" (p. 42). Both fairy tales and horror films provide a safe environment for their audience to confront basic, primal fears of "us" versus "them." For King, "them" consists of those monsters that upset our societal definition of a natural order, typically seen in small-town America, towns that look "eerily as if a eugenics squad had gone by the day before production actually began, removing everyone with a lisp, birthmark, limp, or potbelly" (p. 52). With the exception of the very few "freakish" tales discussed in Chapter Three— such as "Thumbling"—most of the Grimm tales feature a similarly sanitized environment invaded by some metaphorical monster. The tales do not usually begin in a perfect world, far from it in fact, as the heroes and heroines face painful trials at the hands of wicked foes; however, their tales certainly conclude in a near-utopia, with the hero or heroine emerging triumphant to show children that they too can emerge safe and strong from their own trials.

In his chapter "The Modern American Horror Movie," King labels a series of films under the sub-genre of "fairy tale horror," including *Halloween*, *Psycho*, *Alien*, and *The Omen* among others. All of these films "demand a heavy dose of reality to get them rolling.... The audience is propelled into the movie by the feeling that, under the right set of circumstances, this could happen" (p. 179). In *Halloween*, for example, we are introduced to a group of high school students looking to celebrate an annual event before the masked killer returns home, while *Psycho* focuses on the hidden dangers of stopping at a secluded little motel. *Alien* and *The Omen* focus on decidedly less human attackers, but they are still grounded in believable characters and very real fears that we have about diseases/infection and child-rearing. King goes on to claim that only these kinds of fairy tale films effectively combine what he terms "the gross-out" factor (creatively staged kills and splattering blood like the alien bursting from the victim's chest cavity) with emotional resonance: "Blood can fly everywhere and the audience will remain largely unimpressed. If, on the other hand, the audience has come to like and understand—or even just to appreciate—the characters they are watching as real people, if some artistic link has been formed there, blood can fly everywhere and the audience *cannot* remain unimpressed" (p. 186). Tatar (2003) describes the impact of fairy tale violence on its audience similarly, arguing, "The more Hansel, Gretel, Cinderella, and Snow White are victimized by the powers of evil, the more sympathy they elicit and the more captivating they are for children" (p. 21). In both cases, we root for the hero/ine not merely to defeat the villain, but for the villain to be dispatched in a truly horrific fashion. Imprisonment is simply not as satisfying as impalement in the horror and fairy tale worlds.

Although King does not mention the Grimm tales specifically (nor the names of any actual fairy tales, for that matter) in *Danse Macabre*, his criteria for fairy tale horror films can readily be applied to the canon of Grimm fairy tales. Most of the tales discussed in this text begin very much in the real world: Little Red Cap has an ailing grandmother; Rapunzel's parents worry about infertility; Snow White and Cinderella lose their mothers and must compete with jealous stepfamilies; Hansel and Gretel could starve to death at home or left in the woods; and the miller's daughter is a poor lass whose father makes promises he cannot keep. Even "Brier Rose," which introduces a cursed princess and hundred-year sleep from the outset, grounds the tale in the reality that parents, no matter how powerful, cannot protect their children from harm at all times. These tales also include their own unique "gross-out" factors, enhanced by the Grimms themselves to enforce the stronger moral component. In the first, more academic edition of the tales, Little Red Cap does not make that second trip to grandmother's house where they drown another hungry wolf (after having disemboweled the first one). Similarly, in their first version of "Cinderella," the Grimms allowed the stepsisters to escape with their vision in tact; however, their subsequent "child-friendly" versions have Cinderella's doves poke their eyes out one socket at a time. The other tales have their own well-known "gross-out" moments, that involve agonizing torture ("Rapunzel" and "Snow White"), vengeful murder ("Hansel and Gretel"), and otherwise gruesome, horrifying deaths and mutilation ("Brier Rose" and "Rumpelstiltskin").

In describing his list of twenty fairy tale horror films, King cuts their plots down to their most basic elements, beginning each description with the classic "Once upon a time...." In his own writings, King has tackled most of the chilling themes covered in this text, from cannibals and vampires to aliens and devils. However, we can also categorize a number of his works as fairy tale horror, using our own "one upon a time" summaries to link them to all of the canonical tales discussed in this volume:

(1) Once upon a time, a little girl who was closely linked to the color red became lost in the woods where she had to fend off a most deadly predator. Is this "Little Red Cap" or *The Girl Who Loved Tom Gordon*, in which the lost girl loves the Red Sox player?

(2) Once upon a time, a female figure went into a deep sleep, secluded from the world and men. She eventually awoke for the right man who fell in love with her from the first moment he saw her; however, many young men died on her account. This description could relate to "Brier Rose" or *Christine*, in which the dilapidated 1958 Plymouth Fury is discovered and refurbished by a young man for whom she instantly starts.

(3) Once upon a time, a young girl was locked away in a high room by a woman fearing her maturity and interest in men. Her maturity was symbolized by remarkable changes that she could not control. Are we discussing "Rapunzel" and her abundant hair or *Carrie*, the teenage girl whose mental powers spin wildly out of control?

(4) Once upon a time, an older person who appeared completely normal to others was revealed as an evil, deadly foe by a younger person with remarkably similar qualities. Their relationship was a tense, quasi-familial one and brought out the older person's innate rage and violence. In the end, however, the older villain died while the younger version lived and learned. This relationship could be the queen and her stepdaughter in "Snow White" or the disguised Nazi and youth—who pretend to be related at one point—in *Apt Pupil*.

(5) Once upon a time, a young girl's mother died, leaving her alone with her father. They joined a surrogate family only to learn that the new family intended on using her for their own selfish purposes. With some supernatural help, the girl vanquished her foes. Is this a synopsis of the Grimms' "Cinderella" or King's *Firestarter*?

(6) Once upon a time, a brother and sister found themselves alone in a magical realm fending off a carnivorous villain who appeared in two forms, one normal and one otherworldly and powerful. This basic plot is followed by Hansel and Gretel when confronting their stepmother/witch and the siblings of *Silver Bullet* fighting the town's priest/werewolf.

(7) Once upon a time, a strange, devilish figure appeared, demanding that he be given children to go away. His name and background were a

mystery at first, and those involved tried to discover his agenda and prevent his plans. He knew their secrets, but they knew almost nothing about him. We could be describing Rumpelstiltskin's demands for the queen's child or the similar demand made by Andre Linoge, the stranger of *Storm of the Century*.

King and the Grimm Brothers share another commonality with regard to the reception of their work in literary and popular cultures. In *Hollywood's Stephen King*, Magistrale (2003) points out that King's commercial success seems almost to exist in inverse proportion to his critical acclaim: "[T]he academic world has tended to view cinematic versions of Stephen King with the same level of dubious disaffection with which it treats his published prose" (p. xii). More than any other living writer, Stephen King has seen an astonishing number of his works make the transition from text to screen. His professional website (http://stephenking.com) lists over fifty films and television movies based upon his works that have already been filmed or are in development. While a number of these have been well-received over several decades, notably *Carrie* (1976), *Stand By Me* (1986), *The Shawshank Redemption* (1994), and *The Green Mile* (1999)[6], critics have not universally embraced films based upon King's works. Magistrale acknowledges that the lack of critical success is tied in part to some truly poor adaptations and screenplays, such as *Children of the Corn* (1984) and *Maximum Overdrive* (1986), a film that Stephen King adapted himself and has called one of the worst ever made. Magistrale compellingly argues that King also exists as a brand-name broadly used to market films and miniseries that have not been authorized or written by him, such as 1992's *The Lawnmower Man* (pp. xi, xv).

In her detailed analysis of the collection's early sales, Bottigheimer (1993) notes that the first volume of the Grimm tales sold well—roughly 300 copies per year—while the second volume was unsuccessful. This led the Grimms to edit the volumes into a more child-friendly single edition with fewer tales. Intriguingly, a translated version of the tales in England was a great commercial success, but the Grimms received no royalties from those sales (p. 86). The outspoken Grimm Brothers' professional and political rivalries did not help the critical reception of their tales, as Bottigheimer reveals, "In the early years of the tales' published life, reactions to them were mixed at best and heartlessly critical at worst" (p. 79). Tatar (2003) goes on to explain that, for the Grimms, "What really mattered, particularly in the years immediately following publication of the first edition, were the views of the larger literary world.... But none of the people who counted seemed to take much interest in reviewing the book, and those who actually did review it rarely had anything good to say" (pp. 14–15). Among their harshest critics were Friedrich Rühs, a professor of History at the University of Berlin; Heinrich Voß, best known as a translator; Johann Gustav Büsching, who had already come out with his own edition of fairy tales and legends in 1812 (*Volks-Sagen, Märchen und Legenden*); and Albert Ludwig Grimm (no relation to the brothers), whose book of children's fairy tales was published in 1809. Albert Grimm also reworked a number of international tales, including stories of Sinbad the Sailor and *1001 Arabian Nights*, as abbreviated stories for schoolchildren, and his rivalry with the Grimm Brothers was vitriolic and enduring.

RECUPERATING IN THE SMALL COTTAGE

The story of "Mother Holle," like the best horror tales described by Stephen King, begins in the real world. A widow with an ugly, lazy biological daughter and a beautiful, hardworking stepdaughter favors the former while having the latter do the housework and spinning. The poor girl has to spin so much, in fact, that her fingers bleed from the task. One day, she accidentally knocks the spinning reel into a nearby well. When she dives into the well to retrieve it, she loses consciousness and awakens in a supernatural world where trees ask to have their ripened apples shaken free. She comes across the small cottage of Mother Holle, who tells her that she can stay with her, and that she will be rewarded if she does all of the housework properly. The girl does exactly as she is told, and eventually asks to return home to her own people. Mother Holle agrees and rewards her by covering her in gold.

When the stepdaughter returns home, her greedy stepmother decides to send her own daughter to Mother Holle in the hope of being equally rewarded. However, when she arrives in the magical realm, the lazy girl makes little effort to be as industrious as her sister. After one day of labor, she grows tired of work and reveals her true nature, leaving chores undone and the bed unmade. Mother Holle soon becomes so disenchanted with the girl that she sends her back home. Instead of covering her in gold, however, she covers her in a tar that sticks to her for the rest of her life.[7]

The hard-working daughter falls down a well into the secret world of Mother Holle, a demanding, lonely woman who rewards the good and punishes the bad. (Illustration by E. H. Wehnert from *Household Stories Collected by the Brothers Grimm*. London: Routledge and Sons, 1880.)

The tale ends abruptly, and we never learn what becomes of the good stepdaughter or her greedy stepfamily.

In this section, we interpret this tale as one that depicts the sometimes tenuous relationship between authorial control and reader acceptance. Without the reader, the writer's work remains as useless as it is lifeless, mere words on a page serving as its obituary. Thus, the reader wields an incredible amount of authority in determining just how much power to grant the author. The author is far from powerless, however, as the ultimate creator of that which is read. Symbolically, we can think of the stepmother in "Mother Holle" as the author looking for critical and commercial success. On the one hand, she creates the situation that compels the reader, represented by Mother Holle herself, to empathize with the beautiful, industrious daughter. On the other, she has also created a biological daughter whom she loves more. This daughter lacks the popular beauty of her stepdaughter, but the mother's connection to her is stronger and more powerful. This is the real daughter, the artistic creation that does not appeal to the powerful reader, but just might appeal to the critics.

Structurally, Rob Reiner's version of *Misery* (1990) allows for a similar character reading. Paul Sheldon (James Caan) parallels the step-mother/writer who simply cannot love the pretty, popular daughter. He tells his editor (Lauren Bacall) that he is tired of his "bloody spinning" of the Misery Chastain tales, an apparent series of bodice-ripping, romance novels that he believes have kept him from reaching his potential as a real writer. His editor reminds him that the so-called "Misery business" has been good to him, putting braces on his daughter's teeth, paying for her college, and securing him two houses and floor seats to the Knicks games. The character of Misery has worked as hard for him as the stepdaughter who sits at the spinning wheel until her fingers bleed; nonetheless, he is overjoyed to have written her final novel. His true love is reserved for his ugly daughter, an untitled (in the film) manuscript about tough-talking street kids. When Paul is rescued by Annie Wilkes (Kathy Bates), his— and, really, Misery's—number one fan, he finds himself being cared for by a strict Mother Holle figure who bestows praise on the lovely Misery and punishment on his ugly daughter. At heart, this is the story of two mothers looking to protect their favorite child.

After he completes his most recent novel, Paul drives down a snow-covered road into a blinding snowstorm. He loses control of his car and veers off the road. He passes out as a mysterious, hulking figure arrives, pulling him and his manuscript from the wreckage. As he resumes consciousness, he hears nurse Annie Wilkes reassuring him, "I'm your number one fan. There's nothing to worry about. You're going to be just fine. I'll take good care of you. I'm your number one fan." She is wearing a simple frock buttoned all the way up to the collar, a grey cardigan sweater, and a simple gold cross as her only jewelry. For the first part of the film, she acts as a kindly Mother Holle figure honored to take care of the man who has brought her the golden girl, Misery Chastain. In her mind, the two must be related, as she tells him, "I love you, Paul. Your mind, your creativity, that's all I meant." For Annie, who is unaware that her patient has written Misery into a grave, Paul is as pure and good as the character she adores.

The intimacy of reading, of the connections between the author, characters, and reader, is expressed in both "Mother Holle" and *Misery* through similarly isolated settings. In the Grimm tale, the girls both come upon the title character's lone small cottage in the middle of "an eternally vernal world by falling into a well" (Bottigheimer, 1987, p. 32). Other than magical speaking trees and loaves of bread, Mother Holle is their only

After wrecking his car in a blinding snowstorm, prolific author Paul Sheldon finds himself in *Misery* (Castle Rock, 1990)—that is, in the isolated world of Annie Wilkes (Kathy Bates), his number one fan until she learns that he has killed off her favorite character. *The Kobal Collection*

companion, and they are dependent upon her in this realm. Mother Holle tells them both that she will take care of them as long as they do as they are told. According to Roberts (1958), the house, household chores, and reward are all required elements of this archetypal tale. In addition to other housework, she instructs them to shake her featherbed strongly enough for feathers to fly, as that will also make it snow on earth. Thus, we see that she can exert her own limited editorial influence over the outer world, blanketing it in a pristine white cover that will eventually melt away.

Director Rob Reiner and screenwriter William Goldman cleverly use Annie's little house and surroundings to reveal her inner moods, staging the interior and exterior shots in such a way that the outer world seems to change based upon her emotional states. When Paul awakens to find himself in her home, Goldman (1997) writes, "Dissolve to the white of what seems like a hospital. Everything is bled of color. It's all vague" (p. 401). Annie is beaming with pride and anticipation while standing over him. Reiner's cutaway shot shows a bright, sunny day following the snowstorm. The snow is untouched as is her opinion of the world's greatest author. In the establishing shot immediately before Annie discovers that Misery is dead, Reiner shows us a full moon on a clear night, dark and foreboding. The snow has begun to melt, revealing a muddy earth. Annie suddenly enters Paul's room, a woman who has seen the purity of her beloved author completely dissolve into muddy filth as well.

Once Annie has coerced Paul into reviving Misery, he asks her to join him for dinner to celebrate. The outer shot is clear and at night, and we hear Bing Crosby singing "I'll Be Seeing You." As we enter Annie's parlor, we see Paul at a table in front of a shrine to Misery. She has all of the books in hardback and soft-cover, and his autographed picture is framed in the middle, a large headshot that overshadows any of her family pictures. As Paul's writing progresses, a montage of light, day, and the seasons pass around him until a thunderstorm arrives. Lightning flashes and the exterior view of the house is shot at an awkward angle and at night. Rain pours down on the house. Annie enters Paul's room, for the first time looking depressed. Even Paul appears concerned, asking his captor what has happened. She tells Paul, "The rain, sometimes it gives me the blues. When you first came here, I only loved the writer part of Paul Sheldon, but now I know I love the rest of him, too." She then shows him a gun and tells him that she often thinks of using it. She then drives off, leaving him to think that she might soon kill them both.

Paul has managed to get a knife, and he prepares to defend himself upon Annie's return. He falls asleep however, as the rain continues to fall. Suddenly, there is a clap of thunder and lightning flashes over Annie's face as she drugs him. The next shot is, ironically, of sunshine emerging from behind dark clouds. Rather than show us Annie's house, Reiner pans out over the mountains and trees, revealing no other signs of life or community. There is quiet and calm in Annie as well. She tells Paul, "Last night it came so clear. I realized you just need more time. Eventually, you'll come to accept the idea of being here." She then "hobbles" him, breaking both of his ankles with a block of wood and a sledgehammer in the film's most memorable and squirm-inducing sequence. Immediately after delivering this punishment, Annie looks down upon Paul and sighs, "God I love you."[8]

The cover art for the *Misery* film poster shows a tiny, completely isolated cottage covered in snow. Snowflakes continue to fall from above, and it appears to be the only home for miles. Inside, we see a warm glow emanating from a downstairs room. The tagline reads, "Paul Sheldon used to write for a living. Now he's writing to stay alive." Both Paul Sheldon and the daughters end up in worlds that are far removed from their everyday realms, but ones in which their hosts still require them to fulfill their professional responsibilities. Mendelson (1997) notes that Mother Holle never collaborates with either girl; rather she "simply commands and rewards her charges" (p. 123). Similarly, Annie expects very specific work from Paul, and, as the woman in power, she embodies "the reader-response critic pushed to its ultimate extreme" (Magistrale, 2003, p. 65). She also exerts her own kind of authorial control over the bed-ridden Paul, telling him how proud she is of the reconstruction she has managed on his broken legs. Yet, when she discovers that he has left his room, she readily destroys her work and his progress, brutally breaking both of his ankles to keep him confined and under her control.

During the latter part of the film, Paul becomes a reader as well when he finds Annie's memory book filled with newspaper clippings. Her scrapbook reads like a collection of morbid tales with her at the center, particularly when she becomes the head of a pediatric unit. Following the mysterious deaths of several infants, Annie is featured in a series of news articles that follow her being questioned in their deaths to a trial to her eventual release. The scrapbook also includes recent stories about Paul's disappearance, making him a character in her life book. These articles reveal her editorial control in the outer world: Paul learns that he is presumed dead, as she has managed her own media blackout following the car crash. He has vanished from his own world as completely as the girls who journey down the dark well to Mother Holle's realm.

PUNISHING THE BAD DAUGHTER AND REWARDING THE GOOD

The bad daughter/good daughter dichotomy is established at the start of the second DVD Chapter, aptly named "The Misery Business." The picture paired with this chapter on the DVD menu focuses on the book jacket for *Misery's Child*. It is unfolded so that we see Paul Sheldon's serious author photo on the left and the cover art of Misery on the right. He appears pained and miserable. She is sitting blandly and blank-faced under a garden trellis, staring off-center with her hands folded in her lap. A pair of ducks swims in a pond behind her. The chapter does not begin with this picture, however. Rather, the camera begins with an unusual close-up of Paul's old, worn leather briefcase. He tells his editor that it's an old friend he found while rummaging through a closet. She replies, unconvincingly, "It's... nice, Paul, it's got character." Behind her we see a large framed picture of another Misery cover with the heroine tilting her head back in ecstasy as a lover kisses her on the neck. The title is written in French, *L'Amour de Misery*, indicating the world-wide success of the series. The editor realizes that Misery has helped her and Paul financially, and she is not ashamed of the success brought to them by the superficial romance novels. In contrast, Paul clings to the briefcase that will serve as the womb for his new novel now that Misery is dead. This case, he remembers, is the one in which he carried his first book in search of a publisher. He sighs, "I was a writer then." He then tells his editor that the new book could make him proud, declaring, "If I can make this work, I might just have something I want on my tombstone."

When the good daughter returns home covered in gold, her stepmother and stepsister greet her warmly. The stepmother then decides that she would like to see her own daughter equally rewarded. Mother Holle is willing to provide the girl with the same opportunities, but she gives her little guidance and quickly dismisses her for being so lazy. The unsuspecting girl is then covered in tar and sent home, forever damaged. When

Annie notices Paul's briefcase, she also appears prepared to give the new manuscript a chance to please her, assuming that it will be as beautiful and fulfilling as the pure Misery. After reading just 40 pages, however, she informs Paul that the profanity in the work has "no nobility." He responds, "These are slum kids; I was a slum kid. Everyone talks like that," revealing his primal connection to this work, his natural daughter, in contrast to the stilted, refined speech of Misery. Paul's defense of the work and its verisimilitude brings out Annie's wrath for the first time. Neither she nor Mother Holle is open to what they consider the ugly aspects of life, and they both make every effort to expel any such ugliness from their worlds. As Canby (1990) explains in his review of *Misery*, "Annie will forgive Paul everything except his aspirations toward Art" (p. C1).

    While Paul continues to recuperate, Annie returns from town, elated to have found a copy of *Misery's Child*. As she lovingly reads each chapter, she tells Paul that the work is "a perfect, perfect thing" and "divine" like the Sistine Chapel. She explains briefly how she came to love Misery, diving into work after her husband left and reading books to help salve her loneliness: "That was when I first discovered Misery. She made me so happy. She made me forget all my problems. Course, I suppose you had a little something to do with that, too." Magistrale (2003) argues that the film's plot "reflects the spirit of its historical time by inverting the gothic male villain/besieged maiden prototype: The story's female character is no longer a passive victim but rather the agenda-setter" (p. 65). Annie is in control of the author, feeding and cleaning him and giving him pain pills, but she cannot control the characters that emanate from his creative world. His characters enter her world freely, but she, like Mother Holle who always remains in her own realm, does not enter theirs.

    When she finishes Paul's last book in the Misery series, Annie is enraged to learn that the character has been killed. In this instant, Paul becomes the ugly daughter covered in tar, as she exclaims, "You dirty bird. How could you? She can't be dead. Misery Chastain cannot be dead.... You did it! You murdered my Misery! I thought you were good, Paul, but you're not good. You're just another lying old dirty birdy, and I don't think I'd better be around you for awhile." When the tar-covered daughter returns home, she is greeted by a rooster who calls her "dirty" as well, and the meaning of this insult for both Annie and the rooster is the same: Such dirt cannot simply and quickly be washed off; rather, it is a filth that sticks to their very souls. After Annie calms down, she returns and tells Paul,

"I'll get you everything you want, but you must listen first.... I asked God about you, and God said, 'I delivered him unto you so that you may show him the way.'" She then has him burn the unpublished manuscript of his non-Misery book, telling him bluntly, "You must rid the world of this filth."

For Mother Holle, lavishly rewarding the good daughter with gold and praise will not suffice. When presented with the bad daughter, she realizes that she must be punished in a way that removes her entirely as a threat to the good daughter. Thus she is coated in a tar that can never be removed. As the metaphorical author, the mother happily sent her unloved step-daughter away from home, unaware that she would be richly rewarded by the outside reader, Mother Holle. Thereafter, the mother assumed that her most beloved work would be equally praised, even though her audience had already shown preference for an entirely different genre and style. Paul has made the same fundamental error as the mother regarding his own work and is stunned to find that Annie essentially views it as competition for Misery. As long as he believes in the future of his ugly daughter, he cannot bring Misery back to life. When he tells her that he will just keep the book for himself, unpublished, she explains, "As long as it does exist, your mind will never be free." For the Grimms, the lesson for parents is that they must take responsibility for instilling the appropriate work-ethic and values in their children. If they do not, then their children will not be of use in the world. Similarly, Annie feels that Paul must somehow learn this lesson on his own: She can set-up the situation and require the punishment, but he must be the one to light the match.

PROVIDING THE HAPPILY EVER AFTER

Creating the ending to a story must surely be one of the most challenging tasks for a writer, especially in those cases when the relationship between the hero and the villain has become the driving force of the story, and the villain has taken on a remarkable life of his or her own. An appropriate resolution would seem to require that one of them die, typically the villain, and memorably so in order to do justice to the character and to satisfy the audience. For the most part, the Grimms reliably followed this pattern, torturing and killing their villains in ways that let us know that their actions were deserving of the harshest punishments while rewarding their heroes and heroines with everlasting love and happiness. "Mother Holle" is rather unique in this regard, as we never learn what becomes of the good stepdaughter upon her return home. Does she remain in the house with her stepmother and tar-covered stepsister? Does she go into the world and find her very own prince? Or does she wander off a forest path only to encounter a waiting wolf or witch? Likewise, the stepmother is not punished for her actions, while the stepsister's punishment lacks the intensity of that applied to Cinderella's stepsisters. In this particular tale, the Grimms give us an open-ended story with its own kind of cliffhanger.

In contrast to the standard Grimm tales, most of the films analyzed in this text, including *The Silence of the Lambs*, *The Talented Mr. Ripley*, *The Ring*, and *Rosemary's Baby*, provide ambiguous endings in which stunningly amoral villains do not die. Evil seems destined to live on as Hannibal Lecter leaves Clarice Starling hanging on the phone and as Tom Ripley bids Marge farewell to spend her fiancé's money. Samara's videotape appears ready for mass-marketing around the world, while Satan's son, Adrian, gets rocked to sleep by Rosemary. The endings resonate with the audience, because they are believable and terrifying, and because we feel some type of strange connection to these characters. Both Hannibal and Tom are charming, in their own ways, while Samara and Adrian are isolated children with little control over their evil origins and legacies. Importantly, none of these films shows the absolute triumph of their villains over their heroes, however. Clarice has graduated and is now an agent for the FBI, while any happiness Tom hoped to create for himself with Peter is shown to be impossible. Rachel and her son have figured out the bizarre key to their own survival, and Rosemary, the lone innocent surrounded by witches, will no doubt have some influence over her son. In the end (and excluding sequels that might answer such questions), however, we ultimately do not know what happens to them.

In both the novel and film, *Misery* masterfully plays with the idea of cliffhangers and endings. Two stories are featured, the primary tale of Paul trying to survive Annie's growing psychosis and the secondary tale demanded by Annie, *Misery Returns*. Both of these tales also embody, figuratively and, quite literally, ideas expressed in Roland Barthe's 1986 essay "The Death of the Author," in which he asserts, "To assign an Author to a text is to impose a brake on it, to furnish it with a final signified, to close writing. This conception is quite suited to criticism, which then undertakes the important task of discovering the Author (or his hypothesis: society, history, the psyche, freedom) beneath the work: once the Author is found, the text is 'explained,' the critic has won (p. 53). Annie is determined that her favorite author—whom she believes to know through his magazine and television interviews, all of which she remembers by heart—remain assigned to one text alone, and she is an all-powerful literary critic who will not relinquish editorial control now that she has it.

Annie sets up a make-shift studio for Paul with a card table and old typewriter missing the letter "n," telling him that he will bring Misery back to life. He expects her to love his first draft and is surprised when she returns it to him, explaining, "I'm sorry, Paul, this is all wrong. You'll have to do it all over again. It's not worthy of you. Throw it all out, except for that part of naming the gravedigger after me, you can leave that in." Her frustration is rooted in her desire for internal logic to the continuing storyline, and she relates his first draft to the disappointment she felt when she was a child watching "chapter plays" with cliffhanger endings. At the end of one episode of *Rocket Man*, she complains that the hero was shown getting welded into a car with no brakes. The car flew off a cliff and exploded, leaving her excited for the following week. At the start of the next week's episode, Rocket Man was shown jumping from the car before it flew off the cliff, however. As the other children cheered and applauded, Annie says that she stood up, shouting, "This isn't what happened last week! Have you all got amnesia? They just cheated us! This isn't fair! He didn't get out of the cock-a-doody car!" She explains that Paul has begun the new novel with a similar kind of cheat, saving Misery through a blood transfusion even though she was already dead and buried at the end of the last novel. She demands that he begin where the last work concluded and that he follow through fairly. King's Paul Sheldon carefully considers her criticism: "He thought about this, startled—her occasional sharp insights never failed to startle him—and decided it was true. *Fair* and *realistic* might be synonyms in the best of all possible worlds, but if so, this was not that world" (p. 109).

Once Paul creates a storyline that fairly brings Misery back to life, Annie is hooked, and he realizes that the only way that he can remain alive is by creating and resolving mysteries about Misery's life.[9] Each chapter is a cliffhanger for him as well, keeping the killer at bay, and he is like Rocket Man, sealed up in that car, speeding towards the edge and hoping for his own *deus ex machina*. As a writer, he can control Misery's world; as a human victim, however, he encounters great difficulty in determining his own plotline. On two occasions, escape and rescue seem possible but are thwarted by Annie's intrusion into the story. Paul saves up his pain capsules and plans on drugging his captor over a dinner to celebrate Misery's resurrection. Annie knocks over the wine, however, spoiling that plan and forcing Paul to wait for outside rescue. When the town sheriff, Buster (Richard Farnsworth), realizes Annie has been keeping Paul hostage, she shoots him in the back. She sees herself as the writer now, creating her own melodramatic scenario, and speaking in the stilted dialogue of a typical romantic heroine: "You see, I've known for some time why I was chosen to save you. You and I were meant to be together forever, but now our time in this world must end. But don't worry, Paul, I've prepared for what must be done. I put two bullets in my gun, one for you and one for me. Oh, darling, it'll be so beautiful." As she approaches him with the gun, Paul stalls his ending by clinging to Misery's story, the plot that he can control. Mimicking her own halting dialogue, he explains, "And you're right, we are meant to be together. And I know we must die, but it must be so that Misery can live. We have the power to give Misery eternal life. We must finish the book."

The most intriguing difference between the film and King's novel lies in the ending for *Misery's Return*. In the film, Paul views the novel as nothing more than a means for him to remain alive. He despises the character and all that she represents from the beginning of the film through its climax. As he completes the final chapters, Annie exclaims, "Oh, Paul, I'm dying! Does she wind up with Ian or Winthorne?" Sending her from the room to get two glasses for champagne, Paul throws the manuscript to the floor and douses it with lighter fluid that he managed to sneak into the room after she locked him briefly in the basement. She has brought him the cigarette and match that complete his writing ritual. He rips the final page from the typewriter and holds the match to it as she returns. He confronts her, declaring, "Remember how for all those years nobody knew who Misery's real father was? Or if they'd ever be reunited? It's all right here. Does she finally marry Ian or will it be Winthorne? It's all right here." He then lights the last page on fire and tosses it onto the manuscript. As Annie throws herself onto the fire, desperately trying to save the answers to these questions, he bashes her skull with the typewriter. The two wrestle on the floor, and he stuffs the ashes of *Misery's Return* down her throat, screaming, "Here! You want it? You want it? Eat it! Eat it till you choke, you sick, twisted fuck!" He finally kills her by hitting her in the face with an iron doorstop shaped like her pet pig, named after Misery. Thus, she is killed by her own symbolic rendition of her favorite works.

We flash ahead eighteen months later to Paul's meeting with his editor. His new book, *The Higher Education of J. Philip Stone*, has just been published and the early reviews are, as his editor says, raves "with a shot at some prizes." Paul responds stoically, revealing the ever-present difficulty faced by authors, "I'm delighted the critics are liking it, and I hope the people like it, too, but I wrote it for me." The film's ending aligns Paul more closely with the mother who cannot bring herself to love the beautiful stepdaughter in "Mother Holle." In spite of her own daughter's obvious flaws, she loves the ugly, lazy girl and wants her to be rewarded with gold, the equivalent of critical acclaim and commercial success for the writer; however, even when this does not occur, she welcomes the tar-covered daughter back into her home. As the Mother Holle figure and representative reader, Annie could only love the beautiful girl. In describing how Annie responds to the first fair pages bringing Misery back to life, screenwriter William Goldman states, "She touches the pages as if they were *gold*, rubbing gently with the tips of her fingers [emphasis added]" (p. 451).

In the King novel, Paul Sheldon has a change of heart as he constructs the new Misery story. He is surprised to discover himself actually liking her tale and his evolving writing style: "This book, he began to understand, was a gothic novel, and thus was more dependent on plot than on situation. The challenges were constant" (p. 166). On some level, he also comes to respect Annie as a reader, realizing that she represents a wide-reaching group with their own valid criticisms. As he sets the manuscript on fire in the novel, he tells Annie, "Too bad you'll never read it. False modesty aside, I've got to say it was better than good. It was *great*, Annie" (p. 315). By the conclusion of the novel, Paul simply cannot bring himself to kill Misery again, and he has instead set fire to "an illusion with the title page on top—blank pages interspersed with written rejects and culls" (p. 323). While Annie will never get to know what happens to her dear characters, Paul's audience will get to enjoy the ending, or new beginning as it were. The novel's ending suits the ending of most fairy tales and parallels the treatment shown by Mother Holle to the beautiful, hard-working girl. As powerful and precise as Annie the reader and editor, Mother Holle demands that her rules be followed for the reward to be earned. The conclusion for the lazy girl is as final and lasting as Annie's conclusion for Paul's beloved, burned, and—in King's novel—never-published manuscript about street kids.

In *On Writing*, King (2000) reveals that he had yet another ending planned as he constructed this story. His Annie Wilkes was originally set to join the Lecters, Ripleys, Samaras, and Adrians, villains left free to wander the earth. In that never-published version of the tale, Annie was to get her one and only copy of *Misery's Return*, bound in the very skin of its author. King decided to go in a more positive direction, however, when he thought of his audience: "[N]o one likes to root for a guy over the course of three hundred pages only to discover that between chapters sixteen and seventeen the pig ate him" (p. 165). In the final version of the novel, he allows Paul to return to this image, of his essentially being consumed by his work and gruesomely serving as its cover. His publisher urges him to write an autobiography based upon his time with Annie, yet Paul realizes, "It would start out as fact, and then I'd begin to tart it up.... I don't want to fictionalize myself. Writing may be masturbatory, but God forbid it should be an act of autocannibalism" (p. 332). As King wrote Paul's story, he states that he also realized that "[Paul's] efforts to play Scheherazade and save his life gave me a chance to say some things about the redemptive power of writing that I had long felt but never articulated" (p. 165). Thus, his novel gives us the death of Annie Wilkes, ironically caused when she fractures her skull by tripping over the typewriter forced upon her captive author.

Even after he decides to kill Annie officially through the written word, King shows the difficulty he has committing to her death, however. The final section of the novel is called "Goddess," revealing her continued power over the mutilated author. In both the novel and film, Annie continues to haunt Paul even after he returns home. King's version stalks Paul's visions wielding a chainsaw and everlasting fury while Reiner's version concludes with a more ambiguous—but not less omnipresent, and therefore, omnipotent—representation of the goddess. After Paul finally kills Annie, the next exterior shot contrasts all of the previous ones centered on Annie's forest home. Reiner cuts immediately from Paul and Annie's corpse to the New York skyline on a sunshine-filled day. A caption reveals that eighteen months have passed. Now walking with a cane, Paul meets his agent in an upscale restaurant to discuss his new book. He has returned to his own world, but, like the tar-covered stepdaughter, he is scarred and wounded forever. He looks up only to see Annie approaching him with a large knife. Suddenly, we see that the woman approaching is not Annie, but rather a waitress pushing a dessert cart who nevertheless stops by to tell him that she is his number one fan. As the credits roll, Bing Crosby's familiar song from Paul's dinner with Annie plays in the background, a warning to Paul and all popular writers that the Annie archetype can always reach him from far outside her secluded cottage.

Notes

One: The Path of Beast Resistance

1. Neil Jordan would famously visit the idea of gender identity and sexuality again in *The Crying Game* (1992), a complex thriller which was marketed as the film with the year's most shocking secret: The beautiful heroine, Dil (Jaye Davidson), is revealed to be a man.

2. *The Silence of the Lambs* was recognized for Best Picture, Best Actor (Anthony Hopkins), Best Actress (Jodie Foster), Best Director (Jonathan Demme), and Best Screenplay (Ted Tally). Only *It Happened One Night* (1934) and *One Flew over the Cuckoo's Nest* (1975) have achieved the same "Top Five" honors. The film also grossed over 130 million dollars and ranked fourth in domestic box office receipts for 1991, ironically coming in just under Disney's *Beauty and the Beast*. In 2006, the American Film Institute ranked Hannibal Lecter as the number one film villain of all time with Clarice Starling as the number six film hero. And in an unusual coincidence related to this text, Thomas Harris reveals that Hannibal Lecter is descended from one Hannibal the Grim in *Hanni-*

bal Rising (2006), a prequel that describes Lecter's first encounters with cannibalism in World War II Europe.

3. Hannibal Lecter, like Norman Bates of *Psycho* (1960 with Anthony Perkins; remade in 1998 with Vince Vaughn) and "Leatherface" of *The Texas Chainsaw Massacre* (1974; remade 2003), is often said to be based upon the story of Ed Gein. Several years after his mother's death in 1945, Gein was found living in one room of her dilapidated farmhouse. Police found fifteen vivified bodies as well as nine death-masks and various garments made from human skin. In *Cannibal Killers: The Real Life Flesh Eaters and Blood Drinkers* (2005), Peter Haining asserts that Harris likely based Lecter on a composite of several other cannibal killers, including Jeffrey Dahmer, Russian Andrei Chikatilo, and Albert Fish.

4. In the DVD documentary *Inside the Labyrinth*, production designer Kristi Zea states that her designs were influenced by the works of Francis Bacon. Although she does not name specific paintings, I found remarkable similarities between Bacon's *Figure with Meat* (1954), which features a man with two

opened, dripping slabs of beef behind him in the shape of wings, and this particular scene. Additionally, Lecter's center cage closely resembles Bacon's *Figure in Frame* (1950), and the grotesque head in the jar found by Starling could have been inspired by Bacon's malformed *Head I* (1948).

5. In "Lil' Red Riding Hood" (1966) by Sam the Sham and Pharaohs' Ronald Blackwell, this same theme is addressed as they tell the young woman that they intend to keep their sheep suit on until proving that they should be trusted. The song was remixed by Bowling for Soup for the 2005 soundtrack of Wes Craven's werewolf picture *Cursed*.

6. One officer asks Starling in all seriousness if Lecter could be a vampire. This scene with Lecter rising up in the ambulance seems to pay homage to F. W. Murnau's *Nosferatu* (1922) in which Max Schreck's Count Dracula emerges bolt-upright from his coffin for his nightly feeding. See the chapter "Reality bites: The new American film gothic" in Maddrey's *Nightmares in red, white and blue* (2004) for a detailed comparison between Hannibal Lecter and vampires. I believe this scene can also be closely tied to John Carpenter's *Halloween* (1978). As Jamie Lee Curtis' Laurie looks away from the supposedly dead Michael Myers, we see the killer rise up like Nosferatu to strike again. Like Michael, Lecter is also wearing a mask when he startles the audience by rising up behind an unsuspecting victim.

Two: A Rose by Any Other Name

1. This opening gambit has frequently been compared to Alfred Hitchcock's *Psycho* (1960) in which lovely Janet Leigh is unexpectedly murdered after establishing her as the ostensible star of the film. The remainder of the film focuses on her sister and married boyfriend trying to find out what has happened to her. In the DVD commentary track, Williamson states that he wanted a well-known actress for the role of Casey to heighten the dramatic shock when she is murdered.

2. *Scream* contains countless references to other films, but it seems most inspired by John Carpenter's *Halloween* (1978). In addition to having characters discuss the film openly, Williamson lifts some of the dialogue directly from this classic. Both Casey and Annie (Nancy Kyes) say that they are making popcorn while they are on the phone, and Bob (John Michael Graham) curses himself to die when he tells his girlfriend, "I'll be right back." In *Halloween*, the film *The Thing* plays in the background while Michael Myers goes on his spree; in *Scream*, *Halloween* is shown while the killer stalks his victims. Tatum and Annie both find themselves stuck in small openings (a pet door and window, respectively) before being slain, and Billy's last name is Loomis, the same as the psychiatrist (Donald Pleasence) who tracks down Michael.

3. As Casey flees the family room, the camera pans to a picture over the fireplace, and we briefly see the image of some old white buildings that look strikingly like palace ruins surrounded by prickly, dying branches.

4. The "prohibition/violation" function is dramatically realized in Gore Verbinski's *The Ring* (2003; a remake of the Japanese version *Ringu*, 1998, by Hideo Nakata). The characters (and audience) know that viewing a nightmarish underground videotape leads to an inevitable death, but they watch it regardless. For a full discussion of this film, see the following chapter dealing with "Rapunzel" and freaks of nature.

Three: The Hand That Hawks the Cradle

1. It is tempting to believe that a "killcrop" was so-named as its arrival may have led to the destruction of a village harvest; however, etymologically, the word has nothing to do with the English compounds "kill" and "crop." Rather, it derives from the German word *der Kielkropf*, a deformed, ravenous child. According to the *Kluge Etymologisches Wörterbuch der Deutschen Sprache* (1995), while an exact derivation cannot be determined, the word may have been used to describe children born with hydrocephalus, commonly called water-on-the-brain. During Martin Luther's time, such children would no doubt have been viewed as creatures of the devil.

2. This haunting image of a hand bursting through the earth stands as one of the most frightening elements in the film version of Steven King's *Carrie* (1976), directed by Brian de Palma and starring Sissy Spacek as the telekinetic teenager and abused prom queen. Although I do not discuss the American sequel, *The Ring Two* (2005), directed by *Ringu*'s Hideo Nakata, in this chapter, I was amused that Spacek was cast as Samara's birth mother, Evelyn.

3. Nakata's film was based upon Koji Suzuki's 1991 novel of the same name. In a 2004 interview with Caroline Hsu, Suzuki notes that a major difference between our two cultures is that American monsters are typically male, while Japanese monsters tend to be female.

4. From the Publishers Association for Cultural Exchange (PACE) website at http://www.pace.or.jp.

5. Rapunzel is another name for rampion, which derives from the Latin *rapunculus*, the diminutive form of *rapa* (turnip). The leaves and roots are edible, and it is still commonly grown in Germany.

6. Verbinski includes a number of videotapes alongside the unmarked tape, whether as in-jokes or homage, including Robert Aldrich's *Sodom and Gomorrah* (1963); Alfred Hitchcock's last film, *Family Plot* (1976); Tobe Hooper's *Spontaneous Combustion* (1990); and Wolfgang Petersen's *Shattered* (1991).

7. The famed Antti Aarne classification system, for example, breaks fairy tales down into their most fundamental elements and then categorizes them across cultures, such as Russia, Greece, Norway, and others. Asian and Pacific Islander cultures are not included. "Rapunzel" and similar tales are classified as number 310, "The Maiden in the Tower." See Aarne, A. (1995). *The types of the folktale: A classification and bibliography*. (S. Thompson, Trans.). Bloomington, IN: Indiana University Press.

8. Although Japan remained largely closed to Western influence until Matthew Perry's diplomatic trip of 1853, a ban on Western literature was lifted over one hundred years earlier in 1720. This would have allowed fairy tales like "Rapunzel" to enter the Eastern realm. We cautiously point out that, while "Rapunzel" and "The Maiden of Unai" are thematically and structurally quite similar, we have found no direct link between the evolution of these two stories.

Four: The Object of My Reflection

1. Although citations are not typically given for dictionaries, it is important to note that the Grimm Brothers' *Deutsches Wörterbuch* (*German Dictionary*) stands as a monumental accomplishment for German culture. In addition to their work on a comprehensive dictionary—they died before completing it—and the fairy tales, they also developed a German grammar, providing

unity through language at a time when Germany was divided into hundreds of smaller, largely independent principalities that frequently fought with one another. Germany would not exist as a fully unified nation until 1871 under the rule of Otto von Bismarck.

2. In *Vampires, Burial, and Death*, Barber (1988) explains that the dead were often bound prior to their burial in order to prevent them from returning as vampires.

3. Please see McNally and Florescu's (1994) *In Search of Dracula* for a thorough and compelling discussion of the history of Dracula.

4. *The Talented Mr. Ripley* is based upon Patricia Highsmith's novel of the same name, which was published in 1955 and filmed once before as *Plein soleil* (*Purple Noon*) in 1960 by director Rene Clement and starring Alain Delon. Highsmith wrote several sequels to the original novel, including *Ripley Underground* (1970); *Ripley's Game* (1974) which was released as a film in 2002 with John Malkovich in the lead role; *Ripley Underwater* (1980); and *The Boy Who Followed Ripley* (1991). Highsmith also wrote *The Price of Salt* (1952), widely considered one of the first lesbian love stories with a positive ending.

5. In Tod Browning's *Dracula* (1931), a similar scene is staged for the siring vampire and victim. The famed count (Bela Lugosi) arrives to London and stops off briefly at the symphony house. He is escorted to the box seats where he meets Lucy (Francis Dade), Mina (Helen Chandler), and John (David Manners). As the lights signal the end of the intermission, he tells them, "To die, to be really dead, that must be glorious." They express their astonishment, but he silences them, stating, "There are far worse things awaiting man than death."

Five: Mother of the Pride

1. As Gelder (2000) comments, the most significant change concerning the making of the monster lies in his brain: "The film adds a new episode in which an extra character called Fritz, Frankenstein's assistant, is sent to a laboratory to steal a brain for the monster. In that laboratory are two such pickled organs, in large jars boldly labeled NORMAL BRAIN and ABNORMAL BRAIN" (p. 121).

2. Ellis (1983) and Tatar (2003) explain that the Grimms transformed the biological mothers of stories like "Hansel and Gretel," "Snow White" into stepmothers to soften the tales for children.

3. In keeping with Charles Perrault's version of the tale, Walt Disney's *Cinderella* (1950), directed by Clyde Geronimi and Wilfred Jackson, maintains two homely stepsisters, thereby removing this important theme of ugliness disguised by beauty from the tale. We—and the prince—are thus immediately encouraged to dislike them while rooting for the singularly beautiful Cinderella.

4. *Nostromo* is also the name of a 1904 novel by Joseph Conrad that focuses on the corrupting effects of greed. This theme is explored in both *Alien* and *Aliens*, as the Weyland-Yutoni Corporation (with the slogan "Building Better Worlds") sells its crew in exchange for the weapons biotechnology it hopes to gain from bringing back live creatures. The 1978 *Alien* screenplay by Dan O'Bannen opens with a direct quotation from Conrad's *The Heart of Darkness*: "We live, as we dream—alone"; it does not appear in the actual film, however.

5. The Final Solution (*die Endlösung*) was the name used in Nazi Germany to justify the extermination of the Jews during the Holocaust.

6. This particular scene closely parallels a scene in James Whale's *Franken-*

stein (1931). Little Maria (Marilyn Harris) is playing alone by a lake when the monster (Boris Karloff) approaches her from behind. She shows him how to throw flowers into the water to make boats, but the monster does not understand and eventually throws her into the water where she drowns.

7. In "Daemonic Dread," a chapter from her *Remaking the Frankenstein Myth on Film* (2003), Picart expertly analyzes the *Alien* series as an extension and re-imagining of the Frankenstein story, focusing on it as "a narrative concerning our ambivalences concerning power, gender, and technology" (p. 79).

Six: The Devil in the Details

1. Martin Luther wanted to reform the Catholic Church, and he never intended to develop a movement that would break off entirely. At this time, Germany was still not a united country, but rather a grouping of hundreds of smaller states ruled primarily by their own princes. The Peace of Augsburg (1555) temporarily settled the Reformation and Counter-Reformation by allowing territorial rulers the right to choose which religion would be practiced within their own region; however, it also further solidified the splintering of the German-speaking states. For more on Martin Luther and the Reformation, please refer to Collinson's *The Reformation: A History* (2004) and Mullett's *Martin Luther* (2004).

2. This tale alludes to and unites several stories. The hero of the tale is prophesied from birth to marry the king's daughter. When the king discovers this, he offers the parents money for their child and then throws him into the river to drown, echoing the biblical tale of Moses. He is rescued by a miller's apprentice, however, and raised by the

miller and his wife. The Grimm Brothers also give us a ferryman who pilots the boat across the river to hell, clearly borrowing from the Greek idea of the River Styx and its ferryman, Charon.

3. The Antii Aarne folklore classification system places "Rumpelstiltskin" into category 500, "Guessing the Helper's Name," when considering the tale among hundreds of Western fairy tales and folklore stories; however, this system also leaves "Rumpelstiltskin" alone among the 200 Grimm tales to be classified as such. We have decided to go against this conventional system to include the tale in this devilish section, since it shares common threads with the Grimms' other devil tales as well as the Faust legend in its various incarnations. In *The Hard Facts of the Grimms' Fairy Tales*, Tatar (2003) classifies "Rumpelstiltskin" as a spinning tale that looks at the hard labor of spinning. Yet she also refers to the title character as both devilish and a demon. Likewise, Zipes (1993) contends that the Antii Aarne classification "has more to do with the male bias of scholarship than the specific problem posed by the tale, namely female oppression and the change in social attitudes toward the métier of spinning and female initiation" (p. 49).

4. The Dakota, built in 1882, was at one time the largest apartment building in New York City. Dick Sylbert, the production designer for *Rosemary's Baby*, decided that it would be the perfect building to use for the exterior shots of Levin's The Bramford. In the novel, Levin states, "The Bramford, old, black, and elephantine, is a warren of high-ceilinged apartments prized for their fireplaces and Victorian detail" (p. 1). The Dakota gained additional notoriety as the home of John Lennon when he was assassinated by Mark David Chapman on December 8, 1980.

5. Levin's Rosemary offers a fairy-

tale argument to Hutch's claims in the novel, asserting, "Maybe there are good houses, too, houses where people keep falling in love and getting married and having babies" (p. 20).

6. Ira Levin took the ideas of feminism a step further in *The Stepford Wives* (1972), which was released as a film starring Katharine Ross in 1975. In both the novel and film, husbands incapable of enjoying independent, successful wives move to the idyllic town of Stepford to trade in their biological wives for robotic ones that do their every bidding.

7. Both Jones (2005) and Schreck (2001) comment on this particular scene's effect on the audience. Although we never actually see the devilish spawn, viewers claim to have seen its terrifying features, including yellow eyes, hooves, and even horns. Polanski does flashback briefly to the eyes seen by Rosemary during the rape sequence, but he provides no shot of the baby, relying instead on Rosemary's horrified reaction and audience imagination.

8. In *Son of Rosemary* (1997), set 30 years after Rosemary decides to take care of her son in spite of the coven, Levin returns to the conflict between dreams and reality. After setting up a rather convoluted tale that hinges on a comatose Rosemary waking up to reconnect with her son at the start of a satanic new millennium, Levin has her "wake up" again in the very final pages as if both the sequel and the original work were dreams. Guy is still acting, Hutch is alive, and she is not pregnant. Hutch calls to let them know that an apartment has come available in the real-life Dakota, and he mentions an anagram (roast mules) that occupied much of her earlier dream, providing no closure or answers.

9. *Rosemary's Baby* is often labeled a "cursed" film due to unfortunate events that occurred following its release, par-

ticularly as Roman Polanski's pregnant wife, actress Sharon Tate, was brutally murdered by followers of Charles Manson on August 9, 1969. Polanski was in London at the time. A full account of the film crew's difficult—if not necessarily cursed—experiences is provided in Brottman's *Hollywood Hex: Death and Destiny in the Dream Factory* (1999).

Seven: Off the Eaten Path

1. "Hansel and Gretel" gained additional notoriety in 2003 when Armin Meiwes, the "German cannibal," reportedly claimed that he felt he was influenced by witchcraft. According to Peter Haining's *Cannibal Killers: The Real Life Flesh Eaters and Blood Drinkers* (2006), Meiwes' hometown of Rottenburg was "somewhat notorious as the home of Hans Georg Hallmayar, known as the 'Witch-Hunter' of Rottenburg who, in the 1570s, had a hundred and eighty alleged witches burned at the stake" (pp. 300–301). In "Witchcraft after the Witch Trials," Gijswijt-Hofstra (1999) points out that a 1986 survey by the *Arbeitskreis Interdisziplinäre Hexenforschung* (The Interdisciplinary Council for the Study of Witchcraft) revealed that one-third of Germans still believed in witchcraft at that time (p. 163).

2. The magical number of three witches dates back to images of Hecate, the Greek goddess of the crossroads, who is often depicted as having three heads or faces. Shakespeare's *Macbeth* (1606) gives us three witches, collectively called "The Weird Sisters," who serve Hecate. These ladies provide some of the most famous lines related to witchcraft, including "Double, double, toil and trouble;/ Fire burn, and cauldron bubble" (4.1.10–11) and "By the pricking of my thumbs,/ Something wicked this way comes" (4.1.44–45).

3. In addition to Hitchcock's *Rear Window*, *What Lies Beneath* contains references to a number of other Hitchcock films. In *The Lady Vanishes* (1938), a name on a train window serves as a clue to a woman's disappearance. The cryptic words "You Know" appear on Claire's bathroom mirror, and the murdered girl's initials MEF appear across the computer screen in Norman's study. In both *Suspicion* (1941) and *Shadow of a Doubt* (1943), a young woman (Teresa Wright and Joan Fontaine, respectively) comes to suspect that a dashing man (Joseph Cotten, Cary Grant) is actually a murderer, and she could be his next victim. Harrison Ford serves as a modern-day Cary Grant, his heroic film image producing what Zemeckis calls a "misdirect" for the audience. And the seminal shower scene of *Psycho* (1960) is played out in similar fashion in Claire's bathroom, where she first sees the ghost and where her Norman tries to kill her. Zemeckis employs several extended real-time shots that bring Hitchcock's *Rope* (1948) to mind, and Zemeckis even states on the DVD commentary that "every single shot [of the conclusion] was going to be like something that Hitchcock would do."

4. The title *Witchcraft, Ghosts, and Alchemy* neatly ties "Hansel and Gretel" to the major themes of *What Lies Beneath* by linking alchemy, the forerunner of modern science and the supernatural. See D. Ogden (2002), *Magic, Witchcraft, and Ghosts in the Greek and Roman Worlds* for a discussion of how these ideas converged. Ogden describes the Greek sorcerer as an early doctor "who detaches his soul from his body in an ecstatic trance. This detached soul then speaks with the gods in their own language and cures the sick by retrieving their souls from the land of the dead," a description well-suited to Claire (p. 9). Where the witch cages

Hansel and enslaves Gretel, Norman uses the real drug halothane—called "a dissociative agent"—to paralyze Claire when he tries to drown her. This same drug was used in the early 1990s by real-life Canadian serial killers Paul Bernardo and Karla Homolka to keep their victims, including her younger sister Tammy, unconscious. Tammy died as a result of the drugging.

5. Although *What Lies Beneath* clearly pays homage to Alfred Hitchcock in many regards, this bathroom set-up shares much in common with Adrian Lyne's *Fatal Attraction* (1987). A similar plot-line depicts the perfect husband, Dan Gallagher (Michael Douglas) having an affair with a woman, Alex Forrest (Glenn Close), who keeps threatening his ideal life. A final confrontation likewise brings the husband, wife (Anne Archer as Beth), and other woman together in the family's all-white bathroom with another old-fashioned, free-standing bathtub. Beth wipes away a steamed-up mirror to reveal Alex standing right behind her for a quick jolt to the audience, and a fight ensues until Dan races in and drowns Alex in the overflowing tub.

6. Clark Gregg's original screenplay has a much less ambiguous ending that keeps it more in line with the family reunion and prosperity that mark "Hansel and Gretel." In his telling, Claire and Caitlin are joined by Mrs. Frank at Madison's grave, all mothers and daughters having been brought back together. Claire is then shown living in New York, playing a piece that "builds to a dark, passionate crescendo." She clearly has regained the life she sacrificed to Norman.

7. The trailer for Hitchcock's *Psycho* (1960) is incredibly inventive and involving, as Hitchcock himself takes us on a documentary-style tour of the Bates family home and motel. Yet, he also reveals several key plot points, describing

in detail how the second murder will occur, for example, with the psychotic woman charging from her bedroom and stabbing her victim at the top of a staircase. The trailer concludes as Hitchcock takes us into the now-infamous bathroom. Here, he intones, "The murderer, you see, crept in here very slowly, of course, the shower was on, there was no sound, and...." As he pulls back the shower curtain, Janet Leigh screams in terror and the title of the film appears over her horrified countenance. The trailer for *What Lies Beneath* is far less inventive, comprised of scenes taken from the film and dailies like most modern trailers; however, it similarly depends on giving away a few plot points to misdirect us from the true killer's identity.

Conclusion: The Writhing on the Wall

1. My translation from the Grimm preface in *Die Märchen der Brüder Grimm* (1987): "Es war vielleicht gerade Zeit, diese Märchen festzuhalten, da diejenigen, die sie bewahren sollen, immer seltener werden."
2. Ibid. The original quotation reads: "So ist es uns vorgekommen, wenn wir gesehen haben, wie von so vielem, was in früherer Zeit geblüht hat, nichts mehr übriggeblieben...."
3. My translation from Wilhelm's July 1, 1809 letter to Jacob in *Briefwechsel zwischen Jacob und Wilhelm Grimm* (2001). The original quotation reads: "Von einigen Kindermärchen habe ich wieder gehört, allein es waren schon bekannte. Uberhaupt fang ich an zu glauben, das ihr Kreis nicht sehr groß ist und daß wir die meisten kennen, das aber diese allgemein verbreitet sind" (p. 141).
4. From the letter dated September 9, 1819 in *Die Brüder Grimm: Ihr Leben und Werk in Selbstzeugnissen, Briefen*

und Aufzeichnungen (1952). In this excerpt, Wilhelm claims, "Sie warden, wenn Sie es einer nähern Betrachtung wert halten, vieles darin verbessert, ja den ersten Teil gänzlich umgaearbeitet finden" (p. 119).
5. This same argument has, of course, been leveled for years against violent horror films, which often receive a less restrictive rating than films with sexual content. The MPAA rating PG-13 was famously devised following the release of *Indiana Jones and the Temple of Doom* and *Gremlins* in 1984. Both of these PG-rated films were criticized for their violent content which was deemed too intense for younger children.
6. Both Sissy Spacek (Best Actress) and Piper Laurie (Best Supporting Actress) were nominated for Academy Awards for *Carrie*; Raynold Gideon and Bruce Evans were nominated for Best Adapted Screenplay for *Stand By Me*; Morgan Freeman (Best Actor), Niki Marvin (Best Director) and Frank Darabont (Best Adapted Screenplay) were nominated for *The Shawshank Redemption*; and Michael Clarke Duncan (Best Supporting Actor) and Frank Darabont (Best Director, Best Adapted Screenplay) were nominated for *The Green Mile*.
7. W. Roberts examines and categorizes hundreds of versions of the "Mother Holle" tale in his *The Tale of the Kind and Unkind Girls* (1958). Similar tales are found in France, Norway, Sweden, Denmark, Russia, Poland, Yugoslavia, and elsewhere. Although the reward/punishment scenario is expressed in all versions, this particular version with gold and pitch-covered girls appears unique to Germany and tales inspired specifically by the Grimm version. Other versions typically include a box of gold for the good daughter and a box of snakes, frogs, or even deadly fire for the bad daughter.

8. In *William Goldman: Four Screen-plays with Essays* (1997), Goldman emphatically declares that he decided to write the screenplay based solely upon his reaction and interpretation of King's hobbling scene in the novel. Defending the scene to George Hill, Goldman says, "And it is great and it is the reason I took this movie, and she only does it out of love" (p. 387). In the novel and Goldman's screenplay, Annie actually cuts off Paul's feet, a scene so graphic that Goldman says the producers had difficulty finding an actor or director to commit to the film as written. Goldman was at first shocked and horrified by Reiner's softened approach to the scene, but he admits, "What they had done—it was exactly the same scene except for the punishment act—worked wonderfully and was absolutely horrific enough. If we had gone the way I wanted, it would have been too much. The audience would have hated Kathy and, in time, hated us" (p. 388).

9. In Stephen King's novel, Paul interprets his role as that of a modern, male Scheherazade living in fear that he will have to spin 1,001 tales of Misery for Annie's demanding king: "And if what he wrote was good enough, if she could not bear to kill him until she discovered how it all came out no matter how much or how loudly her animal instincts yelled for her to do it, that she *must* do it.... Might he not have a chance?" (p. 66). In a scene absent from the film, Goldman's screenplay also has Annie remind Paul of an interview he gave in which "[y]ou said you can make it so they gotta turn the page. You know, 'I gotta know will she live,' 'I gotta know will he catch the killer.' 'I gotta see how this chapter ends'" (p. 450).

Bibliography

Aarne, A. (1995). *The types of the folktale: A classification and bibliography.* (S. Thompson, Trans.). Bloomington: Indiana University Press.

Adams, R. (2001). *Sideshow U. S. A.: Freaks and the American cultural imagination.* Chicago: The University of Chicago Press.

Ankarloo, B. (2002). Witch trials in northern Europe 1450–1700. In B. Ankarloo and S. Clark (Eds.), *Witchcraft and magic in Europe: The period of the witch trials* (pp. 53–95). Philadelphia: University of Pennsylvania Press.

Ashliman, D. (1997). Changelings. Retrieved August 10, 2004, from the World Wide Web: http://www.pitt.edu/~dash/changelings.html.

_____. (2004). *Folk and fairy tales: A handbook.* Westport, CT: Greenwood.

Badley, L. (1995). *Film, horror, and the body fantastic.* Westport, CT: Greenwood.

Barber, P. (1988). *Vampires, burial, and death: Folklore and reality.* New Haven, CT: Yale University Press.

Barthes, R. (1986). *The rustle of language.* New York: Hill and Wang.

Behringer, W. (1997). *Witchcraft persecutions in Bavaria: Popular magic, religious zealotry and reason of state in early modern Europe.* (J. C. Grayson and D. Lederer, trans.). Cambridge: Cambridge University Press.

Bettelheim, B. (1989). *The uses of enchantment: The meaning and importance of fairy tales.* New York: Vintage.

Blake, R. (2000, February). Dubious talents. Review of *The Talented Mr. Ripley. America, 182,* 18–20.

Blamires, D. (2003). A workshop of editorial practice: The Grimms' *Kinder- und Hausmärchen.* In H. Davidson and A. Chaudhri (Eds.), *A companion to the fairy tale* (pp. 71–83). Cambridge: Boydell & Brewer.

Bliss, M., and Banks, C. *What goes around comes around: The films of Jonathan Demme.* Carbondale: Southern Illinois University Press.

Bottigheimer, R. (1987). *Grimms' bad girls and bold boys: The moral and social vision of the tales.* New Haven, CT: Yale University Press.

_____. (1993). The publishing history of Grimms' tales: Reception at the cash register. In D. Haase (Ed.), *The reception of Grimms' fairy tales* (pp. 78–101). Detroit, MI: Wayne State University Press.

Bowker, J., Bleek, [Dr.], and Beddoe, J. (1869). The cave cannibals of South Africa. *The Anthropological Review, 7*, 121–128.

Broedel, H. (2003). *The Malleus Maleficarum and the construction of witchcraft.* Manchester: Manchester University Press.

Bronski, M. (2000, Summer). Review of *The Talented Mr. Ripley. Cineaste, 25*, 41–44.

Brottman, M. (1997). *Offensive films: Toward an anthropology of cinéma vomitif.* Westport, CT: Greenwood.

_____. (1999). *Hollywood hex: Death and destiny in the dream factory.* London: Creation.

Bunson, M. (1993). *The vampire encyclopedia.* New York: Gramercy.

Bundtzen, L. (1987). Monstrous mothers: Medusa, Grendel, and now Alien. *Film Quarterly, 40*, 11–17.

Cameron, J. (1985). *Aliens.* Unpublished screenplay. Retrieved November 11, 2004, from the World Wide Web: http://www.dailyscript.com/scripts/Aliens_James_ Cameron_May_28_1985_first_draft.html.

_____ (Director), Carroll, G., Giler, D., and Hill, W. (Producers). (1986). *Aliens* [DVD].

Canby, V. (1990, November 30). A writer who really suffers. Review of *Misery. The New York Times*, p. C1.

Carroll, N. (1990). *The philosophy of horror or paradoxes of the heart.* New York: Routledge.

Cashdan, S. (1999). *The witch must die: How fairy tales shape our lives.* New York: Basic.

Cave, N. (Performer). (1996). Red right hand. On *Scream: Music from the Dimension motion picture* [CD Soundtrack]. New York: TVT Records.

Clark, S. (2002). Witchcraft and magic in early modern culture. In B. Ankarloo and S. Clark (Eds.), *Witchcraft and magic in Europe: The period of the witch trials* (pp. 97–170). Philadelphia: University of Pennsylvania Press.

Clodd, E. (1898). *Tom Tit Tot: An essay on savage philosophy in folk-tale.* London: Duckworth.

_____. (1920). *Magic in names and other things.* London: Chapman and Hall.

Clover, C. (1992). *Men, women, and chain saws: Gender in the modern horror film.* Princeton, NJ: Princeton University Press.

Collinson, P. (2004). *The Reformation: A history.* New York: Modern Library.

Crane, J. (1994). *Terror and everyday life.* Thousand Oaks, CA: Sage.

_____. (2004a). "It was a dark and stormy night...": Horror films and the problem of irony. In S. Schneider (Ed.), *Horror film and psychoanalysis: Freud's worst nightmare* (pp. 142–156). Cambridge: Cambridge University Press.

_____. (2004b). Scraping bottom: Splatter and the Herschell Gordon Lewis Oeuvre. In S. Prince (Ed.), *The horror film* (pp.150–166). New Brunswick, NJ: Rutgers University Press.

Craven, W. (1996, September–October). MPAA: The horror in my life. *Films in Review, 47*, 34–39.

_____. (Director), Weinsten, B., Weinstein, H., and Maddalena, M. (Producers). (1996). *Scream* [DVD].

Demme, J. (Director), Bozman, R., Goetzman, G., Saxon, E., & Utt, K. (Producers). (1991). *The silence of the lambs: Special edition* [DVD].

Dika, V. (1990). *Games of terror: Halloween, Friday the 13th, and the films of the stalker cycle.* Cranbury, NJ: Associated University Presses.

Dirks, T. (2006). Review of *Rosemary's Baby. The greatest films.* Retrieved September 15, 2006, from the World Wide Web: http://www.filmsite.org/rosem.html.

Dundes, A. (1982). *Cinderella: A folklore casebook.* New York: Garland.

_____. (1989). *Little Red Riding Hood: A casebook.* Madison: The University of Wisconsin Press.

Dunkley, C. (2002, November 4). H'wood's fright-geist: Studios add new twists to their scare tactics. *Variety, 1,* 87, 90.

Ebert, R. (2000, July 21). Review of *What Lies Beneath. Chicago Sun-Times Online.* Retrieved October 15, 2006, from the World Wide Web: http://rogerebert. suntimes.com/apps/pbcs.dll/article?AID=/20000721/REVIEWS/7210304/1023

Ellis, J. (1983). *One fairy story too many: The Brothers Grimm and their tales.* Chicago: University of Chicago Press.

Fink, G. (1988). The fairy tales of the Grimms' Sergeant of Dragoons: J. F. Krause as reflecting the needs and wishes of the common people. In J. McGlathery (Ed.), *The Brothers Grimm and the folktale* (pp. 146–163). Urbana: University of Illinois Press.

Fulbrook, M. (2004). *A concise history of Germany.* Cambridge: Cambridge University Press.

Gelder, K. (2000). *The horror reader.* London: Routledge.

Gerstner, H. (Ed.). (1952). *Die Brüder Grimm: Ihr Leben und Werk in Selbstzeugnissen, Briefen und Aufzeichnungen.* Munich: Wilhelm Langewiesche-Brandt Verlag.

Gijswijt-Hofstra, M. (1999). Witchcraft after the witch trials. In B. Ankarloo and S. Clark (Eds.), *Witchcraft and magic in Europe: The eighteenth and nineteenth centuries* (pp. 95–190). Philadelphia: University of Pennsylvania Press.

Giles, J. (2000, July 24). Review of *What Lies Beneath. Newsweek, 136,* 58.

Glassy, M. (2001). *The biology of science fiction cinema.* Jefferson, NC: McFarland.

Goldberg, G., Lofficier, R., Lofficier, J., and Rabkin, W. (1996). *Science fiction filmmaking in the 1980s: Interviews.* Jefferson, NC: McFarland.

Goldman, W. (1997). *Four screenplays with essays.* New York: Applause.

Goodey, C., and Stainton, T. (2001, July). Intellectual disability and the myth of the changeling myth. *Journal of the History of the Behavioral Sciences, 37,* 223–240. Retrieved August 10, 2003, from the Wiley Interscience online database.

Gregg, Clark. (1999). *What lies beneath.* Unpublished screenplay. Retrieved October 10, 2006, from the World Wide Web: http://www.hundland.com/scripts/ WhatLiesBeneath.txt

Grimm, J., and Grimm, W. (1981). *The German legends of the Brothers Grimm, Volumes I and II.* (D. Ward, Trans.). Philadelphia: Institute for the Study of Human Issues.

_____, and _____. (1987). *Die Märchen der Brüder Grimm.* Munich: Goldmann Verlag.

_____, and _____. (2003). *The complete fairy tales of the Brothers Grimm* (3rd ed.). (J. Zipes, Trans.). New York: Bantam Books.

Haining, P. (2005). *Cannibal killers: The real life flesh eaters and blood drinkers.* New York: Barnes & Noble.

Harris, T. (1988). *The silence of the lambs.* New York: St. Martin's.

Heiner, H. (2003). Tales similar to Rapunzel. Retrieved August 25, 2004 from the World Wide Web: http://www.surlalunefairytales.com/rapunzel/other.html.

Holben, J. (2002, November). Death watch: *The Ring*, shot by Bojan Bazelli and directed by Gore Verbinski, presents a horrific tale about a videotape that can kill. *American Cinematographer, 83* (11), 50–52, 54–59.

Hsu, C. (2004, May 31). Interview with Koji Suzuki. *U. S. News & World Report, 136,* 64.

Hutchings, P. (2004). *The horror film.* Harlow, England: Pearson.

James, G. (1987). *Green Willow and other Japanese fairy tales.* New York: Avenel.

Jancovich, M. (1996). *Rational fear: American horror in the 1950s.* Manchester: Manchester University Press.

Johnson, R. (2001, July). Playing fathers and monsters: The classical appeal of Anthony Hopkins. *Cineaction, 55,* 24–30.

Jones, A. (2005). *The rough guide to horror movies.* New York: Penguin.

Jones, D. (2002). *Horror: A thematic history in fiction and film.* London: Arnold.

King, S. (1981). *Danse Macabre.* New York: Everest House.

_____. (1988). *Misery.* New York: Signet.

_____. (2000). *On writing: A memoir of the craft.* New York: Pocket.

Levack, B. (1999). The decline and end of witchcraft prosecutions. In B. Ankarloo and S. Clark (Eds.), *Witchcraft and magic in Europe: The eighteenth and nineteenth centuries* (pp. 1–94). Philadelphia, PA: University of Pennsylvania Press.

_____. (2004). *The witchcraft sourcebook.* New York: Routledge.

Levin, I. (1967). *Rosemary's baby.* New York: Dell.

_____. (1997). *Son of Rosemary.* New York: Penguin.

Luther, M. (1912–1921). *Werke, kritische Gesamtausgabe: Tischreden, v. 5.* Weimar: Böhlau.

Lyne, A. (Director), Jaffe, S., and Lansing, S. (Producers). (1987). *Fatal attraction* [DVD].

Maddrey, J. (2004). *Nightmares in red, white and blue: The evolution of the American horror film.* Jefferson, NC: McFarland.

Magill, M. (1991, June). Review of *The Silence of the Lambs. Films in Review, 42,* 185–186.

Magistrale, T. (2003). *Hollywood's Stephen King.* New York: Palgrave Macmillan.

Marcus Aurelius. (2002). *Meditations.* (G. Hays, Trans.). New York: Modern Library.

McGlathery, J. (1991). *Fairy tale romance: The Grimms, Basile, and Perrault.* Urbana: University of Illinois Press.

_____. (1993). *Grimms' fairy tales: A history of criticism on a popular classic.* Columbia, SC: Camden House.

McNally, R., and Florescu, R. (1994). *In search of Dracula: The history of Dracula and vampires.* New York: Houghton Mifflin.

Mendelson, M. (1997). Forever acting alone: The absence of female collaboration in *Grimms' Fairy Tales. Children's Literature in Education, 28,* 111–125.

Minghella, A. (1999a). *The talented Mr. Ripley: A screenplay.* New York: Hyperion.

_____ (Director), Horberg, W., and Sternberg, T. (Producers). (1999b). *The Talented Mr. Ripley* [DVD].

Monter, W. (2002). Witch trials in continental Europe 1560–1660. In B. Ankarloo and S. Clark (Eds.). *Witchcraft and magic in Europe: The period of the witch trials* (pp. 1–52). Philadelphia: University of Pennsylvania Press.

Morgenstern, J. (2000, July 21). Review of *What Lies Beneath*. *The Wall Street Journal*, p. W1.

Mullett, M. (2004). *Martin Luther*. New York: Routledge.

Murphy, G. (2000). *The owl, the raven, and the dove: The religious meaning of the Grimms' magic fairy tales*. Oxford: Oxford University Press.

Murphy, K. (1991, January–February). Communion: On *The Silence of the Lambs*. *Film Comment, 27*, 31–37.

Neumann, S. (1993). The Brothers Grimm as collectors and editors of German folktales. In D. Haase (Ed.), *The reception of Grimms' fairy tales* (pp. 24–40). Detroit, MI: Wayne State University Press.

Newitz, A. (1995). Serial killers, true crime, and economic performance anxiety. *Cineaction, 38*, 38–46.

O'Bannon, D. (1978). *Alien*. Unpublished screenplay. Retrieved November 11, 2004, from the World Wide Web: http://www.screenplays-online.de/screenplay/4.

Ogden, D. (2002). *Magic, witchcraft, and ghosts in the Greek and Roman worlds*. Oxford: Oxford University Press.

O'Neill, T. (1999). Guardians of the fairy tale: The Brothers Grimm. *National Geographic*. Retrieved May 20, 2004, from the World Wide Web: http://www.nationalgeographic.com/grimm/article.html.

Orenstein, C. (2002). *Little Red Riding Hood uncloaked: Sex, morality, and the evolution of a fairy tale*. New York: Basic.

Pavlac, B. (2006). List of important events for the witch hunts. Retrieved August 21, 2006, from the World Wide Web: http://departments.kings.edu/womens_history/witch/witchlist.html

Picart, C. (2003). *Remaking the Frankenstein myth on film: Between laughter and horror*. New York: State University of New York Press.

Picart, C., and Frank, D. (2004). Horror and the Holocaust: Genre elements in *Schindler's List* and *Psycho*. In S. Prince (Ed.), *The horror film* (pp.150–166). New Brunswick, NJ: Rutgers University Press.

Polanski, R. (Director), Castle, W. (Producer). (1968). *Rosemary's Baby* [DVD].

Porter, C. (1998). Rapunzel across time and space. In K. Bernheimer (Ed.), *Mirror, mirror on the wall: Women writers explore their favorite fairy tales* (pp. 273–282). New York: Anchor.

Porter, R. (1999). Witchcraft and magic in enlightenment, romantic, and liberal thought. In B. Ankarloo and S. Clark (Eds.), *Witchcraft and magic in Europe: The eighteenth and nineteenth centuries* (pp. 191–282). Philadelphia, PA: University of Pennsylvania Press.

Ramsland, K. (2002). *The science of vampires*. New York: Berkley Boulevard.

Reiner, R. (Director), Scheinman, A., and Reiner, R. (Producers). (1990). *Misery* [DVD].

Roberts, W. (1958). *The tale of the kind and unkind girls*. Berlin: De Gruyter.

Rölleke, H. (Ed.). (2001). *Briefwechsel zwischen Jacob und Wilhelm Grimm*. Stuttgart: S. Hirzel Verlag.

Rooth, A. (1980). *The Cinderella cycle*. New York: Arno.

Schickel, R. (1986). Help! They're back! *Aliens* storms in as the summer's megahit. *Time, 128*, 54–55.

Schneller, J. (2003, March). Laying down the law. *Premiere: The Movie Magazine, 17*, 72–78, 119.

Schreck, N. (2001). *The satanic screen: An illustrated guide to the devil in cinema.* London: Creation.

Schulze, H. (1998). *Germany: A new history.* Cambridge, MA: Harvard University Press.

Scribner, B. (1992). Witchcraft and judgment in Reformation Germany. In B. Levac (Ed.), *Witch-hunting in continental Europe: Local and regional studies* (pp. 160–167). New York: Garland.

Seifert, T. (1986). *Snow White: Life almost lost.* (B. Matthews, Trans.). Zurich: Kreuz Verlag.

Sexton, Anne. (1971). *Transformations.* Boston: Houghton Mifflin.

Sharrett, C. (1993). The horror film in neoconservative culture. *Journal of Popular Film and Television, 21*, 100–110.

Shavit, Z. (1989). The concept of childhood and children's folktales: Test case— "Little Red Riding Hood." In A. Dundes (Ed.), *Little Red Riding Hood: A casebook* (pp. 129–158). Madison: The University of Wisconsin Press.

Shelley, M. (2004). *Frankenstein; or the modern Prometheus.* New York: Simon & Schuster.

Simpson, P. (2000). *Psycho paths: Tracking the serial killer through contemporary American film and fiction.* Carbondale: Southern Illinois University Press.

Smith, G. (1991, January–February). Identity check. *Film Comment, 27*, 28–30.

Sundelson, D. (1993). The demon therapist and other dangers: Jonathan Demme's *The Silence of the Lambs. Journal of Popular Film and Television, 21*, 12–16.

Tatar, M. (1995). *Lustmord: Sexual murder in Weimar Germany.* Princeton, NJ: Princeton University Press.

_____. (1997). *Grimm's grimmest.* San Francisco: Chronicle.

_____. (1999). *The classic fairy tales.* New York: W. W. Norton.

_____. (2003). *The hard facts of the Grimms' fairy tales.* Princeton, NJ: Princeton University Press.

Toennies, B. (Director), Allen, G., and Toennis, B. (Producers). (2000). *Constructing the perfect thriller* [DVD].

Urbano, C. (2004). "What's the matter with Melanie?" Reflections on the merits of psychoanalytic approaches to modern horror cinema. In S. Schneider (Ed.), *Horror film psychoanalysis: Freud's worst nightmare* (pp. 17–34). Cambridge: Cambridge University Press.

Verbinski, G. (Director), Macari, M., Lee, R., and Weisler, M. (Producers). (1991). *The ring* [DVD].

Walton, P. (2004). *Our cannibals, ourselves.* Urbana: University of Illinois Press.

Whale, J. (Director), Laemmle, C. (Producer). (1931). *Frankenstein* [DVD].

White, E. (2005). "Case study: Nakata Hideo's *Ringu* and *Ringu 2*." In J. McCroy (Ed.), *Japanese horror cinema* (pp. 38–50). Honolulu: University of Hawaii Press.

Willard, T. (2002). Tales at the borders: Fairy tales and maternal cannibalism. *Reconstruction: A Culture Studies eJournal, 2.* Retrieved August 10, 2004, from the World Wide Web: http://reconstruction.eserver.org/022/cannibal/cannibalismintro.html.

Williamson, K. (1997). *Scream: A screenplay.* New York: Hyperion.

Wilson, W. (1999). *The psychopath in film*. Lanham, MD: University Press of America.

Windling, T. (2003). Changelings. The Endicott Studio Journal of Mythic Arts. Retrieved August 10, 2003, from the World Wide Web: http://www.endicott-Studio.com/jMA0301/changelings.html.

Wolff, E. (2000, August). What lies beneath. *Millimeter. 28*, 56–58.

Zemeckis, R. (Director), Bradshaw, J., and Johnson, M. (Producers). (2000). *What lies beneath* [DVD].

Zipes, J. (1988). *The Brothers Grimm: From enchanted forests to the modern world*. New York: Routledge.

_____. (1994). *Fairy tale as myth, myth as fairy tale*. Lexington: The University Press of Kentucky.

_____. (1997). *Happily ever after: Fairy tales, children, and the culture industry*. New York: Routledge.

_____. (Ed.). (1993). *The trials and tribulations of Little Red Riding Hood*. New York: Routledge.

Index